Sharing the Good Times

A History of Prairie Women's Joys and Pleasures

❧ Faye Reineberg Holt ❧

Detselig Enterprises Ltd.

Calgary, Alberta, Canada

Sharing the Good Times

© 2000 Faye Reineberg Holt

Canadian Cataloguing in Publication Data

Reineberg Holt, Faye
  Sharing the good times

Includes bibliographical references.
ISBN 1-55059-208-4

1. Women – Prairie Provinces – History. 2. Women – Recreation – Prairie Provinces – History. 3. Frontier and pioneer life – Prairie Provinces. I. Title.
  HQ1459.P6R44 2000   305.4′09712   C00-911189-1

Detselig Enterprises Ltd.

210-1220 Kensington Rd. N.W., Calgary, AB T2N 3P5

Phone: (403) 283-0900/Fax: (403) 283-6947

E-mail: temeron@telusplanet.net/www.temerondetselig.com

We acknowledge the financial support of the Government of Canada through the Book Publishing Industry Development Program (BPIDP) for our publishing activities.

ISBN: 1-55059-208-4
SAN: 115-0324
Printed in Canada

Dedication

To my grandmothers, who arrived in Alberta early in the 1900s as young married women

To my mother, sisters, and neice.

To Karen, Heather and Erin.

To my women friends – especially those in the Alexandra Writers' Centre Society and my life-long friend, Pat Fenske

Top left, Grandma Mary Reineberg; Top right, Grandma Rose McBride; Bottom, Carl & Ruby Reineberg

Table of Contents

Introduction

Sharing *the Good Times* attempts to create a more realistic perception of early prairie women. Reading popular history or academic history inevitably means addressing stereotypes. Were earlier times in western Canada the *good old days*? Or did all the settlers suffer unbelievable heartaches and travesties in order to develop the country? Was the West a wild and woolly place, or was the land settled by good people and without significant lawlessness?

These happy beach bums and sun bathers enjoy a day at Winnipeg Beach in 1912. Provincial Archives of Manitoba, Foote 1218, N 12198

Prairie women's history is equally plagued with questions related to stereotypes and truth. In "Seamless Lives: Pioneer Women of Saskatoon, " published in *Saskatchewan History* in 1991, author Jacqueline Bliss tackles some of these questions. She delineates three major stereotypes of prairie women: the Victorian lady, the household drudge and the pioneer heroine. Victorian ladies were pure, chaste, fainting females of hearth and home. The drudge image is one of endless work, associated with ideas of stoicism and martyrdom. The stereotype extended to female domestics, homestead women and those at work in sweat shops. Pioneer heroines were superwomen and dedicated helpmates. Sometimes these were also stoics and martyrs who served at the family altar. Some might add to this stereotype or create a new category for the female social activist, in particular the maternal feminist –

generally a married woman with grown children who became a political activist or club woman with a cause.

Bliss makes the case that our history is not so simple. She claims that our fore-mothers' lives moved seamlessly from one role or responsibility to another, and I hope I have added to that perspective. The roles that early prairie women played in building families and homes, achieving political rights, addressing employment inequities and forwarding social reforms for women are enormously significant. Western women are due credit for all that they have endured and all they have done, both on the historical and contemporary scenes. However, I think it is time we considered the happy parts of western women's lives, too.

Some women did have a very heavy burden to bear. Certainly, women whose families came to Canada with no money in their pockets, who settled on isolated farms where land needed clearing but where soil proved poor, and those who did not speak English suffered more than others. Often, numerous children added to that burden. Many, many Canadian feminists and historians have treated this part of the story; for example, Lynne Bowen looked at the lives of the women of the Barr Colony, near Lloydminster, Saskatchewan. In her book *Muddling Through: The Remarkable Story of the Barr Colonists* published by Douglas and McIntyre in 1992, Lynne Bowen suggests that

> *These hard-working women were portrayed as being cheerful and compliant. It was a picture painted by men and reinforced by the reluctance of most women to disagree even in their diaries, which make curiously flat reading. There is a lack of emotion demonstrated, and the cheery acceptance of their lot does not ring true. It was as if they could not admit, even to a diary, how difficult their lives were. The letters written by Alice Rendell, a truly remarkable woman whose talents and fortitude were a genuine inspiration to many, sound like the perky Christmas letters of the modern age that reveal little of the difficult side of life.(175)*

True, Christmas letters generally emphasize the positive, but why would anyone assume that the words of a woman – in her diary or to her best friends or family – are untruths, either conscious ones or lies of omission? Such an interpretation undermines the assumption that a woman has the ability to know her own mind and judge truths for herself or about herself.

The negative part of life is only one aspect of the human story. Surely, everyone experiences it at some time in some way. For my book, I assumed that every women who I interviewed or whose story I learned would have had bad days, bad weeks and even bad years. I was not looking for women who claimed their lives were always happy. If I had found any, I would have been very skeptical, just as one should be skeptical of anyone who claims – whether as an individual, historian or politician – that life is all bad.

Looking at the whole of women's lives is important. Logically, women with many young children have significantly more housework and less time for special interests than single women, newly married women or women whose children have left home. Household drudgery can be related to a specific time frame in life, but that time frame is not the sum of a woman's life. Even in the midst of enormous workloads, women can feel truly proud of the jobs they are doing or the family they are raising. Should we dismiss that pride or those feelings? To me, such days should be as important, personally and historically, as the *depressing* days.

From a statistical point of view, the majority of the women who settled in the West were young, married women or young women who soon married and had children. That stage of life includes raising families. The young families were building homes, and they had just moved away from support networks. Financially, they faced insecurity. In terms of measuring stress factors in their lives, according to our contemporary approaches, they were living during a period of high personal stress. Logically, then as now, women in such circumstances would have more negative factors affecting them than they would 15 or more years later in their lives.

If we are truly considering the quality of life of early settlers, age is an important factor in many ways. An inclusive history does not dismiss the experiences of older women. Often, they have dealt with the stressors they faced earlier in life. They have more possessions and time for interests and hobbies. Yet, most women's histories have dismissed the experiences of the woman who is 40 or 50. Surely they mattered and still matter, whether the year is 1885, 1925 or 2000.

The experience of those women who came with more possessions is also important. Not everyone came to Canada by ship, with little more than a few suitcases in their hands. There were many women from eastern Canada who came west. Countless Americans were settlers, especially to the south half of the prairie provinces, and at times, Americans were the largest immigrant population to specific areas. Allowed a settler's railway car of effects free of transportation charges, sometimes these families dismantled and brought entire farms from the United States. Their extended families were not across the ocean but could be reached by train. For others, the things they brought counted less than participating in cultural and sporting events. In towns across the prairie provinces, women participated in creating and building infrastructures in such areas of interest, and for some, it was a rewarding and heady endeavor.

Increasingly, the physiology and psychology of illness and of healthy, elderly people have told us that attitude matters. Positive attitudes affect health in a positive way. Successful women of the past and those who are today's seniors, but who played a very significant role in the developing west, have managed to develop positive attitudes, despite the ups and downs of life.

I believe it is just as important to hand that perspective to the women of tomorrow, as it is important to pass along the economic, political and troubled social history of prairie women. To do so, I've looked at what has been written. In fact, it was much harder to find stories about the positive aspects of women's lives than the negative ones – but I don't believe the problem was the non-existence of such experience. We simply don't value and save those stories because they don't seem as dramatic or as touching. Also, to retell stories of childhood fun is fine, but to focus on our own happiness as adults might be perceived as bragging. To tell any happy stories at all means risking that you will be accused of wearing rose-colored glasses or ignoring the truth.

When I mentioned my project to people, some special person would inevitably come to their minds. I interviewed some of those women and corresponded with others. I looked at traditional historical sources and interpretations. I read autobiographies, many of them self published with very small press runs and few readers. Yet the insight they give us into the past is still enormously important.

This book is primarily about women's lives and perceptions, but I have not excluded men for a reason. Grandfathers, fathers, uncles, spouses, sons, boyfriends, nephews and male work colleagues are all a part of women's lives – during the good times and the bad times. Men are part of the lives of women who never marry and those who marry. Men, as well as women, are capable of recognizing pleasure and happiness or bitterness and unhappiness in themselves and in others. Because a man has said or written something does not make it invalid, just as it does not make it valid.

In this book, I have also relied on photo history. Photos do tell stories, and at least in the past before computer photo manipulations, some photos did catch a moment of truth. Nevertheless, technology did affect the appearance of subjects. In the early days, camera technology meant there were few candid shots and subjects had to stand still for some period of time. Subjects looked serious. That didn't necessarily mean they were unhappy. As increasingly light sensitive cameras and flash bulbs became common in homes, candid photography shared more happy times with viewers.

I wish to extend my sincere thanks to my editor, Linda Berry, and to all those women I interviewed and who gave me written memoirs and photos. I could not have completed this work without your help. Also, thanks to the many people in museums and other institutions who provided me with so much assistance.

I. Hoping for Happiness

Women came to western Canada with dreams of happiness. Hardships awaited, but good times were just as significant in the lives of those women who settled or were born and raised in the area. From generation to generation, western people did pay a high price in terms of work to live in the Canadian west. Women, and men, suffered from isolation. They did without services and without possessions, sometimes even without the basics of food, shelter and clothing. They came from all corners of the world, and they stayed because they believed happiness and a better life were possible. Their successes, their smiles, the glimmer of joy on their faces, the swell of pride that filled their hearts were part of that story – and as important to their survival and well-being as other necessities of life.

In fact, there were almost as many ways of having a good time as there were women. The situations that created happiness for an individual and her family varied, as did the signs of happiness, pleasure and joy, which were definitely affected by cultural expectations. Festive occasions and festive traditions inevitably differed. Nevertheless, people did enjoy themselves, and women who arrived hoping to find happiness found it at different times and in different ways.

These strong and smiling women appear ready to win, proving their combined strength in a women's tug-of-war contest. Glenbow-Alberta Institute, NA 3959-30

Most early settlers came west as young adults, and their ideas concerning good times were shaped by the land and people they had left. Initially, more men were lured west than women. Sometimes, other relatives made the journey in order for families to remain together. Many couples brought young children, and others soon had large families. For those children of the prairies, ideas about what constituted good times were shaped by the landscape, as well as by their parents and community. Undoubtedly, the youthfulness of the population did affect the type of good times people desired, and which activities would be organized in new communities.

Prepared for either rain or sun and not having to paddle her own canoe, the woman with the umbrella is set for a pleasant day on Lake Wabamun in Alberta. Nancy Allison collection.

But there were all kinds of pleasures. In a land where isolation was common, for some, pleasure came from quiet activities, pursued alone or in small groups. Other enjoyments were boisterous and showy affairs, perhaps requiring special talents. Some were simply the result of being present at a given time in a given place. Sometimes, entertainments and pleasures were the same for women and men. At other times, they were very different and women enjoyed aspects of a unique or traditional female culture.

The personal stories of what women deemed *good times* and of how they felt when happiness knocked at their doors are as compelling and interesting as the stories focused on heartache, hard work and hardship. Like other types of social history, the stories don't fit into a neat chronological order. In the early 1800s, women loved to dance. A hundred years later, a new generation was smiling and swirling joyfully on the dance floor. The music had changed. So had the dance steps and the women's clothing, but the feelings of pleasure were unchanged.

Hours enjoying quiet pleasures, such as needlework, became the lifeblood of sanity and happiness for many women. Friends and neighbors brought enjoyment. A glimpse of a wild animal, a sunset or a sunrise was thrilling. New freedoms brought joy, whether that freedom evolved naturally out of living in a sparsely settled new homeland or was the reward of reaching adulthood, becoming mature, even growing old.

A sense of humor and a capacity to enjoy leisure and pleasure were as common and important yesterday as they are today. Contemporary life has brought new freedoms. Other freedoms were rooted in the popular culture of the 1960s. The Second World War gave women additional professional opportunities. The twenties witnessed more comfortable clothing for women and phenomenal success in sports. The late teens meant improved political rights. But such simplifications exclude as much truth as they include.

The lives of early western Canadian women were more complicated and also more joyful than implied in most of those stories. They saw and embraced opportunities for pleasure. What mattered most was a woman's individual capacity for joy, her creativity in determining how that capacity might be fulfilled given her circumstances, and her ability to rise above or forget – if only for a few hours or a day – her difficulties.

Going on Record

Some women wrote about their joyful times. Men also described the good times within communities. Many of the very early accounts focused on dancing and music, and some acknowledged the presence of

By the 1940s, acrobatics and gymnastics were not taboo for women willing to show their stuff in a backyard, at a beach or at a holiday camp. Milton Moyer collection.

women or their roles in helping to create those good times. One such historical account was written by a man visiting Pembina, Manitoba. In October of 1860, he recounted for *Harper's Magazine* the revelry he had witnessed. Accompanying a group on a scientific expedition sent out by the United States government, he was an outsider to the community, and he knew nothing or little of people's troubles. As an observer, he had watched dancers proficient at the popular Red River jig. The pleasure of the women who were present was only implied, but the two dances that the writer described were anything but serious. Whether they watched and listened or danced out on the floor, people were having a good time – women as well as men.

We crossed the river in a crazy dug-out, of precarious equilibrium, and heard the jiggish fiddle before we reached the house. Opening the door, and entering the log-house where the dance was briskly going on, we were greeted by a chorus of "Ho! Ho! Ho!" The fiddle did not cease its scraping, nor the heels of the dancers for a moment intermit their vibrant thumps on the plank floor. There was a huge mud chimney, with an open fire-place, at the right, a four-posted bed, with blankets only, in the further left-hand corner; one or two chairs, which were politely handed to the strangers; and all round the room, sitting upon the floor as Indians and tailors sit, were men and women, boys and girls – twenty or thirty in all....

Jigs, reels, and quadrilles were danced in rapid succession, fresh dancers taking the place of those on the floor every two or three moments. The men wore shirts, trousers, belts, and moccasins; and the women wore gowns which had no hoops. A black-eyed beauty in blue calico and a strapping Bois Brule would jump up from the floor and outdo their predecessors in figure and velocity, the lights and shadows chasing each other faster and faster over the rafters; the flame, too, swaying wildly hither and thither; and above the thumps of the dancers' heels and the frequent "Ho! Ho!" and the loud laughter rose the monomaniac fiddle-shrieks of the trembling strings, as if a devil was at the bow.

Perhaps it is clear that here we saw the commonalty. The next night Joe Rolette gave a dance in his house, and here we saw the aristocracy of Pembina. There was a better fiddle and a better fiddler, and better dancing. Joe's little boy of eleven, home from school at the Red River settlement, and his father-in-law, of near seventy, were the best of the dancers. The latter was as tireless as if his aged limbs had lost no strength by exposure to all weathers and labor, as a hunter and voyageur, for a long life-time; and little Joe had extra double-shuffles and intricate steps, and miraculously lively movements, which made his mother and little cousins very proud of him. In the intervals of the dance Madame Gingrais, one of Joe's lady cousins, sang some French ballads and a Catholic hymn.[1]

Mary's Story

By 1880, women like Mary Fitzgibbon were travelling to the Canadian West. Another visitor and observer, she liked to write, and she offered a woman's perspective. A visitor to the West, she described the festivities in *A Trip to Manitoba*. In the 1880s, like today, the Christmas season meant parties, and already, there were western traditions concerning how to celebrate. Kisses all around was one such tradition on New Year's Day. Whether the women were beautiful or plain, old or young, kissing was the custom. Not free of racial prejudice or of stereotypical ideas of how the Victorian lady should act, Fitzgibbon was glad that the custom of kissing was dropped in the home she visited, but other women had not been so rigidly pious or snobbish. According to Fitzgibbon, the hostess could not legally serve wine or whiskey, but she "regaled them on great slices of cake, with which they were much pleased."

Snow lay several inches thick on the ground at Christmas, and we had sleigh-drives over the smooth white prairie; one great advantage of Manitoban winters being that when once the ground is covered with snow, if only to the depth of five or six inches, it remains, and there is good sleighing until the frost breaks up in March or April. Sleighing parties

Most sleighs were simple in design. This one, from Banff in the 1930s, is similar to the carrioles of the turn of the century, and has a special place for skis. Such styles were often preferred for Santa Clause parades. In rural communities, hay rides were popular winter social events. Whyte Museum of the Canadian Rockies, V227/226

are varied by skating at the rink and assemblies in the town-hall, where we meet a
medley of ball-goers and givers, each indulging his or her favourite style of dancing – from the old-fashioned "three step" waltz preferred by the elders, to breath-
less "German," the simple *deux-temps*, and the graceful "Boston" dance, peculiar as
yet to Americans and Canadians. The band was composed of trained musicians
who had belonged to various regiments, and on receiving their discharge, remained
in Canada. The hall well lighted, the floor in good condition, and we enjoyed taking a turn upon it, as well as watching the Scotch reels, country dances, Red River
jigs performed by the others.

It was a gay and amusing scene, but, the heavy winter dresses – many of them
short walking costumes – worn by the Manitoban belles, looked less pretty than
the light materials, bright colours, and floating trains of an ordinary ball-room.
The absence of carriages and cabs, and the intensity of the cold, compelled ladies
to adopt this sombre attire. The mercury averaged from ten to twenty degrees
below zero, frequently going as low as thirty-three, and occasionally into the
[minus] forties [F]....

On New Year's Day the now old-fashioned custom of gentlemen calling was
kept up, and we had many visitors, among them the American Consul, Mr. Taylor,
known in the Consulate as "Saskatchewan Taylor," from his interest in the North-
West....[2]

Looking for a Better Life

By the 1880s, many settlers had arrived in western Canada, where they hoped to
build a better life for themselves. Often a dream of having land of their own brought
men to the West, while most women came as part of families.

The isolation, lack of services and other unfortunate realities shocked some newcomers. A number of men and women regretted their decisions. Not everyone who
came with dreams garnered a better living or better home. Some dreams went unfulfilled or took decades to fulfill, but others did succeed in western Canada. Not only
did the newcomers make a living, they made a better than average living, and some
made fortunes, but money did not necessarily mean happiness. Still, there was usually pride and pleasure in success. Women had shared in the adventure, work and
risk, and they felt pride as often and as deeply as men.

Lovisa's Story

One early settler who described her homes and her feelings about them was Lovisa McDougall. Born Lovisa Jane Amey and growing up in Cannington, Ontario, she and fur trader John McDougall (not the missionary) courted by correspondence. John's father had died when he was young. His family was poor and he had to quit school at 13 years of age. He clerked in a store, and in 1875, he chose the fur trade as a way to improve his finances. John and Lovisa married at Cannington in the spring of 1878. The young bride was willing to sacrifice for the life she dreamed of with her husband. Knowing there would be little if any medical or dental help for months on end, and perhaps already plagued with aching teeth, she had them all pulled and replaced with false teeth. Perhaps no other woman sacrificed her teeth to journey west.

Their destination was Fort Edmonton, and like others, they travelled by steamship, by train through the United States and by wagon across the prairies. Because of transportation, the time required for their journey and then the threat of a western rebellion, the couple's plans kept changing.

Lovisa corresponded regularly with her family. For the most part, she was enjoying the trip, despite problems and poor water. Because of the rebellion, they had returned to Winnipeg. When they finally settled in Edmonton by the summer of 1879, the town consisted of the old fort, a hotel, the Methodist church, four homes and two stores. In the first years, there were disappointments and few local women to be Lovisa's friends. She had problems breast-feeding her daughter, born in November of 1880, but she coped, and the couple prospered. In time, the McDougalls contributed to the prosperity and growth of a town that became the capital of the province. John opened a store, was successful in business and made money buying and selling his businesses. The McDougalls became millionaires; John was elected mayor of Edmonton; and he served as a member of the legislature.

As the family's finances improved, the McDougalls moved to new homes. They purchased their last home in 1909 for $30 008.39, including contract and extras. They had journeyed west hoping to make a good living, and they had made a fortune.

In letters to her mother and brother Charlie, Lovisa described her new environment, her homes and how she felt about them. Few women became as well-off as Lovisa, but from the beginning, she had been cost-conscious enough to note the price of basic foods and lodging. Still, her letters told of successes. Her fine homes brought her pleasure, and when moving into yet a bigger house around 1892, Lovisa wrote that family might think they were rich. In fact, her husband was better off than anyone except the Hudson's Bay Company elite, and Lovisa admitted to feeling proud they were "getting on in the world."

Winnipeg, January 28, 1879: Johnnie has made up his mind to stay in Winnipeg & I am very glad. He rented a house all furnished from a Mr. Campbell....It is quite a large house, 3 bedrooms & 2 closets & hall upstairs, a nice parlour, hall, dining room, bedroom, pantry, closet & kitchen downstairs, all carpeted & furnished splendidly. I have the use of everything, dishes, bedding & sewing machine all, so we have nothing to buy but provisions. We pay $20.00 per month but a gentleman has one bedroom rented for $5.00 a month & we are going to let him keep it & that only makes our rent $15.00. I think we will try & get 2 or 3 boarders, because I can get along splendidly with that many & that would pay all expenses. $5.00 a week is what they get & every little hole & corner in Winnipeg is full of people boarding. People here buy nearly everything. They get 18 loaves of bread for $1.00, butter 30 to 25¢ per pound, eggs 45¢ per doz. There is quite a difference in prices here & down home...Johnnie & I seem to take splendidly with nearly everybody....

March 28, 1879: I was just thinking today how nice it is travelling out on the prairie, riding along in the fresh air with nothing to bother you. You cannot imagine what a different feeling one has. Everything around you seems to be your own. I just love camping out as we did last summer and there is no one I ever met that has tried it but likes it. Everybody is so friendly....[3]

Edmonton, August 6, 1879: Johnnie rented a splendid big house yesterday, one of the largest houses here & the best....Edmonton is a lovely place & our house, the one Johnnie is going to build, is on a lovely spot....Yesterday the boat came up with the Governor & a few more of the Government officials from Battleford. They gave them a grand reception at Mr. Hardisty's the H.B. Officers. Flags were flying from the Fort & when the boat came in she looked splendid sailing up the river with so many flags flying....

Johnnie bought Mr. Malton's garden & one of his cows so we were very lucky. We will have lots of potatoes & vegetables for the winter. I have not been down to the Fort yet but it is bigger than Fort Garry & the best in the North West. Mr. & Mrs. Malton [missionaries] are going away tomorrow on the boat. They have a splendid church here, nearly as good as in Cannington, a nice stained glass window at the back & nice chandeliers, etc.

I have not a cooking stove, but Johnnie will send for one with his next supply of goods. If I had a stove & sewing machine I would have everything as nice as any one in Cannington. We have some nice things to put in our house, pictures, organ

Building and decorating a large home and surrounding it with a beautifully landscaped yard was the dream of many pioneers. This fine home was in Arcola, Sask., in about 1905. South Saskatchewan Museum.

& lots of other stuff. Johnnie has subscribed for the *Winnipeg Times* & is to send for the *Toronto Mail or Globe* & some illustrated paper for the winter.[4]

December 27, 1879: Johnny is lying on the bed asleep & I am seated in one of the cosiest rooms imaginable writing on the table beside him. We have made a change in our house; the sitting room we have taken for a kitchen & the kitchen for a sitting room so we would have the fireplace in it & we moved our bed in this room. We have the cheerfulest room now I ever was in, completed, curtained etc.…[5]

Jan 26, 1887: We had a surprise party here & had a big time. 60 took supper. There were 2 fiddlers besides Mr Watson & Mrs Walker for the piano besides several lesser lights. They danced in the kitchen & dining room. We had Johnnie's room for smoking & the sitting room for the ladies, supper was served upstairs.[6]

Family Ties

In some aspects of life, the experiences of women in the late 1800s or early 1900s were little different from those of women in areas of the west that were settled or homesteaded much later in the twentieth century. For most, family was important, and much of a woman's happiness was centred in family-related activities. Even in the 1920s and 1930s, family structure and family dynamics were surprisingly diverse. There were many non-traditional families or families that were not based on two biological parents and their shared offspring. In fact, the blended family was

Of these seven sisters in the John Armstrong family, three travelled with their parents from Shawville, Quebec, to join the girls' four brothers homesteading near Botha, Alberta. The oldest of the sisters to make the trek was 27; the youngest, Mamie (centre, bottom) was about 13. Patricia Lyster Fenske collection.

common long before divorce became a fairly accessible option, but the reasons were definitely different. With fur-trade *country* marriages, lack of legal ties meant some families were abandoned. Later, many of those women entered into traditional marriages. The other all-too-common reason for blended families was the death of a mother or father with young children.

Generally, there were more challenges and complications for blended families, but the new families were not necessarily unhappy. Far from it. A new mother or father could bring happiness into an otherwise devastated family. The extended family was also important to feelings of well-being, and in many cases other members of a homesteader's family made their way to the same region. The story of one such family began before they moved to Alberta, but a happy home life – in surprisingly difficult circumstances – became the family's heritage.

Lucy's Story

Lucy Chiesa (nee Rocchio) was born in 1915, at Gallo, Caserta, Italy. She came to Canada in 1923 as a girl with her father, stepmother and siblings. Lucy had been able to attend school only a little until she was 10 years old, but once she could attend consistently, she loved school. Like other immigrant children, Lucy learned and spoke English at school. At home in Mountain Park, Alberta, the blended family spoke Italian and held dear their Italian heritage.

Because money was scarce for the family, Lucy quit school and took on many adult responsibilities by age 15, by which time, she and her family were living on a homestead near Edson. Still, she didn't want to stop learning. She borrowed notes from other students. She read and studied at home. Without denying occasional problems, she saw her stepmother and family in a positive light, and the years on the homestead were some of the happiest in Lucy's life.

The Italian family had good food on their table, though the delicacies were not expensive. Lucy's mother knew how to use the new shoots of dandelions for delicious salads, and sometimes they had homemade wine. Eventually, Lucy had her own home. Returning to Mountain Park with her new husband, who was a miner, she enjoyed getting together with other wives. They talked and crocheted and exchanged patterns.

Lucy did all of her own sewing. Her daughter was born in about 1935, the midst of the Depression, but eventually, Lucy was able to give her skating lessons. When Lucy's daughter was about nine, she was in an ice carnival, and Lucy made the costume. There was work, so much of it, but there was also pride and pleasure in that work, and the early years on the homestead were some of her happiest.

I delivered milk. We helped dad build the house; we peeled logs. Oh, it was beautiful. That homestead was a Godsend..[At first, the house had a dirt floor.] It wasn't finished, but it was partitioned for bedrooms, and when we got our first rough lumber floor…well, we felt we were millionaires. You can't imagine how happy we were. You know, in those days, anything that was an improvement was a big improvement.

In the morning, in the spring time or in the summer, we got up early, because the cows were pasturing around and we didn't have the homestead fenced.…We were singing all the time, my sister and I, all the time. We were happy. And we had a cow. It was a Jersey cow, and she had great big, long horns…She was a lead cow. We thought, "Well, the cow will hear us sing or hear us yell. She will move her head a little." But no way, she wouldn't move until we were practically on top of her. Then she would get up and clonk, clonk, lead all the cows home…Some mornings we would see deer…a moose. We enjoyed the country.…There was a creek running through it. Everything. I liked the work. I liked the family.…I liked my animals, the cows.…And soon we were selling about 25 quarts of milk. That was a lot of money in those days. And only nine cents a quart, but we lived off the land.…

My mom was a good cook. She had beans soaking every night. There's a lot of protein in beans, you know and, then my dad was a good hunter. He hunted moose and rabbits, and she made lovely, lovely stew – moose stew or rabbit stew. She kept the rabbits in water and vinegar over night so they would loose that strong taste.

She would make stew or spaghetti sauce, and we would make homemade noodles. You never tasted anything better....She was a happy mother and a happy lady. I was a little bit jealous of her daughter, because Mom kind of favored her. But that's only natural. I grew up to get used to those things. My dad talked to me [about how important their stepmom was to the family]. He was a good man....

There was singing all the time....in the evenings and in the lamplight. I think we knew every cowboy song that came out. We did. Dad used to go singing in the Old Country. They used to get him to go serenading. The guys would have girl-friends, and they would call Dad all the time because he had a lovely voice. Dad played the guitar....He sang the Italian [songs].

A saw-horse teeter-totter could entertain young adults as well as children. At home on the farm near Alderson, Alberta, the Parkkari family enjoy themselves in June, 1912. A musical family, their talented members played everything from fiddle and accordion to pots, pans and spoons. Glenbow-Alberta Institute, NA 2083-3

We laughed all the time. Oh, we quarreled and fought, too, but I can say we were always singing. My cousins would come from Cadomin and we would sit at night and we would sing and sing. But what else are you going to do in the lamp-light?...

We made our own entertainment. Our own entertainment was singing or maybe going upstairs — it was a big eight-room house — to read stories. My friend used to keep this *McCall Magazine* for us. There were continued stories, and we could hardly wait for the magazine to come so we could keep up the stories. But in the afternoon in the summer time we always had a siesta. That's what the Italians have. We would go upstairs and we would read or just talk for a couple of hours or an hour, but it wasn't until all the work was done....And sometimes we would go to the creek to paddle. We were a nice bunch....We were busy mostly working all the time, but we were happy doing that....

Some friends lived maybe ten miles from where we lived, some Italian people, and Mom liked to talk Italian with friends. She would take us brood over, and we would walk ten miles and stay overnight and visit these friends....And then they would come sometimes, too, and stay overnight at our place....

My aunt would come from Cadomin. She would come to our place, and her and Mom would get together and they would make stew and go out and pick mushrooms. My aunt was another good cook, and everything they would cook, you could smell it all around you, and they were laughing and joking all the time. My aunt worked hard. Her husband died and was buried in Edson, so she came twice a year to fix up his grave and she would come to our house and stay....

Berry-picking expeditions could be fun. Often, part of the outing with family and friends was a picnic. Also, most pickers enjoyed eating fresh berries and the journey itself. Saskatchewan Archives Board, S-B 1004

In the spring or in the summer, there were blueberries galore. We would pick them by the tubs full and sell them to the bakery for books. We did. We bought our old books with blueberries....Mom would pick and pick and so would us kids. And on the way home, she would always run into a fresh patch She was a great one for wandering. "Oh here's another patch. Don't hurry. I have to pick." The pails were full. And she would pull up her apron and we wouldn't come home until that was full, too. We made pies and she canned some and made jam....

When they first moved, even to the mining camps, she would save all the flour sacks when we used all the flour....And she used the flour sacks for sheets. She used the flour sacks for slips, and for our bloomers — we didn't call them panties then, we called them bloomers — [she put in elastic] and she always managed to have a little bit of lace to put on them. You couldn't bleach the Robin Hood or Five Roses Flour off....but it bleached off with time....

When you are young, you figure "Oh, we haven't got this or we haven't got that." You go to town and you see girls all painted up and fancy shoes and everything, and us, we were just so plain on the farm. You don't understand. My Dad said one time, "You don't know but those people depend on us. We gave them vegetables and we gave a lot of food and milk." Some of our friends didn't have wood, and Dad said, "Come to the farm. You can cut all the wood you want." [He explained to his family] "Can't you see. We are lucky."...

I loved to read. But mostly, [I did] fancy work. When I got married and we went to these teas — I didn't get many things for my wedding gifts. I didn't have nice table cloths or anything crocheted. So when I got invited out and they had embroidery....I thought, I'm going to start doing that. I started doing everything myself. I got flour sacks, washed them, stamped them, embroidered them, learned to crochet. I crocheted everything. I knitted. I sewed, and I enjoyed it. I did everything myself, and pretty soon, I had a lot of fancy things, too.

We [women] didn't work then in those days. We were home. My husband worked afternoon shift in the mine. He didn't come home until 12:30 in the evening, so I stayed up and waited up for him, and I did all those nice things. I learned it all myself. I got a little book and I just practised....But I liked housework. Believe me, I was born a housekeeper. Everything was neat.

[When I was young and] we made bread, it was a ritual....And Mom would say, "you put something on your head," and "put an apron on." We had nice homemade aprons. We never wore slacks in those days. They were all skirts. [Mother said]

"Don't you run around and let dust get in the bread." So two of us would be mixing, and Mom would put in the liquid and we would punch away. Mary, me and Mom and the other little sisters. When my aunt came we were all in the kitchen. There was another Italian lady…she had six children, so there would be….I don't know how many in the house all together, and the women would all be in the kitchen.…Anybody that came, there was always bread and cheese. They didn't need any fancy stuff.[7]

Many Sources of Hope

A few children came west without parents. Some of the child settlers were Canadian and sent west to other relatives who had ventured into the wilderness. A few ran away from whatever circumstances created unpleasant lives. Especially once they could board a cross-Canada train, children of fourteen or fifteen and very young adults stepped aboard for the west. Child "immigrants" also came as part of programs sponsored in Britain, first for orphan children, and later as evacuees during the Second World War. The jobs for girls and young women tended to be in domestic service, and often the girls were given a place to stay or a home as part of the job. Some found themselves in difficult circumstances, overworked and abused. For others, being a domestic meant making money of their own, being able to buy clothes for themselves, having money to attend movies and social activities, in fact, stepping up in the world.

Both before they arrived in the West and after settling here, many such children or young women had little opportunity for an education on which to hang at least some of their hopes. Being without parental or family support could leave them feeling hopeless. That any of these young girls were able to develop positive attitudes as adults, that they found things in life to enjoy and that they passed the ability to enjoy life on to their own children is amazing. For some of them, religion and cultural traditions provided the needed sense of security and hopefulness.

Annie's Story

Born in 1900 in Montreal, Annie Larose had seven siblings. When she was only four years old, her mother died. Later, her father remarried, this time to a widow who had 24 children of her own. After she moved to a homestead near Harris, Saskatchewan, with her oldest sister, there was no opportunity for Annie to continue her education, and her formal schooling did not extend beyond grade four. Yet her daughter Edna Quilichini (nee Larose) of Biggar, Saskatchewan, remembers feeling that her mother had an amazing life. There were other disappointments, too, but marriage made a significant difference in her life. In the years to follow, oral and musical traditions played important roles as the centre of a strong family life, and they were part of the good times for the entire community.

Annie was a religious woman, but she enjoyed a good time, and she shared her enthusiasm for the things she valued with her children. According to Edna, the third of Annie's eight children, somehow, Annie always adopted and maintained a positive attitude.

She [Annie] and her sisters – two years older and 2 years younger – got jobs working for people in Biggar. They made beds, swept floors, and as my mother said, were not always treated kindly. At any rate, my mother got married when she was 16. My father was 26. When we asked her how she had met him, she said ["]he sat beside me at a show["].…My dad had taken out a homestead and been a bachelor for several years. He had come out west from Toronto and became a farmer even tho he had never been out of the city.…They went to Edmonton for their honeymoon and one of my mother's fondest memories was their stay at the McDonald Hotel.

Financially, they had good times and bad, especially during the Great Depression. In spite of her inability to attend school, my mom was always learning and very determined her children would get as much education as possible. One of the first experiences I remember was that of having to kneel together with my brothers and sisters, night and morning, and recite our prayers. They were not short and I don't know how she had learned them.…They included the Our Father, the Hail Mary, the I Believe in God (the Creed), the I Confess (Confiteor), the Acts of Faith, Hope, Love and Contrition, the Ten Commandments of God, the Six Commandments of the Church, the Glory Be to the Father. To this day, I have trouble omitting any of them.

My mother and dad were very musical and one of the sounds we heard was that of my mother's singing. She knew the words of many songs – especially French folk songs, and we knew them too. My dad had a gramophone and lots of records. One of our most fun things was to dance with Mom while Dad played records. That was our evening entertainment. The most common social event in our district was a dance, and we went as a family. My dad could chord on the piano and often did. These were very enjoyable. The women took a cake or sandwiches and the men paid 25 cents to pay the orchestra.[8]

Building and Rebuilding

For most women, home was more than a place to rest your head. It could be part of a woman's dream for herself and her loved ones. It could become a symbol of what was working or not working in life. For those who had lived in desperate conditions elsewhere in the world, finally having a home on land of their own – or on land that might one day be their own – was a wonderful thing. Even the dream of having such a home could sometimes make work less tedious. For those who walked and travelled thousands of miles in wagons over cart paths, and even those who brought their belongings by train, it was a relief to find their own land and begin building their new homes.

Some women were fortunate. They came with fine dresses and good china, expecting similar nice things in the Canadian West. However, although homes in the West became more and more pleasant, until the late forties, conditions were sometimes quite basic. Usually, the young women had the physical strength to endure whatever inconveniences they found, and they had confidence that things would get better. For most, conditions did improve, at least in terms of housing, but always, having a sense of humor made life easier.

Holmes on Homes: A Humorous Perspective

Married in 1916 during the First World War, Peggy Holmes came to Canada in 1919 as an English war bride. She liked nice things, and she had brought a lovely trousseau and Royal Doulton dishes. More importantly, she brought with her a sense of humor, optimism and adaptability.

Most homesteaders lived in very basic housing, but women dreamed of nicer homes. Although women didn't visit show homes, special catalogs were available for leisurely and enjoyable hours of dreaming. City of Edmonton Archives, Eaton's Plan Book of Ideal Homes.

The couple settled near St. Lima in Alberta's Peace River country, and later they moved to Edmonton, where Peggy became a well-known broadcaster and writer. Her two autobiographical books, *It Could Have Been Worse* and *Never a Dull Moment*, revealed the ups and downs of her life. Instead of feeling bitter, she recognized the ironies of life. She laughed warmly at herself, at her circumstances and at other people's humorous stories.

In the spring of 1921, Peggy and her husband Harry headed for their homestead in the north. With a glowing picture of their new home in mind, they were anxious to arrive. The Peace River country of the 1920s surprised them, and they were horrified to find that they had no house. It had burned and everything had been pilfered. So the couple stayed in a nearby abandoned shack where the homesteader had left a note: "Have given up the unequal struggle. Help yourself."

Peggy and Harry scavenged for essentials and built their new home on the site of the burned building. They called their sturdy little house "The Gables," and slowly they continued to make improvements. They purchased a chemical toilet, but a real bathtub and hot running water remained an unfulfilled dream. They moved to Edmonton, and after several other housing disasters there, things finally turned around. The couple had money to spend on a luxury – building their own house.

Elegance was Peggy's dream, but she was prepared for the hard work to achieve it. In the building of their house, they had help from friends. When finished, their new home had a steep-pitched roof, maple flooring, brick fireplace, built-in bookcases, and dozens of fine touches, but there would be more about her new home that would bring joy into Peggy's heart.

We'd started life in our new home with high hopes for the future – I couldn't conceive of wanting anything more. There we were living in the house of our dreams, my parents happily settled in their own business. All I had to do was add the finishing touches.

On advice from so-called helpful friends I called in an interior decorator to help me choose curtains. The poor man was doomed from the moment of his arrival. I knew there would be trouble as soon as I saw him; [he] was such a fussy little man and obviously had completely different taste from my own. Sure enough he suggested swathes of frilly white violet and nets. No way! I wasn't going to have my nice new windows all netted up like someone's frilly undies. He departed in a huff and I set out for the fabric sales and the bargain counters.

Poking around sale stalls is one of my delights. I love to find a bargain. Sure enough, the sales did not let me down. There at the back of a stall, I found some real fabric; a heavy shot silk in deep orange. Made up, these curtains were a huge success, and neighbors and passersby used to remark on the glow and sheen of the material. In fact when we sold the house fifteen years later, the new owner was so taken with the curtains that she asked me to leave them. I feel sure the frilly ones suggested by the decorator would have been dishrags long ago.

A new house always means extra furniture, and I spent many happy hours haunting antique shops and second-hand dealers looking for bargains. I had a favorite haunt, Reed and Robinson's Antiques and there I found a very nice Jacobean oak tea table for five dollars. It was a lovely piece of furniture with elegant twisted legs, and I carried it home with pride and stood it in the dining room.

For homestead women, a trip to town was a treat. So was shopping, whether at a store or outdoor market. In 1916, this Eastern European woman browses at Dufferin Avenue Market in Winnipeg. Provincial Archives of Manitoba, W. J. Sisler 21, N 9633

Standing back to admire the effect I suddenly thought, "That's a daft height to pour tea from," so I called in my friendly handyman and asked him to chop off five inches from each leg. He shuddered. Pointing out that it was a treasure, he begged me not to ruin it, but did succumb when I asked him to lend me his saw so I could do it myself.

With five inches removed from the table's undercarriage it made a very fashionable coffee table. In fact, a couple of weeks after the operation a visitor fell in love with it and offered to purchase it for twenty-five dollars. Of course I refused....

Funnily enough a friend who needed a fireside stool offered to buy the leftover legs from me. I laughingly gave them to her, casting five inch legs, not bread upon the waters.[9]

II. Love Lights Shining

Romance may be as old as the hills and prairies, but in the Canadian West in the early settlement days just finding a girl was a chore for a young man. If he found one who made his eyes light, he faced serious competition. For many romantically inclined women, courting left vivid memories, some of the best of their lives. Often, young women of marriageable age had many potential suitors vying for their attention. That situation had as much to do with population statistics as it had to do with their desirability, since the population was predominantly male until the First World War.

This suitor seems to be popping the question in the hay. With little accommodation available to early travellers, some newlyweds spent part of their honeymoon with nothing but a bed of hay for their mattress. Provincial Archives of Alberta, Ernest Brown, B 177

With an almost two to one ratio in some places, such as in Regina during the early 1900s, most young women could count on popularity, good times and marriage proposals. Then by 1916, in the midst of the First World War, the ratios changed drastically.[1] The city decreased in size, and men only slightly outnumbered women. However, with the war and with the uncertainly of life, there were other reasons for courting and good times to be fervent preoccupations.

At this elegant Manitoba wedding in 1908, Antonio Beliveau wed Louise Prud'homme. Provincial Archives of Manitoba, Beliveau, Antonio, 1, N12148

Just Courting

With good reason, bachelors wanting to change their marital status did not miss church, picnics or dances. All were great ways to meet women. Even in church, there was the possibility of meaningful glances, and churches sponsored countless functions where women were present. Most churches had picnics, but so did schools, community groups and businesses.

Picnics and dances were a relief from the work in people's lives, but for the unmarried, they also held the possibility of a budding romance that could bloom into true love. In winter, family and community hay rides and bobsleigh rides offered opportunities for snuggling close. Even in the early days of the Red River settlers, for winter parties, young men set off in sleighs to gather up the girls.

Most courting was done in earnest, but that made it no less wonderful. In the Winnipeg area in the early days, the parlor was the room used for formal courting. Not only would a suitor have to meet the family, he might have to accept the presence of a chaperone while he sat watching the woman of his dreams as she sang or played the organ, piano or harp. Even less entertaining would have been watching her while she did handicrafts such as embroidery or other needlework.

However, in the West, there was usually much more freedom for young couples than elsewhere. Some traditions were very friendly, such as Yuletide kisses for girls and women, a long-standing custom at Fort Garry [Winnipeg]. These Christmas and

New Year's kisses were meant to be neighborly, but undoubtedly, they might lead to flirtation.

In many families, daughters chose who they would marry. Mothers and fathers who could supervise them were often busy and tired, but there were fewer people in an older generation to provide supervision. So rigid and eagle-eyed supervision of courting just did not work that effectively. Sometimes, wealthy families did send daughters away to finishing school or to relatives in eastern Canada, the United States, or Europe so a suitable match could be made. Yet, increasingly, the prairie provinces became settled, and rigid, old ways lost ground. Families simply wanted their daughters to be happy.

Young men and women found each other. They walked together and talked together. They played sports such as tennis. They went on sleigh rides and to skating parties together. They sat side by side on Ferris wheels and at fairs, and when, for a donation to a worthy cause, a young man might kiss the young woman in the kissing booth at the fair, he did. Courting was an exciting time in women's lives.

A prairie farm in about 1910 was the setting for this tennis match. Since rackets were small and nets were portable, tennis was a popular game with many young couples.
Saskatoon Public Library, LH 1382

Norah's Story

Norah Driscoll (nee Matthews) was the daughter of Claire and Inspector [R.G.] Matthews of the North West Mounted Police. The family was in western Canada in the late 1800s, and Norah's experience reveals that not all courting was grave and formal. Rather, the times allowed for fun and flirtation and for a young woman to change her mind.

Norah was born in Ontario in 1876. Her father was appointed an inspector for the North West Mounted Police in 1886, and the family moved west, first to Winnipeg, then to Regina in January 1887, and then to Fort Edmonton in May of the same year. As a young girl, Norah, along with her sisters and mother, had suffered cramped or rough quarters, but life had been interesting and filled with adventure. Activities were wide-ranging and included staging plays and skits for the entertainment of themselves and others at the police posts. In 1889, the family was transferred to Lethbridge where they spent four years. By then, Norah was 17 and of marriageable age. Surprisingly, she was allowed to go camping with a co-ed group of friends, but the affairs of the heart were usually very innocent at the time.

W̄e spent four happy years there [Lethbridge] at the age when I was growing into womanhood, and having beaus! We had a tennis court and all became good players, taking part in local tournaments and going to tennis dances etc.

My Aunt visited us again from Butte and made things lively for us. Mother was always kind and hospitable to the many homeless young bachelors and it was I suppose inevitable that I should have my first proposal of marriage when only 17, but mother shooed him away. Father had a rule that none of us should be engaged before 20 years of age. Consequently I became engaged on my 20th birthday to an entirely different person, after having three or four affairs in between. Girls were very scarce in those early days.

In 1892 our happy life in Lethbridge came to an end when father was transferred to Fort Macleod. Again there were no quarters available in the barracks, and we had to remain in Lethbridge for some months until in the Spring of 1893 when a house was found for us not far outside barracks, and we reluctantly moved. Macleod was a much smaller place and we were going to miss all our friends, and besides starting another school did not appeal to us. However, father bought a tennis net and we made a tennis court so that was some consolation, and as I was then about 17 [I] was permitted to go to all the grand balls and was soon having a gay time, interspersed with visits to Lethbridge, and having our friends visit us, and then happy when Inspector Morris was moved to Lethbridge and we moved into his quarters in barracks, not nearly as commodious as our quarters in Lethbridge but still we managed very well and lived there until 1898.

Our greatest joy was our annual camping trip to the mountains, to Waterton Lakes where old Kootenai Brown's shack was the only sign of habitation – now a very large and prosperous summer resort for Lethbridge and other towns in the South. We also camped in the Crows Nest Pass on the spot where the terrible Frank slide took place a few years later, and a hundred lives were snuffed out in the little mining town that had sprung up on the site where we camped.

And another delightful camp was in the Livingstone Range at Bull Park. I had just become engaged to be married so this has particularly happy memories for me, and we were quite a party. My friends Eva Murcott and Lily Deans of Lethbridge, Inspector Primrose, John Cowdry and R.C. Mathews, who afterwards married my sister Clare. Lily Deans and Inspector Primrose also married some time later. We had a wonderful camp and the fishing in the river was the best we ever had anywhere.

On breaking camp, we came down to the North Fork where there was quite a large settlement of young English ranchers who played polo etc. They were having a dance and gymkhana to which we were all invited. So this was my introduction to the ranch life of which I was to become a part when I married. I met many who were later on to become good friends and we all thoroughly enjoyed the polo gymkhana and dance after. That was our last camping trip I think.[2]

Advice to Lovers

When it came to affairs of the heart, some women got their advice from an unexpected source. Emily Ferguson Murphy became famous for her work as a respected magistrate in Edmonton and for her political efforts on behalf of rights for women.

Emily had a less serious side, too. She was well known for her sense of humor but as years passed and she saw so many problems in her courtroom, she became increasingly serious. Still, her laugh was a roaring sailor-style laugh, and she enjoyed wild hats and masquerades. She moved to the prairies with her husband Arthur and their two daughters. They settled first in Swan River, on the border of Saskatchewan and Manitoba, but by 1907, they had moved to Edmonton, Alberta.

Already, Emily was a well-known Canadian writer of books and articles, and many of her articles were about the lighter side of life – including romance and marriage. Her humorous articles included titles such as "Winsome Widows," "Old Maids" and "How to Choose a Wife" for the magazine *Modern Women*, but she wrote for countless other magazines, too. Sometimes, she used her own name and other times she used the male pseudonyms Earl Yorke and Earlie Yorke. Her advice to young lovers was always interesting and often surprisingly frank and *liberated*, given the time period.

February, 1906, To Kiss or Not to Kiss: During these later days, the world seems to be hopelessly divided over this momentous question. The kiss has fallen into sad disrepute – in theory. In practice – well, that's another matter. How do I know the world is hypocritical? Never you mind how I know. I know all right....I know – because I – because I happen to know.

...along comes a whirl of girls with their "Anti-Osculation Societies" and "Bachelor Girls Prohibitory Clubs." Who ever thought it. I always knew our sex was given to little duplicities.

Here is what some of the girls swear to: – "Realizing that kissing is very demoralizing and detrimental, but still delicious, and that it is exclusive (I wonder what they mean) and contagious, we the undersigned students of Northwestern University, solemnly swear that we will refrain from all kissing."

The witches! They haven't a word to say about receiving kisses. They know right well that the only exception to the divine maxim "It is better to give than receive" is to be found in the kiss of love....[3]

Dressed as an Amazon for the Edmonton Horse Show parade in 1919, women's rights activist Emily Murphy didn't seem a likely source of advice for lovers, but she did many unusual things in her life. As well as writing, she loved parades, wild hats, dressing in costumes and riding her beautiful horse, Major. City of Edmonton Archives, EA 10-2039

Cupid and Cupidity: Every girl should marry and it is well that she should marry for love. In marriage, money should not be the *first* consideration, but it ought to come in a close second.

Not every hug or snuggle meant a couple would marry. Being confidantes or good dance partners might be the limits of a still-valuable relationship. Photographed near Fort Saskatchewan, Alberta, the enlisted woman and Milton Moyer were just friends. Milton Moyer collection.

In matrimony, happiness is not a matter o'money, but the happiest couples have money....

Personally, I like substantial qualities, such as character, a fine physique, and good manners, but unfortunately this is a trinity of traits, hard if not impossible to find....

A woman is so much a man's superior that he should have plenty of money to cover his shortcomings and multitude of sins.[4]

A Married Flirt: What is flirtation? It is the froth of love: a light friendship; a transgression of the law. "Thou shalt not play at courtship...Do all women flirt? Nearly all....

This kind of flirtation takes dramatic talent and a keen, hard-knit knowledge of the world of men. This is why married women are the most successful with the game. Indeed flirting is much more difficult than it is generally conceded to be, although some there are — in truth there are many, who contend the game is well worth the candle....

This dream begins early and springs eternal in the feminine breast. Even the veriest miss, not yet in her teens, dreams of a golden day when some great, big man will melt away before her very eyes all for love of her. She would have her lover at her feet rather than in her heart.

The only flirting a married woman should do is with her husband.

"True but trite," says my reader....

And really flirtation with one's own husband may be wonderfully fascinating and thrilling. A woman may plan wonderful situations if she has only the brains and heart to plan them.

But a caution in your ear, Madam. *Never* flirt with him in company. Such a proceeding has been rightly defined as washing one's clean linen in public.[5]

Dancing Up a Romance

Writer Jack Peach was born in Calgary in 1913, and he became known as a local historian. He knew the community's past from the stories he had been told, his research and his own experience. Very occasionally, he wrote about romance. He was realistic about it. He didn't believe that people had been more moral and less amorous in days of old. In one of his columns for the *Calgary Herald*, he wrote about the city's lovers' lane. Finding privacy was difficult, he admitted, but not impossible. There were some unsettled hills overlooking the community, and they were fine places after sunset. The road to Bragg Creek had possibilities, however, uncontrollable factors such as the high cost of gasoline might affect where a couple could go or not go. The Weaselhead area was closer, but wherever they went, couples had to be on the watch for prowling police cars. Not surprisingly, the romantically inclined determined the risk of being caught was worth the price.

Peach also wrote about one of the community's most romantic-looking couples, and he knew how important they were to other lovebirds. In his own growing up years, he had spent long, wonderful evenings at Penley's dance hall. But the story really started with the Penleys themselves.

Born in 1888 and moving with his family from Ontario to Saskatchewan in 1907, John Penley worked his way west, arriving in Calgary in about 1912. Already, he had set his heart on being a dance instructor. Eventually, he purchased the Christopher Robinson Dance Studio, renaming it Penley's Dance Academy. Pursuing his career seriously, he travelled to New York for courses in ballroom dancing from expert instructors. While he was there, he met a young woman just as passionate about dancing. From New England and born in 1900, young Wahnita Barker had established a name for herself by wowing audiences. The two proved to be perfect dance partners, and in 1918, John convinced Wahnita and her mother to help him run his dance studio in Calgary. They agreed, and once his dance partner was in Calgary, John proposed. Just before he left to serve in the First World War, the young couple married and honeymooned in Winnipeg. Keeping the studio going was not easy in the years John was away. Nevertheless, soon Penley's was the place to go for dance lessons during the day and the joy of dancing during the evenings. The dance hall was a hit, and the Penleys were the best dancers in town. In the summer, they took their love of dancing to summer villages at Sylvan and Chestermere lakes.

The two dancers built Penley's into almost a legend. Calgarians by the score met future wives and husbands at Penley's. When I was in my teen years that was the place to go, with parental blessings!

Gentleman Jack Penley would have reminded you of Fred Astaire, lithe, slim, with sparse, smooth hair and a shy smile. Beneath it was an iron resolve, for Jack said, "I wanted a place where not only could a person take his best girl, but also feel quite safe and sure of a good time if they wanted to take a sister or a mother." He laid down strict behavioral and dress rules and you abided by them or were not welcome. The result was a phenomenal success for the Penleys and Calgarians at what became an institution held in the highest esteem for generations.

During the Second World War many entertainment spots were off limits to thousands of high-spirited young people of the armed forces. Penley's dances always were in bounds and many lasting romances began to the music of the orchestras that played there.

Not only were the Penleys a romantic-looking couple on the dance floor, their dance hall in Calgary gave thousands of young couples an opportunity to swirl around in each other's arms. Glenbow-Alberta Institute, PA 2585-2

Mart Kenney, perhaps the most famous of them all, called Jack and Wahnita "two of the smoothest dancers I have ever seen...."

In the 1920s and early '30s attendance was in full spate and couples really "touch danced" in those days, to the dreamy waltz and to new and traditional steps: fox trot, two step, and the Latin American import, the tango.

The sights and sounds were memorable: wailing trombones, sobbing saxophones, the "big band" sounds, everyone in party clothes, the Penley pair and their teachers, such as Kathy McHugh and Jean Gauld, coaxing the shy ones onto the romantically lit dance floor....In Calgary, nimble toes and Penley's were synonymous all the way from 1912 to 1964.[6]

Showers and Weddings

An engagement was the beginning of good times for family and friends of the starry-eyed betrothed. Well-prepared young women had begun working on their hope chests while they were still young girls. Some collected dishware and silverware. Most could at least afford to crochet the edges of tea towels and pillow cases to put away, but usually, they could also depend on the women of the community to help them become ready to set up house.

After the engagement was announced, it was time for a shower. De-

Wedding and baby showers provided necessities and luxuries for new brides and new mothers. As well, they were important social gatherings for women. In 1932, these telephone operators worked for Alberta Government Telephones. For the wedding shower, their gift appears to be a silver tea service. The doll may be a decoration, gift or teasing reminder of future roles. City of Edmonton Archives, EA 160-1705

pending on whether the community was large or small, half a dozen to 40 women might gather in someone's home. First there were games. One style of game meant determining the names of songs that corresponded to the stages in a man and woman's relationship from the first sparkle in their eyes to being the old folks at home. At some showers, the women sang favorite songs. Other times there were charades, or the amateur actresses in the group dressed in wedding clothes to present a skit related to romance and marriage. Sometimes everyone brought their favorite recipe for the bride-to-be, and usually before the day was over, she was given a recipe for marriage.

To host a shower, the woman of the house needed cups. Early settlers often had few, but knowing they might someday host a horde of ladies, collecting tea cups became important. In fact, tea cups were common gifts for young brides. Luxury and practical items of every sort were showered on the lucky bride, and gifts were often handed from person to person around the circle so everyone might see them. Then, coffee, tea and cakes or cookies were served before the women returned to their everyday lives. Such showers brought pleasure not only to the bride-to-be, but to all the women attending, who had been able to catch up on community news or simply enjoy the company of friends.

Often, weddings were considered the best of times, not just for brides and grooms and their families, but also for guests attending the celebration. A wedding dance was a time to meet members of the opposite sex and to begin anew the flirtations and romantic liaisons that might lead to yet another wedding and dance.

The celebration of the fur trader weddings and the countless weddings that followed on the prairies might be brief or might last for days. In his book *Women of the Red River*, W.J. Healy captured some of the early local wedding customs.

One evening last summer while the material for this book was being collected [ca. 1922] it happened that there was assembled in a house in Kildonan a group of members of the Polson family connection and a few others of old Kildonan families. They were asked to give their memories of the Kildonan wedding customs. Their recollections are here set down. Marriages in Kildonan were always on a Thursday. On the Monday before the Thursday of the ceremony in the church the invitations to the wedding were given verbally, often by the father of the bride, who went from house to house. Only in the late years of the old regime did it become the custom not to invite everybody in Kildonan to every Kildonan wedding. On the Monday of the invitations the cooking for the wedding dinners began. "Old Man" Harper and John Auld were mentioned by the older people as men who were always engaged to do the roasting. Oxen and sheep were killed, and great roasts of beef and mutton hung on the spits before the open fireplaces.

Roast beef, roast mutton, boiled potatoes and plum pudding were the staple fare at the wedding feasts. The festivities began in the house of the bride's family the day before the marriage, with dancing and feasting. On the Thursday named for the wedding the bride and groom went to the church accompanied by all the invited guests in a long procession. In the earlier years it was usual to walk to the church. When horses and carrioles and cutters became common in Kildonan the wedding parties used to drive to the church. Young men used to make arrangements weeks ahead with the young women who were to be their partners at the weddings. Rev. Dr. Black met the bride and groom at the door of the church and went in with them.

The ethnic dress at early Ukrainian weddings, such as this one in Samburg, Saskatchewan, would eventually give way to western European and American styles. However, the Ukrainian tradition of celebrating over a number of days survived longer, as did the reputation for great wedding dances.
National Archives of Canada, PA 88459

The return of the wedding procession was generally taken advantage of by the young men who desired to give an exhibition of the speed of their horses; but it was a rule never violated that the bride and groom must not be passed on the road from the church. On arriving at the house of the bride's parents the first of the wedding dinners was served; it always took several tables to accommodate the wedding guests in relays. Usually the house of a neighbor was cheerfully given up to the dancers; often two neighboring houses were used for the dancing, as well as the house of the bride's parents. The dancing was kept up during the afternoon and evening, and sometimes continued for three days. The dancers danced in moccasins; it was usual for them to provide themselves with fancy moccasins ornamented with bead work and colored silk work to wear at weddings and there are traditions which are jocularly mentioned of a vigorous dancer having worn out more than one pair of moccasins at a wedding.

Next came the "kirking." On the Sunday following the marriage the bride and the bridegroom accompanied by the two groomsmen and the two bridesmaids drove to the church and sat together in a pew in the front of the church. Their horses were decorated again with the many-colored ribbons which had bedecked them on the marriage day, and the bridal party were arrayed in their best clothes. They drove back from church to the home of the bride's parents; but there was no racing on Sunday. The Sunday dinner after the "kirking" was one of the chief feasts of the whole wedding celebration, which was not yet ended. The bridegroom lived at the house of the bride's family until Tuesday, when he and his bride were convoyed by another bridal procession to his father's house, where they were to live until the house for the newly wedded couple was ready for them. It was now the turn of the family of the groom. There was another wedding dinner followed by dancing and merry-making, and so the wedding festivities came to an end at last.[7]

What's Funny About Love?

Most women took love very seriously. However, even in the early days, men made jokes. Bob Edwards was the writer and editor of Calgary's *Eye Opener* newspaper, and he was considered one of the finest humorists in the West. He took shots at women, at their manners, causes and fashions, but he took even more shots at men. Undoubtedly there were women who disdained him, but others laughed. In fact, when one woman first arrived in Calgary, she read the *Eye Opener*. She determined to meet the man who could "write like that." She did; she loved him, and she married him.

Known for his drinking escapades, Bob Edwards made his drinking buddies the target of hilarity. One of those cohorts, an imaginary newspaper editor from Midnapore, was Peter McGonigle. He had graduated from Toronto University with a B.A., Boozilogical Artist, and the character became the perfect mouthpiece for Edward's humor.

Edwards wrote a society column to cover Peter's courting and marriage to the imaginary Miss Phoebe Delaney of Calgary. Whether he based the lovers on his own experiences when struck by Cupid's arrow is uncertain. Bits and pieces of the love story were reported week after week, and local readers became as hooked on the escapades of the couple as contemporary enthusiasts have been hooked on soap opera love. Once Phoebe's father even ordered McGonigle out of the house because he was "under the influence of bugjuice."

June 16, 1906: The engagement of Miss Phoebe Delaney of Calgary to Mr. Peter J. McGonigle of Midnapore is at last announced. The wedding has been set for March 17, to be followed by an extended honeymoon to Macleod via Okotoks, High River, Nanton, Staveley and Granum. The happy couple would thereafter take up residence in Midnapore, where Mr. McGonigle has extensive business interests. Midnapore society is all agog over this delightful society event and many balls, routs, dinner parties, pink teas and receptions will be gotten up in their honor.

Mr. McGonigle gave a charming pink whiskey to his male friends last Monday afternoon in the spacious parlors of the Nevermore Hotel, when he formally announced his approaching marriage. A pleasant time was had by all....The function...is still in progress....The guests are engaged in a delightful game of progressive poker, the prizes being round and flat object d'art of various hues....

Mr. And Mrs. Peter J. McGonigle returned a couple of weeks ago from their honeymoon and have taken up residence in the charming flat above the printing office....Mrs. McGonigle will receive for the first time next Wednesday afternoon. Mr. McGonigle has only had one mild toot since his wedding....

The first tiff of the happy couple came from the family Bible aforesaid, for which Mrs. McGonigle had paid $1.60 in Calgary. On looking over the good book and idly turning over the pages she discovered that her Peter had been using the leaves for cigarette papers, probably because they were so thin. On close scrutiny she found that her husband, whom she thought so noble, so high-minded, so god-like, had smoked up all the gospels and about half of Ezekiel....[8]

War and Weddings

To most, wedding celebrations might be a wonderful time, but getting married was serious business, especially so when trouble was on the horizon. As it would at other times and in other places in history, world politics affected wedding celebrations in western Canada. Before 1950, men had left the West to serve in the Boer War, the First World War and the Second World War. The wars hastened decisions to marry, increased the number of weddings during those years and decreased the size of most weddings.

For writer Jean Leslie of Calgary, a young woman at the time, the Second World War brought the marriage of many of her friends and acquaintances. Jean captured the story of some when she wrote about friends and their experiences.

At 10:00 o'clock [on Friday, July 12th, 1940], a radio broadcast had carried the story that compulsory military training for home defense would commence for all single men between the ages of 21 and 45 and that any man single as of July 15th would be considered single for the duration of the war. The strong inference was that men called up or enlisted after that date would receive no dependant's allowance even though they had since married….this was just at the end of the 'dirty thirties' when couple's went together sometimes six or seven years trying to save enough money to marry…so the thought of receiving no dependant's allowance was a very serious one….

In 1940 there was but one…registrar, David Ormond found over 100 people waiting in line when he arrived for work. Two of those were Doris Patton and Ronnie Moore who found, when they got to the window, that Doris, being under 21, must have at least one parent present. "The office was to close at noon so you can imagine our panic as we dashed home through flooded subways to get Mother," Doris recalls. They had gone together for two years but had postponed marriage because of her youth and Ronnie's penurious salary. "We knew from the way the war was going that Ronnie would soon enlist and although we hadn't actually heard the broadcast, when we discovered that Ronnie's sister and our close friends were all being married that day we felt it must be the best thing to do."

All across Canada license bureaux, jewellery stores and ministers did a roaring business….[In] Edmonton the staff at the vital statistics branch worked overtime with one of the stenographers reeling after acting as bridesmaid 20 times in one day. John Singleton, janitor at Knox United Church in Calgary, acted as best man at three weddings there.

John Ragan worked a night shift as a linotype operator and had not heard the news broadcast and as there were no Sunday newspapers he was unaware of the 'stampede' until his fiancé [Lillian Regan] phoned from her work place on Monday saying she had had several phone calls suggesting it would be best for them to move up their wedding date from August. He was over 'call up age' and had three younger brothers and a sister already in the armed services but Lillian's mother, no doubt concerned about her daughter's plight if she were to find herself without dependant's allowance, persuaded them to marry on that deadline day.

"Our minister was away on a convention but we managed to get Rev. Rex Brown of Knox United Church, who had married many couples over the weekend. The Bay had phoned me just that morning that the wedding dress I had ordered had come in, but now that we were to have just the family with my young sister and my twin brother to stand up for us, I let the beautiful long white gown go and wore a little blue dress with matching blue shoes that I already had."

"I took the night off and it was all over before I knew what happened," laughs John Ragan....

On Monday, July 16th, Ottawa announced that the new regulations had nothing to do with men enlisting or being called up and [did] not affect regulations concerning dependant's allowances.

"But," laughed the Ragans and the Moores, "somehow a lot of us were married by then. For those of us who had gone together for some time it worked out great, others may have 'repented at leisure.'"[9]

Honeymoons

After the wedding came the joys of first days and nights together. Some couples simply couldn't afford a honeymoon. They got married and went home. Once there, the night's silence might be broken by party-goers, prepared to shivaree them. Newlyweds loved it or dreaded it, but in at least one Saskatchewan community, a new wife was already so lonely, she thought she couldn't bear it. The party antics made her feel welcome, and she stayed. In an area near Moosomin, Saskatchewan, shivarees became so rowdy and out of control, the more conservative neighbors decided to halt them. Near Findlater, Saskatchewan, the noise so frightened a young bride new to the community that she burst into tears. The group insisted on coming in. The bride sobbed; the groom said it was only his friends; and finally entering into the fun, the new wife went up stairs, put on her wedding dress, came down again, had a good time, made lunch for her visitors and became a favorite in the community. Community by community, traditions varied, as did the intensity and even existence of shivarees.

Once railway tracks crossed the West, many honeymooning couples boarded the train. In about 1914, after their wedding, Sybil Meyers and Edward Kopstein travelled from Winnipeg on the CPR. Large hats and long dresses for women were still stylish, but the men's clothing gives an added air of elegance. Provincial Archives of Manitoba, Foote 1639, N15817

Newlyweds with the money for a honeymoon sometimes left for far-off places, including the United States and Europe. However, before the days of good roads, good cars and train travel, more than one couple found themselves spending their first nights together in unusual circumstances, like one young couple who slept under their wagon and in a haystack on their way home.[10]

Aldis's Story

The story of her wedding and honeymoon held fond memories for Aldis Olson (nee Hallgrimson). She and Rae Olson, a young flying officer in the Air Force, married in 1944. After the church service, her parents held a reception at their home for the young couple. Finally, they set off happily on their honeymoon.

With gentle humor, Aldis conveys the unexpected developments. Her story suggests the shyness of many women concerning that momentous change in their lives. Getting married was wonderful. Going on a honeymoon could mean some embarrassments. To start, the couple got stuck in Dafoe, Saskatchewan, while awaiting a bus to Regina.

We examined the room. There was an old, brass bed, a dresser and a wash stand with a basin and a jug of water and towels. I opened the bed, and the sheets were snowy white and ironed. Everything was neat and clean, including the little rag rug by the bed, though it was threadbare, probably from too much washing.

We would rest and catch the train to Regina in the morning. The good old C.P.R. was never late. We were getting into our new night clothes when I discovered I couldn't get my arm into the sleeve of my robe. Someone had neatly sewn the sleeve shut. I looked up at Ron, sitting there beside me on the bed. He was totally engrossed, trying to untie what looked like hundreds of knots in the string of his pyjama bottoms.

He gave up and looked at me, and we started to laugh our heads off, rolling around on the bed. I wondered what our host [would think]. Likely, "Air Force people! They're all crazy!"

In the morning, I heard a rustling outside our door. There was a ten pound lard pail full of hot water. "Great service," I thought, as I'd expected we'd have to wash up in the cold water of the jug.

We were dressed and ready to go in time to catch the train. As we came down the stairs at the back of the restaurant, we realized the place was jammed with people in Air Force uniforms. They were from the bombing and gunnery training base a few miles north of Dafoe. They were drinking coffee and Coke, talking and

For her honeymoon in the early 1940s, this central Alberta woman travelled to Banff. On the way, the couple stopped in Calgary and visited St. George's island, where huge dinosaurs were already fascinating visitors. Walt and Faye Holt collection.

laughing. No doubt they were waiting for the train or bus to take them away on leave, too.

Someone spotted us, and all of a sudden, we were looking down on a sea of faces staring up at us. Total silence came over the place for a minute. It was the longest minute I ever spent. I wanted to turn back and run up the stairs, but there was nothing to do but brazen it out and try not to trip on the stairs. A giggle came from the back of the crowd. When we reached the bottom of the stairs, Ron set down the luggage and straightened up in his officer's uniform. The man in front of him gave him a snappy salute. The whole crowd then saluted in unison. Ron returned the salute, I thought, a little sheepishly. I couldn't help but smile....

We slipped into a booth and ordered toast and coffee from the waitress. We were no longer embarrassed....

Earlier, when we had discussed where we would go on our honeymoon, Ron had said, "I've saved up five hundred dollars for this trip. You have often mentioned that you wished you could go to Portland to visit your Aunt Sara and your cousins. Now we can do that."

Only a couple of naïve kids like us would visit relatives on their honeymoon, but we didn't know that. So it was settled. In 1944, five hundred dollars was an enormous amount of money, and we knew what we would do with it....

[Later on their trip...]

Back on the train, the porter had started to make up the berths. I took my overnight bag to the women's room to change. I was almost ready to go back to the berth when one of the women giggled.

"We must have a new bride in our midst." She pointed to the confetti on the floor and said, "Look! Confetti!"

I hurried out of there with dark thoughts of how I would get even with my bridesmaid and friends who had tampered with our luggage. We were lulled to sleep by the clickety-clack of the wheels on the rails.

I woke in the morning and peeked out between the drapes. All the passengers were up and dressed. Their berths had been made up and the sun was shining brightly. I couldn't hide in the berth so I woke Ron, put on my robe and walked to the end of the car as sedately as possible.

When I came back, my embarrassment was soon forgotten. We were in the Fraser Valley. The flat, fertile valley and the mountains in the distance, north and south, were breathtakingly beautiful.[11]

Keeping the Love Lights Burning

Pre-marital romance was exciting, but keeping the romance in marriage, especially when life was filled with so much work, required thoughtful and loving spouses. The old childhood rhyme claimed, first there was love, then marriage, and then came the baby carriage, but no rhymes and few stories have told of the good times throughout the years of a long and rewarding marriage.

Because they had to travel for their jobs, some couples have always faced the challenge of separation in terms of keeping love alive. Before telephones kept travelling spouses in touch at any time of the day or night, committed couples depended on love letters, just as much as unmarried lovebirds who were miles apart.

On hot days, when dresses were long and underclothes plentiful, pregnancy was no laughing matter. However, even then, and for this latter-day photo when women's styles included shorts, jokes about large-bellied men and pregnancy did entertain women. Stettler Town and Country Museum.

Some such letters between spouses are not only romantic, they hint at full and loving relationships. A few even imply the importance of sex in the lives of such couples – including those in western Canada – though they lived over a hundred years ago during the Victorian age.

Mary and Jim's Story

The family of Scottish-born James Macleod immigrated to eastern Canada in 1845. While serving in the army during the 1870 First Riel Rebellion, 34-year-old James met and fell in love with 17-year-old Mary Drever at Fort Garry [Winnipeg]. Enthusiastically, the young woman sent to Scotland for a wedding dress, but she was so young, and already James' career was taking him back and forth across Canada as Assistant Commissioner in the North West Mounted Police. He arrived at Fort Whoop-up in 1874. Two years later, Mary finally wore the wedding dress, but by evening of their marriage day, James had to return to duty and leave on a tour of his assigned territory.

The couple didn't see each other again or celebrate with a honeymoon until early 1877. For the trip from Chicago to Fort Pelly, which combined pleasure with official duty, they travelled by train, stage coach and dog team in still wintry conditions. This set the tone for much of their marriage, as James travelled frequently for his work.

Fortunately, James was a letter writer. Not only are his letters filled with history, daily duties, weather, road and living conditions, they speak of his deep love for his wife and family. Even the endings to letters spoke of love and he signed off, "Your very own," "Your devoted husband," "With fondest love and kisses," "With fondest love and kisses all around," "Kiss the dear little ones and imagine yourself kissed 1000 times."

They revealed a very different self from the professional man who loomed large in history. Still, what reassurance and happiness the letters must have brought to Mary. James died in 1894, and after little more than 20 years of marriage, Mary found herself alone. She lived almost 40 more years, but the letters were a reminder of how much her husband had loved her.

Fort Macleod, June 4, 1882, My own dearest Mary

It is impossible for me to tell you how much I miss you my darling girl and our two little pets. Hithertofore when we used to be apart I always had so much to occupy my mind that it was not quite so unbearable as it is at present, but now I feel our separation most <u>horribly</u> as if my betterhalf had slipped out of me. I hope to goodness I shall feel better over it. I suppose the feeling is partly caused by my getting older, and more and more infatuated with my perfect wife....I am now writing in our old dining room where I have been the greater part of the day reading papers and thinking of the happy days we have spent together in it, those delicious evenings when we used to spoon on the easy chair and talk and chatter and hug and kiss to our hearts content. My sweet, sweet bird were we not happy in our little nest and then the journey in comes back to me where you would drive with me in the blazing sun – the night the first on the Belly River where I bid you good night after you had all gone to bed, and the delicious drive between the South Fork and Cutbank!! [How about] we take this journey over someday and won't I tease you, and wont you in your pretty blushing way pretend you don't remember and don't know what I am talking about. I sleep in our old bed now and try and try to content myself but it is no use. It is you and not the springs that make it so nice. But with the two it was Paradise in bed!! I will [get] my ears boxed by my blushing and offended beauty pet, and try not to think about it. This place is kept much cleaner than it used to be....

Fort Macleod, July [14], 1882, My own darling wife

...I again walked over the ground where our tent was pitched [in 1877], and didn't I long for my pet. Nothing of interest happened on the way out, but it was a dismal journey and very much more so by comparison with the delicious journeys I have had over the same road with my own pretty love. I think I have revealed to you before in one of my letters that I get [spooneyer] as I get older. I wonder if you will think me an old goose when I tell you that I walked over and over the ground upon which we camped at our different stopping places. I think you can spot one or two places which are especially to be remembered. Do you remember the hill just this side of Red River where we walked abroad, and you were in such a state of mind [worrying that someone] should see us in each others arms right in the road. Would that I could fold you in my arms this moment — my sweet darling. I am so lonely without you and the dear old bedroom where I continually loiter is awfully cold and unsatisfactory....Oh dear sweet darling pretty bird[,] life is not worth living without you[,] 'tis almost unbearable after such a taste of Paradise as I have had to feel so much alone....

I do hope and pray I shall hear good news about my precious Nel [daughter who has been sick] by next mail. Written with fondest love to you and the little ones...hoping that I may hear good news of yourself my sweet darling love[,] I am as ever your devoted Jim[12]

III. Every Day and Festive Days

Hospitality mattered in the West. For those living in towns and cities, there were many opportunities to enjoy the company of others. Some rural women living in very isolated areas faced loneliness. Farm men made more trips to town or to neighbors, but farm women sometimes felt desperate for company and enjoyments. For them, seeing a new face and visiting was a particularly welcome break from day-to-day life. As a result, even strangers who ran into unexpected difficulties and needed shelter or a meal were welcomed. With neither help nor a hotel for miles, few rural people dreamed of turning anyone away, even if the kids had to give up their own beds or the barn was the only place to sleep.

Being a good hostess was a point of pride to many women. It seemed there were no circumstances when a woman couldn't come up with something to serve visitors for a light lunch or a meal. "Will you stay for potluck?" "We haven't got much, but you are welcome to what we've got," were customary invitations, and often, the coffee pot remained on the back of the stove all day, in case of a visitor.

Hearty meat and egg sandwiches were standard in most rural homes, but an English or wealthy hostess might serve

Community gatherings, such as sports days, picnics and dances offered many forms of fun. Long skirts did not prevent women from entering races. During this fair at Three Hills, Alberta, in about 1909, the women faced an additional challenge. They had to thread a needle before reaching the finish line. Glenbow-Alberta Institute, NA 772-12

fancy or crustless sandwiches. Those with English, Chinese or Japanese background preferred tea. Americans liked coffee, but everyone accepted that coffee, tea and a light lunch were a customary part of enjoying each others' company.

Often church was as much a place for friendship as for worship, but many people also set aside Sunday afternoon or another time and day to go visiting. At-home days and calling cards were popular in some towns, and a hostess might set herself a schedule for being at home to receive visitors every Wednesday or the last Tuesday of every month. Such scheduling was seldom a hit in rural communities, where it was considered *swank* and a neighborly visit was always welcome.

Communities built halls in which to have dances, meetings and card parties, or they used their local schools for the gatherings. They met in each others' homes for potluck parties, card parties, birthday parties, anniversaries, and for religious and other traditional festive occasions. Children were always brought along, and once they were tired, they were put to sleep in whatever space was available, in beds, on benches, on piles of coats in corners.

For *The Story of Manitoba*, published in 1913, F. H. Schofield described how it had been during even earlier days in the province's history. Although he gives a man's perspective, the part women played in this tradition of neighborliness and community social activities is very clear.

The nearness of the houses was conducive to the frequent exchange of social visits on the long winter evenings, and hospitality was unbounded. Entertainment of various kinds, long talks about the dangers and hardships, which they had passed through, tales of their ancestors in the far-away homeland, and the recital of the old Celtic legends and folk-stories filled many a long evening in a pleasant manner. There were no "days at home" or card parties in the old time. A lady went to visit her friend when it was most convenient, and she was sure of receiving a welcome, if the neighbor was at home. For many years the musical art of the settlement was confined to playing the violin, probably because the instrument was so easily carried; and although much time was spent in practice, the class of music produced was not very high.... The instrument was in such common use that violin strings were forwarded as a part of the consignments of goods for the northern districts.

During the summer months the people were too busy for much amusement; but the gun and the fishing rod furnished sport for the holidays, and "bat,["] a game of ball in which leagues and professional players had no part, gave recreation during the long evenings. Driving parties were very popular in the winter. Processions of perhaps twenty cutters and carrioles would set out for a long drive over the snow to the home of some, friend, where all the party went in for an informal dance, concluding the visit by singing in a hearty way some of the old and well known songs. The gayly painted carriole, the fine horse, the bells and ribbons, and the swift dash across the snow made carrioling [a] favorite pastime among the French and Metis. One of the occasions which brought out carrioles in large numbers was the celebration of midnight mass at the cathedral of St. Boniface on Christmas eve; and the congregation gathering from all quarters, with the bells on the carrioles ringing clearly in the frosty air, created an excitement in the midst of what was really a solemn occasion....

The 24th of May was always celebrated, and people came to Fort Garry from points as far away as Lake Manitoba and Portage la Prairie, sometimes even from Pembina, and St. Joe. Horse races were the principal events of the day, and many a horse was ridden from Fort Garry down what is called Main Street to-day. Competition was keen, but a race was run on its merits, the best horse invariably being declared the winner. Dominion Day was not known then; but the 4th of July was celebrated by friends from the United States with the proper salute, sports, and horse races.[1]

Nothing Like a Picnic

Picnics were hits for both women and men long before motorized vehicles made travelling in the prairie provinces reasonably easy. They provided good times for everyone in the family, from toddlers to old folks. Picnics could be small and simple outings for family and a few friends, or hundreds of people could be in attendance. Early in the century, iced tea or lemonade were available at some picnics, but ice was a problem. Sandwiches, buns, sliced ham or turkey, potato salad, brown beans, bean salads, coleslaw, pies, cakes and cookies were good old-fashioned stand-bys. At an outstanding picnic, people might find hot corn on the cob, homemade marshmallows or fried chicken.

Sunday was a good day for church and family picnics at a lake or in the countryside. June was a favorite month for school picnics, and in late summer or early autumn, any day of the week could be a fine time for berry picking and a picnic.

The entire family might go berry picking, but generally it was the work and pleasure of women and children. From the very earliest days on the prairies, indigenous women picked saskatoons essential in the making of pemmican. Long after the Depression, to have fresh fruit in the summer and canned fruit in the winter, families set out in search of the biggest and sweetest berries. Most had their favorite patches, and to keep morale up throughout the day or afternoon, there would be a

At many community picnics, tables were filled with food provided by individual families but shared with everyone. Other times, small groups had their own picnic lunches, but activities included everyone. Given the crowd and tent in the background, this small picnic in 1913 at Beaver Creek (Sask.) appears to be part of a larger community celebration. Saskatoon Public Library LH 491

picnic and snack breaks. Sometimes the contest of "who could pick the most" became a serious one, and the woman usually won. The taste of newly picked berries and the fun of the picnic created pleasant memories.

Huge community picnics became annual events. They were organized as part of ball games, horse races, local rodeos and sports days. Labor Day, Victoria Day and Farmers' Day meant picnics and sometimes even parades. Businesses sponsored picnics for employees, and political parties sponsored them for supporters. At some picnics, there were booths where picnickers could buy lemonade or kiss a pretty girl, with the price of the kiss going to some worthy cause. However, no picnic was a picnic without food, food and more food, whether provided by the local women or the host of the event. When huge crowds were expected, a band might play into the small hours of the morning so everyone could enjoy the pleasure of a dance. As the evening wore on, often, there was still more food. Sandwiches and squares left the children full and happy, and coffee kept their parents awake for the journey home.

Not only was there mounds of food at a community picnic, but countless combinations of activities were offered. In the summer of 1884, people came for 25 miles to the South Antler and Winlaw area for a picnic. There were no foot-races or prizes, but picnickers set tables and shared picnic baskets, and by the next year, pony racing and dancing were added to the fun.

Young women, as well as men, played scrub and ball at picnics, and women made the pies for the pie-eating contests that men entered. At large picnics, a wide variety of competitions and races for women became popular. Short distance running races were standard, but races that required care rather than speed were big hits. The spoon race meant making it to the finish line while carrying an egg on a spoon in one's teeth. Some hopped to the finish line in sacks, and some entered three-legged races. Co-ed team races requiring participants to place a large ball against their necks and holding it in place while passing it without the use of hands to the next team member who was of the opposite sex was particularly fun for men and women interested in romance. Women of all ages entered nail-pounding contests and tug-of-war, but when dresses were long, wheel barrow races were not for women.

Party Time

Some events were tied to seasonal and religious celebrations, but in many communities gatherings were planned for once a month or even for every weekend. Because so many of the settlers were young adults who had energy and mobility or young adults with families who needed other adult company, most house parties featured their shared interests. Card parties with potluck suppers were common, especially in winter when indoor activity was key. Playing cards was an entertainment for people of all ages. Crib boards were easy to make and easy to carry, so that die-hards could be prepared for a game any time, any place. Donkey and old maid were easy enough for children. Men liked poker. A favorite game for those of German descent was euchre, but whist, hearts, 500 and canasta were widely popular with men and women – or at least those who played cards. In communities with large numbers of Baptists or Methodists, card playing was frowned upon and some even considered it a serious evil.

At Pheasant Forks, Saskatchewan, strict Methodists were never in on the dancing or card playing, but they had good times. Occasionally, they held box socials, for which women filled boxes with fine lunches and men bid. For young people, a romance might be at stake, but for others, it was a fund raiser, since good food and conversation were always in demand.

About once a month or every six weeks in the winter, the Methodist neighbors planned surprise parties. Since the host family didn't know about the party, there was no extra work for the lady of the house, but guests would come from as far as 15 miles away. The party-goers took the lunch. On cold winter evenings, the journey home could result in frosted toes or fingers, so if the temperature dipped too drastically, party-goers from far off sometimes stayed the night.

In most prairie communities, dances were the social highlight of the week or month. There were barn dances, dances at community halls, dances in church basements, at people's homes, and when there wasn't an overhead structure to protect dancers from the elements, a quickly built dance platform or hard-packed ground proved good enough. Enthusiasts saw few reasons to forego a dance.

Prairie women weren't slouches when it came to "cutting a rug." Whether dressed in the long, swishing dresses of the turn of the century or the popular styles of the 1920s, whether the music meant a square dance, a waltz, a tango or a two-step, dancing brightened the lives of thousands of women. Music was provided by the fiddler in almost every community; even if other musical instruments were not available, someone could always fiddle up a tune for dancing.

In the early 1900s at Yorkton, Sask., these three women had fun dressing in costumes for a fancy dress party. Glenbow-Alberta Institute, NA 2878-61

Mrs. Kennedy's Story

The wife of buffalo and fur trader Alex R. Kennedy was comfortable with life in her homeland in 1874. Unlike many such women, she was willing to travel with her husband when he returned to Winnipeg with furs and tanned buffalo hides, despite the fact that the journey lasted 54 days. Mrs. Kennedy took the adventures for granted and warmly remembered special occasions and parties.

[In 1875] we returned to Winnipeg. In crossing rivers we would take four cart wheels and cover them with buffalo hides making a kind of raft, and with these we would cross with babies and fur. We stayed in Winnipeg all winter and then came out to Fort Saskatchewan (Victoria east of Edmonton) in 1876....

The traders would bring in prints, tea, sugar, ammunition, ribbons, and beads. We have made our home here since 1878. We had a log store....the first store in the district....We were more contented and better satisfied, I think, in those days than we are now. There was plenty of game and wild fowl, chicken, deer and buffalo.

When we left Battleford in 1874, we left two or three carcasses of buffalo for the Indians. The last time we had buffalo meat was in 1881....People were more religious in those days than they are now. It did not matter how far the church was people would go to it. In those days Indians would go to church on Sunday. People were more sociable then. There was more kindly feeling, and everybody knew everybody else there in the country. Some of the luxuries of those days were buffalo tongue, buffalo bosses and beaver tails, and sometimes we would have a big plum pudding or boiled rice with raisins in it.

If you went to give a party you would send the boys out on horseback around to everybody and ask them out. If it was in the winter people would come in sleighs drawn by Hudson Bay dogs or in all kinds of rigs. There would be a fiddler. People would begin to come along by sundown. The table was set with roasted duck and so on and eating and drinking would be going on all the time. There would be tea to drink, very seldom anything else but tea. Shortly after sundown the fiddler would start and dancing would begin. All enjoyed themselves in smoking, talking, eating and having a dance. There would be a pack of cards. This would be kept up until morning. If it was a wedding we would keep it up for three days. We would keep on dancing. We started the dance on Wednesday, on Thursday they would get married and keep it up till Saturday. We were all the same, rich and poor together. All had the same friendly feeling in those days.[2]

Holiday Festivities and Feasts

Special holidays meant good times for the entire family. The fall harvest was celebrated at fall fairs and Thanksgiving, but even more important festive occasions were all the other traditional, religious holidays.

The holidays, their dates and the traditional activities associated with them varied with the homeland and cultural background of families. The exact dates for Christmas festivities varied for Eastern Orthodox and other Christians; but for most of the population, there were Christmas and Easter celebrations. Jews observed Passover, Hanukkah and other dates of religious significance. The Chinese celebrated New Year's on a different day than most other western Canadians.

Special church services, gatherings and sometimes concerts were part of the religious observances, but the good food and special, traditional dishes were highlights of the day. Food was in the realm of women's work and women's culture. Cooking for such occasions was a great deal of work, but to many, the role was a form of participation in the religious and family life that was treasured. Even the baking of bread became more than part of physical well-being. For important religious observations, bread – whether leavened or unleavened, a plain loaf or a braided one – was essential as a symbol.

As was the case with other immigrant cultures, Ukrainian women handed down the recipes and methods of preparing and decorating the special foods from one generation of women to the next, and bread was just one such food. Braided Easter breads were of particular importance, as were the beautifully decorated Easter eggs. Their range of festive foods was extensive, and at Christmas, a tradition of 12 meatless and milkless foods usually included such dishes as *kutia, borsch, pyrohies,* cabbage rolls, fish, torte, stewed fruit.

Although some of the foods were unique to their culture, the work of Ukrainian women to prepare festive foods was not significantly different from that of women from other cultural backgrounds. English and American traditional festive foods for Christmas included turkey, but goose, chicken, fish or wild meat became options. Perhaps dessert was a suet or plum pudding and shortbread. Even those women who had very little money somehow found ways to prepare the family's favorite festive foods.

Often, additional family and friends were expected as visitors, so traditional celebrations meant extra cleaning to do and bedding to wash. Many men made trips for purchases, and they were the ones to arrange outdoor entertainment, cleaning ice for skating or getting a wagon ready for a hay ride. For most women, the fact that traditional holidays meant significantly more work did not negate the value of them nor women's ability to enjoy them. Women looked forward to seeing the extended family, and knowing how much their families would look forward to the festive foods, good cooks enjoyed doing much of the extra baking and cooking.

Those who were well-off had more extravagant celebrations with more guests, and they gave more gifts and more expensive gifts. Those not so well-off spent many a night planning and making home-made gifts, but the task brought a unique kind of pleasure. Sometimes, gift-making spread over months while a woman knitted or sewed something special. Adding to the joy of many other celebrations were the cards and letters to and from loved ones. Some families made their own greeting cards; they wrote long letters, usually focusing on the happier parts of their lives; they were thrilled when the mail brought word from their extended families and friends. Often, the treasured lines of a letter were read and re-

The traditional importance of women in creating a festive and joyful Christmas is conveyed through this image from the Medicine Hat News, December 20, 1894. Glenbow-Alberta Institute, NA 1754-11

read on other days throughout the year, and gifts added joy to the occasions, whether the gifts were useful, decorative or food for the mind and soul.

Monica's Story

Monica Maggs Hopkins and her husband Francis "Billie" Hopkins ranched near Priddis, Alberta. Her letters to family in England told of the ups and downs of prairie life, but they also told what was enjoyable and important to her in Christmas and New Year's festivities.

Enmore, Priddis, Alberta, Jan 4, 1910,

Dearest Gill

The happiest of New Years and all the best to both of you. We loved the parcel of books that arrived just the mail before Christmas. We didn't open them until Christmas morning; books are a real joy to get here and your selection, was delightful, suited all our tastes. Joe retires into *Robbery under Arms* every evening now, and there is never a peep out of him. It will take him weeks to read for he is a slow reader; fortunately Billie read it first or he would have been annoyed at having to wait so long. I haven't read it, just glanced through it but I don't think it is much my style, I prefer the less "bluggy" ones. Thank you so much for them, You certainly need not have apologized for sending books in place of some things more useful. We would rather have books than anything, so send along as many as you like, and as often as you wish.

We had a very nice Christmas Day, though I was disappointed at getting no home parcels or letters. We had quite a lot of English parcels from friends but they were not quite the same; still they made our breakfast table look very festive. Joe had never seen parcels on a breakfast table before. I rather doubt if he has had many presents before and he was quite thrilled at those we gave him and very distressed that he had none for us but he has not been to Calgary since he was in to meet us. Billie, the young spendthrift, had all sorts of things for me and made my pipe, slippers and book for him look very humble.

I had a tremendous spread, had been cooking for days, and the old hens came up to scratch. I take back all the nasty things I said about them in my last letter. After a huge dinner we went skating on the creek. Joe, as most Canadians, is a really good skater, I can manage to keep going fairly, but Billie is a perfect menace on skates; he wobbles in every direction, his arms going around like windmills. He goes where his skates take him, clutches at all and sundry, and finally sits down

Creeks, rivers, sloughs, lakes and freezing weather meant ample opportunities for skating and skating parties. This foursome glides across the glimmering ice of a slough near Fort Macleod, Alberta. Glenbow-Alberta Institute, NA 1128-1

with the most awful whack, is up again and off in another direction. I keep clear of him for a very little thing up ends me. We had a jolly time and returned home ravenous to eat huge quantities of cold turkey, pudding, mince pies and trifle, and after washing up we sat down to eat fruit, nuts, and chocolates, and to read your books. It was a happy thought on your part to send them. Thank you again.

On Boxing Day, Joe drove to Priddis and, oh joy! returned with my missing parcels and parcels for Billie from Ireland. Just as we had unpacked everything and the room was knee deep in paper all the Mortons arrived. Such a mess, but I bundled the paper away and left them to look at our gifts while I got them a meal. As it was a cold day I gave them hot soup as a starter and then cold scraps of everything that was left over. They only stayed about three hours as they had a long drive and the nights are very cold. It's down below zero nearly every night now. My parcels from home were lovely. Mother and Father still think that we are more or less on the verge of starvation, that we can only get the absolute essentials out here in the way of wearing and household goods and I have no intention of disillusioning them at present....

Yesterday Billie and I went fishing. We walked up the creek to where there is a deep pool and Billie chopped a hole through the ice — it must have been a foot thick. We dropped our hooks baited with raw beef down the hole and almost at once we were hauling up some lovely large mountain trout. If the fish are going to bite they will do so right away; if they don't bite you might as well go home and get warm. We caught eight nice ones and they are a welcome change, not that there is

About 1890, with the help of an ice boat, wind and sail, this couple enjoyed ice fishing on Devil's Lake, later renamed Lake Minnewanka, in Alberta. Whyte Museum of the Canadian Rockies, NA 66-1635

any monotony in our menu now. We have hanging in the storehouse a side of beef and one of pork, a number of partridge and prairie chicken, and about a dozen roosters....[3]

Unique and Special

Many festive days weren't on the annual calendar. The West, like other places in the world, had its unique special occasions, and early ones were celebrations for both indigenous people and newcomers. For indigenous women, there were pow-wows, Sun Dances and Thirst Dances. Treaty signings were celebrated events, but with missionaries and settlers came new reasons and traditions of revelry. Some were tied to important religious dates; others were simply traditional gatherings. Whenever royalty, prime ministers and governor generals visited, festivities were planned. On a national level, the redrawing of territorial boundaries and the resulting new political status for the western provinces lead to impressive celebrations, especially in the capital cities. In later years, politicians and their backers celebrated winning elections, and women celebrated the granting of the female franchise as special times to remember. But none of that would have happened – or would have happened in the same way – without provincial status for Alberta and Saskatchewan.

Achieving provincial status was one of the most highly celebrated events to follow the signing of the treaties. Women planned events of their own. They decorated venues and joined in the larger celebration. They played a less noticeable, formal role than men when it came to speech-making, but it was a heady time. Parades

For the royal visit to western Canada in September 1901, everyone dressed in their best. The ceremonial clothing of this Blackfoot group is evidence of the fine, decorative handicrafts of the women. Glenbow-Alberta Institute, NA 539-2

were staged, with decorated carriages carrying dignitaries. There were balls and dancing, and someone had to entertain the prime minister, his wife and entourage.

Wife of a Lieutenant Governor

A small number of women were in social positions where they influenced and participated in the most lavish social life and entertainment the prairies had to offer. Henrietta Drolet Forget moved to Battleford (Saskatchewan) in about 1877. By 1898, her husband A. E. Forget was appointed lieutenant governor of the western territories, which continued until 1905, when the provinces of Saskatchewan and Alberta were created and the boundaries of Manitoba were redrawn. Mr. Forget became lieutenant governor of Saskatchewan, with Madam Forget now official hostess for the new province.

Well-educated and socially at ease, she entertained lavishly. She had staff to help with the work at Government House, but her relationships with them were sometimes warm and informal. She was an active and honored member of numerous women's clubs. However, the most significant festivities that required her involvement were the ones for the 1905 celebration.

With similar celebrations happening in Edmonton, many prairie women worked hard to make the festivities a success. In advance of the momentous occasion, people built archways over streets and hung the arches with banners. Storekeepers decorated their store fronts and flew flags. Inside buildings, bunting and streamers added festive touches.

The Province of Saskatchewan was officially recognized on 4 September 1905, but celebrations lasted for days. Special excursion trains stopped in Regina and Edmonton where streets were soon crowded. Prime Minister Laurier and Lady Laurier arrived in Regina, and there the carriages of the Lauriers and Forgets became a viceregal cavalcade to the official ceremonies and the swearing in of A. E. Forget.

Privileged ladies within the community enjoyed a luncheon at Government House. For others, there were parades, including a children's parade and one by church members. Bands played and marched. At the exhibition grounds, Mounties performed a musical ride to an appreciative audience, followed by other sporting events. At the athletic grounds, spectators watched a lacrosse match between Regina and Brandon. There was something for everyone. With five to ten thousand people watching, a breathtaking display of fireworks concluded one of the evenings, but for some of the women, the highlight of the celebrations was the Inaugural Ball, which lasted until 2:00 a.m.

For Saskatchewan and Alberta, one of the largest and most extravagant celebrations of the early nineteenth century was in 1905, when the territories achieved provincial status. As part of the celebration, these school children and women joined a parade of about 2000 people who marched along McDougall Hill in Edmonton, Alberta.
Glenbow-Alberta Institute, NA 1711-1

The Leader, Regina, 6 September 1905

No more fitting climax to the celebration could have been arranged for than the grand inaugural ball at the Auditorium rink in the evening. At the moment the Ball was opened by Their Excellencies the scene was brilliant and long to be remembered. The rink itself had been converted into an extremely handsome hall, a score of arc lamps and hundreds of incandescent lamps made the building bright as noon-day, while at either end electric mottos added to the brilliancy of the scene. Over the entrance burned the words "God Save the King," while at the opposite end in the supper room flashed "Confederation" in a half circle, and below it "Alberta and Saskatchewan." Hundreds of yards of bunting took away all appearance of barrenness in the huge structure, and the curved arches supporting the roof, hidden as they were by sheaves of wheat and evergreen bedecked with miniature flags, presented an attractive appearance....

The dance in progress was beautiful beyond description. The many beautiful dresses worn by the ladies, the brilliant scarlet of the R.N.W.M.P. uniforms, the sombre hues of the 90th Regiment uniform, and the dress suits of the gentlemen made a varied and ever changing picture, which was enjoyed as keenly by the spectators as the dance itself was by those participating in it....[4]

Mrs. Strong's Story

Like Regina and Winnipeg, for Edmonton women who were financially stable or even well-off, social life in the area offered a range of pleasant experiences long after the days of the fur-trade and the soirees at the Big House, the chief factor's home. By the end of the first decade of the 1900s, they had celebrated provincial status, but there were many parties to attend.

In her early twenties, Madge Isabel Strong (nee Scott) became a widow with a one-year-old son, so life was not always easy, but she enjoyed her social life in Edmonton.

Most of the new comers came with the intention of living as they had known in the cities where they had lived before and it [Edmonton] was a very gay place.

We had dinner parties, balls, parties of all kinds, bridge and golf was attempted to be played on a level below the Legislative Buildings. Skating was in a large rink called the Thistle which having a removable floor was also used for concerts and dances....Very soon the Pantages theatre was opened where we had vaudeville and good plays....

On special days of the month the women of the city occupied themselves by having 'at homes' and the 'at home' days were marked on our calling cards. It was the proper thing to leave one for the hostess, one or two for the man of the house, this being one for oneself and one from one's husband and one each for the daughters over 18.

Lunches and teas were given by the Women's Canadian Club which Emily Murphy had inaugerated (sic) and was their president for the first two years. Some chapters of the I.O.D.E. were formed and most of us belonged to one or the other. The First Consumer's League was formed but our only worthwhile job was having all bread in the city wrapped. Churches were rapidly being built in the West and work for those was also necessary.

Private balls were very popular the Murphy's giving two and a wonderful time was had although in many cases we walked to the dances and back holding up

This elegant reception celebrated the tour of Governor General and Lady Grey in 1909. The October event was at City Hall in Regina.
Saskatchewan Archives Board, R-B 3159

our gowns and carrying our slippers and fancy bags. Our first outstanding event was the ball given in the Thistle rink for Earl Grey and party when he came to lay the cornerstone for the Legislative Building. A committee decorated the rink on the most elaborate scale and it was beautiful, the tiers on each sides being almost hidden by small evergreens and sitting out places was arranged by teepees and rugs. Emily Murphy introduced the young ladies to the Governor General and her younger daughter Evelyn was one of them whom my brother had taken in his new car.

A few wonderful years passed and then came the war.[5]

Plain Food and Favors

When the Depression hit, times were dramatically worse for everyone in the West. Just the same, not all good times ended. In the thirties as in the earliest days of settlement, good times once again centred around what people could do with little or no money and little or no transportation. Ball games, card games and community picnics fit the bill. Many groups had hard-time dances – they were either used to raise money for the poor, or they cost next to nothing or accepted a food donation as an entrance fee.

Newspapers recorded the hard lot of most in the West. Surprisingly, they also gave another side to the story. In some cases, life went on with small rather than large adjustments. Women still wanted new recipes, and female food columnists provided them. Crafters wanted new patterns for knitting, crocheting and other projects. Newspapers provided some free of charge. Some women wanted entertainment ideas for surprise parties, card parties, Valentine's Day and Christmas.

During the 1930s, Kathleen Esch, B.Sc., wrote food articles for the *Edmonton Journal*, and her articles for each date tell what was possible or trendy at the time. March 3, 1936, recipes included: Short Rich Pastry, Chocolate Pie, Prune Whip Pie, Cheese Souffle, Bannan and Pimiento Salad, Butter Cookies, Macaroni Souffle, Stuffed Tomato Salad, Griddle Cakes, Apple Dumpling *à La Anglaise*, Yorkshire Pudding. For Christmas, Dinner Number 1 cost $2.50 to serve six. The two options for Dinner Number 2 cost $5 to serve six. The first had oyster cocktail for an appetizer and roast beef and potatoes as main course; the second option featured roasted chicken and suggested Bavarian cream and nuts for dessert. The very elegant and gourmet Dinner Number 3 cost $10 to serve eight.

December 13, 1935 Merry Christmas Dinner To Fit the Pocket Book. You cannot dodge the fact that keeping cheerful is as much a part of your job as cooking. Women who possess this nobleness of spirit (and there are legions of them) have been known to make the leanest of Christmases into a jolly holiday....

Christmas Dinner No 1

Frosted Apple Cider, Veal Birds Noel, Rich Brown Gravy, Glazed Sweet Potatoes, Small Buttered Onions, Pickle Relish, Cranberry-Apple Sauce, Waldorf Salad (celery, apple, walnut), Mince Pie, Coffee. [Note: Veal Birds appear to be thin slices of veal stuffed with dressing]

March 10, 1936 A St. Patrick's Bridge Party....Cover your bridge tables with covers of green and white checked gingham. Playing cards with shamrocks, Irish hats or pipes on the back are easily obtainable....Here are charming favors for both men and women. They are easy to make....Start with a paper drinking cup....

Here are several tricks which will make the party truly a "Blarney Bridge." Tell everyone that they are to stop as soon as the first hand is bid. Then have each player change hands with the player to his left....Later there is another pause, when the hostess announces that for the next four hands the object will be to avoid taking tricks....A very appropriate prize would be a nice piece of green glassware.[6]

Welcome to the Community

As late as the 1930s, the community life of every day and festive days was surprisingly similar in rural and isolated communities for those who were very early settlers in the West, for latter-day homesteaders and for second generation farm people. Simple pleasures that could be created with little money, little time, few facilities but a great deal of individual or community enthusiasm were considered tried and true recipes, whatever the decade. High Prairie, Alberta, was an area to see much of its settlement following the first decade of the twentieth century. There the life lived by Sophie Smith and her family was very similar in its joys and pleasures to those of other families decades earlier and also more than a decade later in other areas of the West.

Smith Family Story

Sophie Smith and her family moved from Canton, South Dakota, to the Canadian west in 1911, part of the second large immigration wave that settled the prairie provinces. The first year the family lived in Red Deer. Unfortunately, the following year, Sophie's husband died. Looking for a better life, she, her 33-year-old son Henry and her younger daughters set out for Alberta's north. Years later, daughter Edith Van Kleek (nee Smith) wrote about the experience and about life on the homestead in *Our Trail North*. When they set out the four girls ranged in age from 8 to 15, with 11-year-old Edith as the second youngest.

The journey seemed a horrendous ordeal. By the time they reached High Prairie, the heavy piano that they so valued had been damaged. "The beautiful tone sounded flat. It was never the same again....Maybe they dropped it in the lake at Grouard as they did one piano we heard about. Maybe the piano that broke the ramp was ours!" Nevertheless, often, around the evening campfire, they sang, and Sophie who "was a good alto singer...joined us if the song was one of her favorite hymns. The sound of our voices floated out into the night."[7]

In her book, Edith gives glimpses of her own life, the lives of her mother and older sisters, and the life of the community. Edith never denies how hard her mother worked or the challenges that the family faced. However, she does reveal that good times were part of their lives from soon after their arrival in the district.

The Fall Fair: About 6 weeks after we moved to the homestead the Agricultural Society put on a picnic and Fall Fair, at the school. We could hardly wait for the day to arrive, we were so anxious to attend After elaborate preparations of grooming and selecting clothes to wear we started out....

We spend a wonderful day at the fair getting acquainted with homesteaders who understood what we were going through to get established. In the school house, exhibits were arranged on homemade tables around the outside wall; grain, vegetables, baking and sewing. Sheafs of grain and samples in saucers too, showed what the country could produce. There were large smooth potatoes....

The vegetables were beautiful and the baking was mouth watering. The sewing was simple garments a homesteader would use, and there were darning and patching exhibits. There were hand knitted socks and crocheting and tatting which added beauty to the tables.

There was a booth at the fair where they sold oranges, lemonade and home made candy. The fruit had been ordered from Edmonton and came a long way....

Those in charge of putting on the fair really outdid themselves with elaborate preparation. They had bought or rented a battery run movie projector and were to have a moving picture show! (It must have run on a battery; there was no power.) The show cost 5 cents each to defray the expenses and everybody paid their nickel and went to the show. Few had seen moving pictures. (We used to go every Saturday afternoon in Red Deer.)....

Stella was especially popular. She was sixteen years old, pretty, and jolly....The boys of the community didn't need any pushing to get acquainted with Stella, there were so few girls around that age. We had a houseful of company every Sunday after that.

Music and Reading: The weather all summer and fall was beautiful which helped when there was so much to do. Goodness knows it rained enough all spring! Early in October we moved into the new house, and one happy day Henry arrived from Grouard with our piano, and a load of bachelors to help unload it. Our home was complete again.

What fun we had with music for awhile! We had two big old music books the size of sheet music with over 300 pages each; one was favourite songs and the other instrumental old favourites. There were the hymn books and a pile of sheet music our older sister, Anna, used to play.

Mamma had more time now and she gave us music lessons. The piano was going all the time. Mamma had to set up a strict schedule of hours of practice. We

With its own orchestra, the Babb family lived about seven miles south of Byemoor, Alberta, on Farrel Lake. Retta Babb (right) is playing mandolin, but more commonly, women were pianists in local bands. Glenbow Alberta Institute, NA 2691-16

didn't learn to play all the music we had but we learned to sing every song, picking out the tunes on the piano of the hard to play ones.

We sang a great deal together during the day and Henry would join us with his violin in the evenings. There was no radio or T.V. to demand our attention.

When we weren't playing the piano or singing we were reading. We took the *Edmonton Journal, The Red Deer Advocate, The Winnipeg Free Press*, and the *Family Herald* and *Weekly Star* and we read them all. At first we had only candles for light but when the days began to get shorter, Henry brought some gasoline from Grouard and set up our hollow wire gas lamp, which was a marvel in the community, being the only one.

Henry also bought books in Grouard....[He] bought Buffalo Bill stories in Grouard and Kit Carson and Billy the Kid. Mamma was disgusted. She never read any of them; only the Bible was her reading material. She tried to get us to quit these sinful books and read the Bible but we didn't think the Bible could compare with "Buffalo Bill at the Torture Stake," or hair raising adventure stories.

Henry brought home the *Popular Magazine*. That was more difficult to read, as well as the *Saturday Evening Post*, but we read parts of them anyway and the result was we became marvelous readers.

Summer Work and Play: We used to play Flinch in the evenings and on Sunday afternoons, and Art [neighbor] would play the game with us, because it whiled away the time. Mamma and Henry never did this. Mamma never sat idle. She would mend clothes in the evening and on Sunday she read the Bible....

We liked flinch. The family had played the game for years. Flinch is an old French game played with a deck of 225 cards numbered from 1 to 15....You have to be very alert to play this game successfully, not get 'flinched' and you have to be lucky too, to have the opportunity to play off this flinch pile.

We played so much flinch on the homestead we wore out the cards and made another deck from cardboard.

We didn't have the fascinating dice games children have today. We wouldn't have been allowed to use them if we had had them. "Dice are wicked, and used only by gamblers!" Mamma firmly believed....

The Christmas Program: The second big social event of the community was the Christmas Program at the school. We were asked to contribute to this

Here the Beam family, who homesteaded in the Cochrane, Alberta, area prior to 1900, enjoys a card game. The family had a ranch home and one in town so the children could attend school. Creating decorative touches, such as this lace valance and fancy shade for the hanging lamp, were rewarding pursuits for many homemakers. Bert Sheppard Stockmen's Foundation Library & Archives, SFL 40-01-034

Christmas concert, so Mamma taught Alice and me to sing Juanita in harmony. Alice had a clear sweet soprano voice and I sang alto. Mamma played the organ.

The only music in the community was a couple of violins for fiddling a few dance tunes and one family had a gramophone that had been played so much it was worn out.

When Alice and I sang Juanita we received a standing ovation. One homesteader couldn't keep back the tears he was so moved. He had never heard harmony singing. They wanted an encore, but we had prepared only the one song.

They asked us to sing the same song again, so Mamma went back to the organ and we obliged. You could have heard a pin drop in that crowded room while we sang.[8]

IV. Impressing an Audience

Pleasure came from watching as well as from doing, and the range of public events and performances that became available for people's enjoyment was surprising, even at very early dates. There was something for everyone in the family at fairs, parades, rodeos, circuses and Chautauqua. Most families enjoyed music – whenever, wherever and however it found its way into their lives. Plays, operas, orchestral music, ballets were not for everyone, but for devotees, being part of such performances or sitting in an audience and soaking up the performances were times of pure joy. Arranging such moments was more difficult for rural people. Rural communities offered very small audiences for the talents of friends or family members.

In Calgary, the Penleys had both a dance school and a dance hall. These young women were students of the ballet program in the 1930s. Ailsa McLaughlin (right) later became ballet mistress for the Ice Capades. The outstanding national company, the (Royal) Winnipeg Ballet, had its debut performance in June 1940. Its school had opened two years earlier, and students had performed for the royal visit in 1939.
Glenbow-Alberta Institute, PA 2185-2

However, for town and farm people alike, holding the ticket for a major event or performance meant feeling anticipatory delight.

Town and city women had many more such pleasures available to them, simply because of numbers and proximity. Sometimes, for rural people to attend a concert or fair, they had to plan a journey in which they stayed overnight with friends or family, or they planned to arrive home when dawn was breaking. In the long summer evenings, late journeys were little problem. In winter, not only darkness but freezing temperatures made the journey risky, whether the family travelled by cutter or in a Model A.

As a result, especially in winter, those from the country counted more on the talents of family members and nearby neighbors than on the travelling acts and performers featured in towns. Rural families went together to special events or became good at creating their own fun. Eventually, plays and music reached them in new formats. Radios and gramophones brought joy to those hungry for music, comedy and drama.

For some, the world of entertainment meant more than being present for a local concert or play or listening to one on radio. Like the talented elsewhere in the world, many prairie men and women wanted to perform. They wanted to make others laugh, cry or feel incredulous. They loved weaving spells and they enjoyed seeing the eyes of others light up in awe.

Though the territory was a vast one, men and women with like interests were drawn together, and together, they created new worlds of entertainment and amusement for others around them. Soon, those with talents and avocations had opportunities, and people who needed and wanted the relaxation or inspiration inherent in seeing another perform found it in large and small communities across the prairies.

Music

One of the first entertainments on the agenda of newcomers was music. Some brought their musical talents. A few brought instruments. Others brought only their love of music, but music found its way into pioneer homes and communities in dozens of ways. Settlers who had no musical instruments could always sing, and singing became the music of everyday life during the early settlement years.

Hymns were a mainstay; but folk songs from around the globe brought happiness into prairie homes. Even when there wasn't an organ, piano, fiddle, accordion or other musical instrument for accompaniment, people sang. Whether or not they had good voices or musical talent was not an issue in a sing-along or when singing hymns on Sundays. Also, during the long winter evenings, singing was a way of pleasantly being together as family and as friends. Sing-alongs were part of the traditional festivities of Christmas, but hayrides were not hayrides without singing. Campfires weren't complete without campfire songs. Whether the singers were accompanied by a musical instrument or led by a truly good singer just didn't matter a great deal. Simply singing, simply being present while the songs were sung, was joy enough for some.

But instruments did make the music better, and some settlers were surprisingly inventive in creating musical instruments out of whatever was around them. A few could hand craft flutes and other instruments, or they could pick up spoons or place paper against a comb and put it to their lips. In fact, from the earliest days, voyagers had brought small instruments such as fiddles with them, and they were common throughout the West. Tiny mouth organs, or harmonicas, arrived in travellers' pockets, and they provided music at neighborly get-togethers. Those of European background brought or acquired zithers, dulcimers, mandolins and autoharps, all of which were available by mail order. Still, banjos, fiddles, guitars, harmonicas, pianos and organs were much more common. Men, more often than women, played fiddles and harmonicas. Women often played the organ at church or piano at home. Organs were too expensive for most single families, but the numbers installed in early Winnipeg (from two in 1879 to 46 by 1912) hinted at how important organ music was to the religious life of the community, and as such to women.

Also, music festivals became popular very early. By 1908, Edmonton hosted Alberta's

The Vernons performed in Banff in 1925. Women saxophone players were a rarity, but this woman's costume, flare and musical ability were captivating. Many prairie people travelled to the tourist town, and entertainment there was more worldly and sophisticated than elsewhere. Whyte Museum of the Canadian Rockies, V263, NA 71-4014

first music festival. That year, a group met in Regina to form an association in Saskatchewan, and the next year, the province's first music festival was held. In the first years, most of the contestants were male, but many women enjoyed being in the audiences. Women did compete in mixed choral choirs, and a very few became members of philharmonic societies that competed. Eventually, the festivals became geared towards developing youth talent and offering youth competitions, and women proudly supported their children in those endeavors. However, women were also successful in various roles in competitions, and in 1931, Mrs. H. McKenzie, with her Choral Society from Biggar, Saskatchewan, became one of the conductors to experience success.

What was far more important to both sexes than who was playing the music, what instrument was played or where performances might be heard, was the fact that music was part of women's lives. Sometimes, it found its way into their lives in surprisingly strange circumstances and also in surprisingly wonderful ways.

Eugenie's Mother's Story

At the turn of the19th century, before Alberta was a province, even getting to her new home had challenged Eugenie's mother. In the years that followed, there was endless work; prairie wildfires threatened; sickness struck; money was tight, but these were run-of-the-mill problems for prairie settlers. *Going without* was a common condition. Belongings weren't essential to happiness, but women like Eugenie's mother desperately yearned for things other than family and the beauty of the landscape to nourish her spirit and soul. Music had brought immense pleasure in her youth, but on the homestead, she had only her own voice with which to share the joy in music with her children.

The newly built Anglican church eventually acquired an organ, and Eugenie's mother took her turn playing it on Sundays. Organ hymns nurtured the soul, but they weren't the same as the rhapsodies she had known in her youth, and an organ at the church was no substitute for a piano in her home. To Eugenie's mother, raising her children without Beethoven's sonatas and Gilbert and Sullivan's operas meant raising little barbarians. But the dream of a piano in their living room was not an easy one to fulfill.

Finally, the time came when Eugenie's father arrived home from town with an enormous box in the wagon. While her husband and the hired man carefully unloaded the precious cargo, Eugenie's mother rearranged the furniture. A mahogany giant had entered the family's life, and the pioneer woman's spirit could again be nurtured by complex harmonies, concertos and light opera.

Music surrounded the family on cold winter evenings and drifted beyond their walls on warm nights when the windows were left open. Household tasks seem easier when the player piano brought Beethoven into the room. The children pumped the pedals enthusiastically, and melodies and enchantments hovered in the air of their wilderness home.

To do without music became unthinkable. Then, one day, as her young son pumped the pedals of the player piano and filled the silence with Beethoven favorites, Eugenie's mother turned anxiously from the window. Once again, the smoky pillar signalled a prairie fire. This time, the family knew what it must do if there was to be any hope of saving treasured possessions such as the piano. The children wet gunny sacks in the water trough and dragged the sacks to their mother, while the men battled closer to the inferno. As if the family was entitled to more than one miracle, once again, the fire veered.

Despite their exhaustion that evening, their son pumped the pedals of the player piano. Around the family was the lingering smell of smoke, but also hovering in the air were the strains of *Moonlight Sonata*, reassuring them that they had defeated the fire demon.

The family's player piano brought pleasure to others too. Visiting neighbors sat spellbound by its magic, and they visited more often. One special friend of Eugenie's mother had a musically gifted son, and when they visited, he unlocked the piano keys and treated everyone to his own rendition of popular tunes.

Sharing the joy of music mattered. Once telephones linked the rural families of the community, it became possible to pass the musical enchantments along the thin wires to listeners down the line. Occasionally, to lift her friends' spirits, Eugenie's mother would phone, place the telephone receiver at the piano, and then sit pumping the piano's pedals. At the time, phones were party lines shared by many, and a clicking sound meant a rubberneck was listening in. As the years passed, Eugenie's mother learned that, often, half a dozen lonely and music-starved women sat alone in their kitchens, holding the telephone receivers to their ears, to enjoy the concerts from her treasured player piano. The operas, rhapsodies, sonatas, Beethoven and popular music embedded on the little cylinders were carried to them along the humming telephone lines. The land was no longer silent and the women felt less isolated.[1]

Bands and Dances

Bands were big hits in the West, and most popular of all were the dance bands. People of all ages loved dancing, but those who simply wanted to enjoy the music were welcome at dances, too. A newly erected barn was the place for a barn dance, and the dance was a fine way to say thanks to all the neighbors who had helped to build it. As well, happy couples waltzed and two-stepped on platforms built outdoors and without the protection of a roof. For a small picnic, dancers might even whirl across hard packed ground.

Having a local band was essential if a rural community was to sponsor a dance or newlyweds were to celebrate their nuptials with wedding dances. Religions did prohibit dancing for some people, but to most, wedding and weekend dances were considered the week's big night out. Memories of the music, dance partners and good times were savored all week long.

What they most needed was music! Not surprisingly, small local bands comprised of a few talented individuals with instruments provided the music for dancing in communities throughout the country. The most common instruments were fiddle, banjo, guitar and accordion, but some musicians had saxophones, trumpets and other instruments. Often, at rural schools and community halls, groups raised money to buy a piano, and as often as not, the community's best piano player was a woman.

Single and married women played other instruments and sang in the bands, but especially for the many bands comprised of family members, a mother or a daughter was at the keyboard. Pianos stood in parlors of many a music-loving family, and together, the family spent evenings sharing their love of music. They acquired a variety of instruments. Neighbors living close by brought over their instruments, and soon, the group was known as the local band, always in demand and especially for dances.

Since the dances were for all ages, their music had to have wide appeal, a mix of golden oldies and new songs. The bands played square dances, fox trots, polkas, the

Popular Songs Between 1870 and 1900

Then You'll Remember Me
Out in the Cold
Old Folks at Home
When You and I Were Young Maggie
Danny Boy
The Red River Valley
Daddy Wouldn't Buy Me a Bow-Wow
I Guess I'll Have to Telegraph My Baby
Warrior Bold
Just Because She Made Dem Goo-Goo Eyes
The King's Highway
Cleansing Fires
My Gal Is a High Born Lady
Sweet Marie
The Clang of the Wooden Spoon
Strike Up the Band
The Lost Chord
O Fair Dove, O Fond Dove
After the Ball
Waltzing Matilda

waltzes of the day and *old-fashioned* waltzes, but their repertoire usually included the schottische and whatever musical and dancing fads were popular.

By 1896, there was already an Old Timer's Ball in Edmonton. As well as other favorites, the band played the once-popular reels and jigs, but it also rolled out music for the gallop and cotillion. When it came to music, Edmontonians were broad-minded, and the city welcomed the talents of women musicians.

Popular Songs from 1900 to 1930

Some of These Days
School Days
The Darktown Strutters'
    Ball
It's a Long, Long Way to
    Tipperary
Keep the Home Fires
    Burning
When Your Boy Comes
    Back to You
For the Glory of the
    Grand Old Flag
K-K-Katy
Tumbling Tumble Weed
When My Baby Smiles at
    Me
Shine On Harvest Moon
When It's Spring Time in
    the Rockies
Take Me Out to the Ball
    Game
Snuggled On Your
    Shoulder
The West, a Nest and You
Rose Marie

Ma Trainor's Story

Calgary was as musical as any community in the West, and bands and dancing had always been popular. Although it wasn't common, by the early teens, a female newcomer to Calgary decided she wanted her own band. Musically, she very well trained, and she knew exactly what she wanted to do. By the 1920s, she was making a name for herself. By 1940, her band became widely known and enormously popular.

That name was Ma Trainor, her band The Hillbillies or Calgary Hillbillies, as they were also known. Ma's real name was Josephine. She began her music career very early in life, taking music at the Notre Dame Academy and being good enough to teach music at two post secondary educational campuses that became the University of P.E.I. and St. Francis of Xavier University. Josephine moved to Calgary in 1912 with her family. As soon as she was settled, she determined that it was time to start her own orchestra.

At first, she gave the group her own name, Ma Trainor's Orchestra, but their music appealed to local audiences, and eventually, the name was changed. Although very likeable and friendly, Ma was in the music business, and she was a business woman. During the First World War, her band entertained servicemen stationed or training in the West. By the 1920s, her band had gained popularity, and over the next 20 years, the band travelled throughout southern Alberta. Again, for the Second World War, Ma Trainor and her band played for enthusiastic servicemen. With drummer, guitar player, fiddler, two saxophone players and herself as pianist, The Hillbillies were a hit. Despite the name of the band, Ma Trainor's musical abilities were far-ranging, and for 15 years, the Palliser Hotel in Calgary featured Ma Trainor as orchestra conductor. Yet, her hillbilly band reached a far wider audience, especially when it was invited to perform regularly on CJCA radio, which broadcast the gift of music to those in isolated areas, too.

Opera and Orchestras

Some of those new to the prairie provinces had enjoyed opera as part of their cultural heritage or had enjoyed opera and fine orchestral music in other places they had lived in the world. For those who had moved to small, rural communities, attending an opera or philharmonic concert was virtually out of the question, but in the larger cities, enjoying both did become possible at a surprisingly early date, especially in Winnipeg. There, dedicated opera buffs were thankful for the pioneering work of professionals in the fields.

Edmonton, Alberta, was far enough west and north to be an unlikely centre for opera and orchestral music early in the twentieth century, but the location and small population were not insurmountable obstacles to "Auntie Van."

Auntie Van's Story

Beatrice van Loon's father was a professional musician; the five daughters of the family inherited talents, and were well taught when it came to music. By age 4, Beatrice was beginning to sing in public. By 10, not only was she performing at concerts as a soprano, she was learning harmony and taking violin lessons. With lessons from highly respected musicians, she graduated to orchestral performances, and by 16, she conducted an operetta. For it, she was to direct 100 children and a 50-piece orchestra. It was a formidable task, but the young woman was undaunted. At 17, in Chicago, she won a singing contest against all-male contestants; and soon she led an all-girl orchestra travelling throughout the United States, taking over the role of conductor when the former one became ill. It was this five-piece orchestra that first brought her to Edmonton, where they played for eight weeks at the Macdonald Hotel in 1919.

During that time, Beatrice was conductor, but at times, she played violin and sang, impressing her audiences with arias, ballads and light opera. Fortunately for the city's music buffs, she met James Carmichael, and in November of the following year, the two married. Although she decided not to perform professionally after her marriage, she was in constant demand as a musician, and she became the guiding light behind Edmonton's operatic and orchestral scene. She was instrumental in the performance of *Faust* at the MacDougall United Church by the Women's Musical Club. By 1935, she became one of the founders of the Edmonton Civic Opera Society, and Beatrice was involved in the group's presentation of both grand operas and light operas at the Empire Theatre and other stages. Over almost 30 years, until her death in 1964, she had been involved in more than 50 such productions, but the society had also provided music scholarships and raised money for the war effort.

To Edmontonians, Mrs. Carmichael was a powerhouse when it came to musical culture. But, more than anything, to local people whose talents and interests she had fostered, Beatrice was "Auntie Van," an amazing woman with talents and skills that were truly exceptional, in early Edmonton and on the prairies. Only a small part of her story appeared in the *Edmonton Bulletin,* 2 November 1929.

Talented Musician Didn't Know Where Edmonton Was; But Stayed When She Came

Mrs. J. B. Carmichael is Unofficial Professor of Music at the University

Directing two orchestras, playing first violin in the symphony, teaching vocal and violin lessons and being a charming hostess in her own delightful home on 106 street, are not matters of any real importance in her opinion. If it were suggested that no Edmonton musician is doing more for the musical development of the city and district at the present time than she, she would consider it an exaggeration, if she considered it at all....

She is recognized as one of the finest musicians in the city. With an unusual voice, as well as mastery of the violin, her conducting is on par with that of the city's best men leaders, as demonstrated to thousands who have listened to the University Radio orchestra in the last four years, or have heard the University students' orchestra at various campus affairs.

The war, which played a part in shaping the career of so many thousands, laid a stern hand on Mrs. Carmichael's dreams in 1914, when she was about to set sail for Germany to sing in German operas. For four years she had studied with a famous teacher in Chicago and New York. She had at her command eight roles in German opera. Then, just as she was about to sail, the war broke out....

Every year Mrs. Carmichael motors to the east, and there studies the newest developments in music and the conducting of orchestras.

"Hobbies?" she says laughingly. "I guess music is my hobby. On Fridays I take the University Orchestra for two hours practice. It's wonderful to watch those students develop and gradually gain confidence and technique. Some of them have never played before joining the orchestra. I have about forty of them. Then on Wednesdays I have the radio orchestra composed of finished musicians who put on programs of the finest type of music over CKUA once a month. Monday and Tuesday I teach...And Thursday? Well, Thursday I cook. It's the maid's day out."

This busy woman finds time for golf and bowling and is never too busy to sing or play for benefits. Yearly she puts on a concert for the Victorian Order of Nurses and produces and opera at the University....

Being the only woman member of the Symphony doesn't seem so important after all...when viewed in light of her other achievements.[2]

Radios and Musical Machines

Radios were invented in 1901, and the first Canadian enthusiasts picked up broadcasts from the United States. In western Canada, spring of 1922 brought local radio broadcasting to Winnipeg and Calgary. In Saskatchewan, on 29 July 1922, Regina's CKCK hit the airwaves, and the next year Saskatoon and Moose Jaw also had local stations. Ears in all three provinces were glued to radios for entertainment as well as for news. All stations carried some local talent, and Regina repeatedly featured the Ding Dong Bell Orchestra. By the late 1920s, broadcasts responded to the interests of a wide range of listeners. Women enjoyed following the ups and downs in the life of Ma Perkins and her clan. When the Edmonton Grads were the heroines of the west, many of their games were broadcast. By 1937, the Happy Gang was broadcast on C.B.C. It was the noontime entertainment to thousands across the prairies, offering them family entertainment, comedy and music. As part of the program, eight new songs were scheduled each day, five days a week, but the words that brought casual listeners to attention were: "Knock! Knock! Who's there? It's the Happy Gang! Well, com'on in!" And the good times rolled on, year after year, for 22 years.

Listening to recorded music was a joy for the home bound. For an audience of one or a few, radios and gramophones allowed people to pick and choose their favorite type of music and enjoy it even when they were by themselves. Player pianos were impractical for those on limited incomes, but gramophones and phonographs brought the world of recorded music within the grasp of many. Logically, it was an indoor pursuit, especially in the winter. The precious machines stood in the parlors and were cleaned and attended with great care. Nevertheless, just occasionally, wanting the joy of music outdoors during the summer, owners would take their gramophones outside, letting the music floated through the countryside. A few daring families carried the wonder machines outside in winter in order to have music for skating parties, but to most families, the precious machines were simply too expensive to take such risks.

By 1895, Mrs. H. J. Kenyon, who lived in Pheasant Forks, Saskatchewan, had enjoyed a wide range of such entertainment. The community was mostly Methodist. Neither cards nor dancing were acceptable entertainment, but music and reading were important in the family. The family did bring books of interest on their immigrations from England: a complete set of Dickens' works, Bibles, an eight-volume set of Bible study books. Also making the journey with them from England were hymn books and other music books.

During the winter evenings while Mother & I would be sewing or knitting, Father would read aloud to us. I can remember him reading *Martin Chuzzlewit* and *Pickwick Papers* by Dickens. We would put in many hours this way which would otherwise been lonesome or boring.

I remember too a concert we went to at Pheasant Forks in 1894. There were the usual recitations & songs, but the light of the evening was a gramophone loaned for the occasion by Mr. R. H. Hall. To us it was a marvelous (sic) instrument, with a big horn. The music was not of the sweetest tone, but it was the first we had ever seen or heard, probably one of the first made. It was something of a sensation.

Our local concerts at Lorlie had music on the mouth organ. We had some really good players. A combination of mouth organ and autoharp made very good music too, & met with much applause. We didn't have much to make music with but we certainly made the best use of what we had. It was sweeter than a good deal of what comes over the radio these days....

My father was very much interested in music & singing & we often had folks gather in the home for an evening singing. Father would use a tuning fork to get the right pitch....

Later we had the school organ, he trained a group in the singing of a simple Cantata called "Teddy's Button," which was given to the public in the school house. It was really quite an event in 1900.

After my marriage in 1902 we bought an organ. My husband was an expert player on the mouth organ. My brother [had] bought me an autoharp soon after I came to Canada....

My husband's father, Samuel Kenyon, brought an old fashioned music box out with him from England in 1882. This was quite a source of entertainment in the home...[3]

Vaudeville programs such as this one in Winnipeg proved successful because they offered a range of entertainment forms, including humorous skits and popular songs of the day. Glenbow-Alberta Institute, NA 2365-32

Adding Drama to Life

Just as it does today, early drama took a number of forms. Travelling shows stopped at larger communities in the prairie provinces. Skits or short plays, short ballets or dance routines, and comedy acts could all be part of one evening's entertainment. For vaudeville acts, costumes of the entertainers ranged from simple to very elaborate. In the days when men dramatically outnumbered women, performances relied more on bawdy humor; smoke swirled in the air during intermissions; and drinks often followed – sometimes with the entertainers themselves, sometimes with shady ladies who thought the men might be enticed to spend even more money on the night's entertainment.

By the late 1800s, the interests and preferences of ordinary women who had settled in the West were increasingly important to the businessmen who booked acts for the theatres. A home-grown variety of performance had taken root as well. Mounties, soldiers and railway builders acted in plays, and since there were few women to fill the bill, men played the roles of women in the early productions. With the increasing organization of music and drama enthusiasts, men assumed executive or administrative positions, whether on a volunteer or paid basis, and women helped, sewing costumes, getting props or doing whatever else needed doing.

But talent knew no sex, and the interest in watching talented performers was equally unbiased. Especially in rural areas, dramas featuring both men and women were staged at schools, town halls and community halls. Enthusiasts in large communities such as Winnipeg found funds to build beautiful buildings in which to stage performances. For entertainers, the new buildings provided convenience and appropriate staging options. For theatre goers, they offered comfort and luxury.

At one point, Winnipegers could choose from amongst 14 theatres with vaudeville or serious dramatic performances. The Bijou, Orpheus and Pantages enticed entertainment seekers. By the early 1900s, one of the most elegant and popular of the theatres was the Walker Theatre.

The Story of the Matinee Girl

Harriet Walker (nee Anderson) moved with her husband to Winnipeg in 1897. In his work, he booked touring circuits for performing companies from the United States, and Winnipeg looked like a good market. One of the most successful early actresses to perform in Winnipeg had been Fanny Reeves, and in 1879 and 1880, she had impressed local audiences. At the time, theatre work was not considered an ideal occupation for women, but Fanny projected the image her local audience had wanted. She was sweet, demure, beautiful, forgiving, and she had a fine voice and a warm laugh. However, the physical location of the stage where she performed was still a bit too shabby and smelly for many local women. Nevertheless, most citizens believed women's attendance was a civilizing factor for unruly male patrons.

By the turn of the century, Mrs. Walker was instrumental in bringing women into the theatre. She did so under her own name and under the guise of Rosa Sub, the Matinee Girl.

Matinees were scheduled by most theatres as inexpensive opportunities to see the latest productions, and women and children most frequently filled the audience. Rosa went with her boyfriends, and then she wrote her reviews in letters to the *Town Topics*. The paper had a circulation of 10 000, most of them women. To early readers, Rosa was a giddy youthful personality, but exactly who wrote the letters was a mystery, and some even speculated it was a boy, not a girl; but as timed passed, the personality of Rosa matured. The reviews began to sound more and more like a woman

The Old Maid's Convention was staged in about 1905 in Regina. Its political overtones outshone the theme related to spinsterhood and marital bliss implied in the title. Saskatchwan Archives Board, R-B 1257

who knew theatre from her own experience and knew in theory what the best in the atre achieved. The reviews might begin as fluff, but they became informed, critical comment on what was good or weak in the performances.

Eventually, regular readers of the Matinee Girl realized that Rosa was Harriet, a woman who had gathered her background in theatre, first during her American childhood when she played the roles of children, later as part of a comic opera troupe and still later when she toured with her own company.

The mystery of Rosa's identity had been solved. The writer was a respected journalist who was a member of the Canadian Women's Press Club and also the publicity manager for the Walker Theatre. In 1907, the Walkers had opened the famed theatre that carried their name. The fine gowns of women and formal attire of the men attending, the vaulted ceilings, gilt-trim, chandeliers and plush seats brought elegance and comfort to theatre-goers. The first performance, *Madam Butterfly*, was a lavish production and a memorable one. However, in the years to follow, women also attended performances at the Walker Theatre for an evening of laughter, awe and suspense. They were entertained by Harry Houdini, the Marx Brothers, Charlie Chaplin, Sophie Tucker and countless performers who imaginatively transported them beyond their day-to-day lives and into other worlds.

Another kind of respect for Harriet grew out of her leadership in the drama community. As stage director for the Winnipeg amateur Operatic Society, she supported talented women performers in finding the audiences their talents deserved, but she also helped local women get appointed to leadership and administrative positions in the drama-related societies of the city. By 1921, equality in opportunity for women was increasingly becoming a part of the dramatic arts in Winnipeg.

There were other ways Harriet supported women in the community, too. The Women's Parliament of 1914, in which Nellie McClung played the role of provincial premier, was staged at the Walker. And Harriet and her daughter became two of the performers in a play which helped to caused such a stir that it played a role in garnering the vote for Manitoba women.

The Most Successful Travelling Show on the Prairies

In large and small communities, to men, women and children alike, Chautauqua meant days of enlightenment and magic. From beginning to end, the circuit tour of Chautauqua was a fascinating week for everyone in the hosting community. For children, even watching the tent boys set up the big tent was fun, and some earned their tickets by helping out. More fun for them was the children's parade, where they dressed in whatever costumes their parents could devise. The children proceeded down the street warming the hearts of their mothers and grandmothers and everyone in town. Not only was there the fun of participating in or watching the parade, children who won in a particular category won a free ticket into events at the big tent. The younger and less experienced women of the Chautauqua troupe also organized games for the children, but their contagious enthusiasm meant they

In 1922, the Chautauqua brought family entertainment and lectures to Manitou Lake, Saskatchewan. Personnel for the Canadian circuit included young men and women from both the United States and western Canada, and they enjoyed a summer of good times together. Saskatchewan Archives Board, R-A 4657

had soon involved even the adults in such children's games and sing-songs as "Farmer in the Dell" or "Oranges and Lemons" or bean-bag relays.

But the *talent* of entertainers was the big draw. Performers included musicians who could play the 75 handbells and other easily transported musical instruments such as violins, accordions and flutes. Music ranged from hymns and the popular songs of the day to classical pieces by Mozart and Beethoven, yet many of the performers were multi-talented, playing music for one part of the program and acting in a play for another.

Fairs and agricultural exhibitions were fun events for the whole family. By evening, romantic couples gravitated towards the Ferris wheels, such as this one at the Brandon Fair in 1916. A man might win his sweetheart or wife a prize, buy her a candy floss or even a walking cane with a Kewpie doll attached. Provincial Archives of Manitoba, Jessop 118, N3159

The dramas, with their fine costumes and performances, were always a hit. Although most communities included local people who would put on plays and concerts, the professional productions drew huge crowds. For rural people, Chautauqua was a reason for the entire family to come to town for a day or two. Even the featured lecturer was well-received and the lecturer made people feel in touch with what was happening in the larger Canadian and North American community. One such lecturer, Miss Agnes Laut, a Canadian writer who had moved to the United States, presented enlightening facts and figures on topics such as "Canada at the Crossroads."

With the growing success and reputation for providing a wholesome, inspirational and educational good time for the entire family, Chautauqua became the highlight of the year for people in need of relief from daily challenges, chores and troubles. Evening sessions were 75¢ to $1, and nights featured such acts as a Broadway comedy, a "gala entertainment," Royal Serenaders, a lecture entitled "The

Inexcusable Lie," Half an Hour of Familiar Melodies, the King of Jesters, *Pollyanna* and the grand closing concert. Afternoon admissions cost 25 to 50¢ and could include featured musicals, popular entertainers, a lecture on India, the play *Jack in the Beanstalk,* music from Old Mexico and a lecture on Galilee.

However, the Depression brought the end of Chautauqua. Not enough people had extra money to spend on tickets, and local guarantors were too financially pressed to sign contracts. According to Sheilagh Jameson in *Chautauqua in Canada,* despite dust clouds swirling around him and a poor crop the year before, one local farmer in Saskatchewan did sign as a guarantor because "It's not the men who need Chautauqua so much. We go to town and see each other more often. It's the women who stay at home all the time."[4]

Still, in the 1930s the last Canadian Chautauqua performance closed. The financial crunch of those years was part of the problem, but more positive developments also lead to its demise. There were improved roads for everyone, and isolation diminished for rural people. A lucky few even had cars, though many of them were transformed into Bennett buggies. Radios had appeared in homes, and without the price of a ticket, they brought the world to everyone. In towns, movie theatres drew audiences that had once looked forward to the arrival of Chautauqua. The silver screen offered comedies and entertainment as ready escapes from difficult circumstances, an escape many preferred to the morality lectures of the earlier time.

Wowing the Crowds

Fairs, exhibitions, rodeos, stampedes, circuses, horse shows and horse races were summer highlights no one wanted to miss. Who wouldn't love them? Women, men and children watched the entertainment and competitions with enthusiasm, but often, attending meant a chance to win a prize, to go on thrilling rides or even an opportunity to have a photograph taken. It could be a family outing or a chance to meet friends, but almost always people thought it was worth the price of the ticket.

Eventually, each community would refine the type of summer show it was best at, and many of them staged fine parades through main street as part of the events. Women decorated floats and waved from them. They marched and rode horses along the parade routes, and many, many more women who enjoyed the costumes and decorations waved back to those on parade.

Although all communities depended on horses in the early days, horse culture would remain important to some long after motorized vehicles provided transportation. For them, rodeos, stampedes or a wild west show attracted crowds. Other communities had the most success with fairs or exhibitions, and horse races or other

Barnstorming and aviation shows were almost always a hit, but few involved women. This comic aviation act, performed at the Calgary exhibition in 1920, brought Hollywood performers to cowtown. Viola Dana delighted the audience with her antics as a frazzled female. Glenbow-Alberta Institute, NA 1258-23

popular amusements were staged in conjunction with a variety of agricultural, baking and craft-related contests. The displays made women marvel at the talents of other women and gave them ideas for craft projects to complete and enter the next year. Circuses also travelled circuits in western Canada, and the various performances brought magic of one form or another into women's lives.

The range of women performers at the special events was truly amazing, and the talented and daring entertainers and competitors inspired generations of women who followed them. At aviation shows, male flyers entertained women with their barnstorming and, for a fee, offered short flights. Women flyers also performed. Texan Kathleen Stinson was the most renowned, but she later returned to teach flying for the military during the First World War. Still, more often, crowds were cheering for impressive women riders and rodeo performers.

Cowgirl Stories

They could ride 'em and rope 'em as good as any cowboy on the prairie. The female ropers and riders who awed western Canadian audiences came from both the United States and Canada. Most grew up on ranches where they became skilled in handling horses, livestock and roping, learning from fathers, brothers and even mothers. Some received their early performing experience in one of a number of wild west shows that travelled the country, including stops on the Canadian prairies. But the most noted Canadian performances were at the first Calgary Stampede in 1912 and the Winnipeg Stampede of 1913. For years, Calgary had staged an exhibition and horse show, but American Guy Weadick recognized that the community was right for an annual large-scale rodeo, and, an excellent promoter, he got the show off the ground. Competitors for most events were male, and the hundreds of women in the audience saw thrilling performances by them, but the two stampedes also showcased some women competitors, and they were crowd pleasers!

For the cowgirls, it was about both sport and showmanship. Both Canadian and American women were successful riders and ropers in competition. For the first Calgary Stampede in 1912, Flores LaDue – cowgirl, vaudeville and wild west show performer, and wife of stampede organizer Guy Weadick – impressed her audiences as a world champion lady fancy roper. Although also an enormously talented fancy roper, losing to her in the roping was American Lucille Mulhall, who had been billed as champion lady rider in her father's wild west show. A fine trick rider, she was an unbelievable all round cowgirl, and she entered the cowboy steer roping contest. Not surprisingly, she received almost a full minute of applause by roping a steer, throwing it and tying it – just as any male steer wrestler would, but by then she was an old hand at the event. In a 1904 competition in the United States, she had once roped, thrown and tied three steers in just over two minutes.

For the 1912 Calgary Stampede and the 1913 Winnipeg Stampede, American Lucille Mulhall (top and bottom) and Alberta's Tillie Baldwin gave impressive performances to thrill local audiences. Balanced with one foot on each of her horses for the Roman Standing Race, Tillie is in the lead against her two male competitors. Provincial Archives of Manitoba, August, Winnipeg Stampede 1913 6

At the Calgary Stampede, American Miss Carver and her diving horse impressed western women – even those who were expert riders. The performance meant diving into 3 metres (10 ft.) of water from a platform 15 metres (50 ft.) above the tank. Today, the act would be deemed too dangerous for both horse and rider. Glenbow-Alberta Institute, NB 16-417

Dolly Mullins and Arlene Palmer thrilled spectators with their trick riding. They stood on their saddles, performed acrobatics on their mounts, and, performing as a Cossack rider, Palmer did some of her acrobatics at a good gallop. The cowgirls' relay race showed how fast women were willing to ride. Given two horses for the two mile race, each contestant was required to change horses every half mile, revealing how quickly they could saddle and unsaddle their horses. Bertha Blanchett came out the winner, completing the relay in five minutes six and one half seconds. Competing in Winnipeg in 1913, Fanny Sperry became world champion lady bucking horse rider, but other women also became well-known performers and competitors.

Stastia's Story

Stastia Carry had many striking outfits including fancy beaded costumes, cowgirl clothes and gypsy outfits. Performing in vaudeville, rodeos and circuses, her impressive feats of riding could awe even the best cowboys in an audience. In the 1920s, she and her husband toured with their circus, and to them, well-trained and beautiful horses were fairly commonplace. Elephants were a little more exotic, but Stastia was a competent elephant handler.

Her ties with the Canadian prairies became formalized when

Some cowgirls would not receive acclaim, but their riding was noteworthy. At Hardisty in 1920, Wilda Bones is the steer rider, while Billy Gutowski gets out of her way. Rodeo was a popular pastime in the area. Bert Sheppard Stockmen's Foundation Library & Archives, SFL 40-01-285

she met Jim Carry. Also performing with America's Wild West Show in the twenties, Jim was equally talented. The two swept each other off their feet and were married.

Eventually, they created their own travelling show, A. J. Carry's Wild West Hippodrome Attractions. There was a danger in her work that Stastia never really faced until, one day, the elephants stampeded. She was injured, and life changed. At the same time, entertainment styles were changing. The couple left the business and settled in Black Diamond, Alberta, but Stastia never lost her flare or ability to entertain others. She lived life on her own terms. She smoked. She never denied herself the pleasure of chocolate and candies. She told bawdy jokes when she had good ones to tell. She continued to surprise people, but somehow, they always respected her, too. And she left an important legacy, one of thrilling men and women who loved the spectacles created by acrobatics and wonderful costumes, by amazing feats of riding and roping, by just the vision of giant elephants and fine horses in the circus rings or corrals where the summer's entertainment unfolded. It was a legacy which embraced enjoyment, that encouraged performance by talented individuals and endorsed daring and hard work to achieve one's dreams.

Dreaming Along with the Silver Screen

Movies were late to the entertainment scene in the Canadian West. However, before movies made their debut, there were visual presentations that excited imaginations. Travelling speakers and magic lantern shows brought the world to the

Movies, such as this one at the Empress Theatre in Edmonton, became an increasingly popular form of entertainment. For the silent films, theatres hired pianists to play the accompanying music. Glenbow-Alberta Institute, NC 6-6007

prairies and made money doing it. Sometimes the presentations were in churches, sometimes in community halls and sometimes even in railway cars.

Eventually, for about $55 at the turn of the century, anyone could order equipment and a lecture *outfit* (similar to a slide projector) from any catalog. For an additional $7-16, there were a variety of slide sets, sometimes including colored ones. Much of what was available in North America focused on serious topics including history, the military and religious instruction. Of interest even to Canadian farmers was the series on the Chicago stockyards, but for entertainment-seeking audiences, travel slides were a popular option, and one such set presented life at the circus tent.

Even more exciting for families looking for entertainment were moving pictures. Once again, equipment, as well as educational and entertainment titles, were available from the United States. For those who had never seen a silent movie, one topic was just as fascinating as another. In 1901, there were films on the Passion Play, the American presidential assassination, the funeral of Queen Victoria and the life of a fireman. Yacht races, railways, buffalo, native people and Niagara Falls had all proven worthy of being shot for the silver screen.

Once dramas were fairly widely available for showing in smaller towns throughout the prairies, stories of love and romance became popular with women. When it came to laughter and pure pleasure, Charlie Chaplin and Buster Keaton movies and Keystone Cops were hits. Audiences loved America's Sweetheart, Canadian-born Mary Pickford. Women swooned over Valentino in the twenties and Gary Cooper in the late twenties, and in the thirties, thousands of prairie mothers curled their daughters' hair in ringlets like beloved Shirley Temple. By then, hundreds of movies and magic worlds vied for the interest of women everywhere.

A few prairie women were drawn to the silver screen in a different way. Some became actresses. More surprising was that a few were also drawn into the business of running movie theatres and were responsible for a great deal more than selling tickets or treats. In a very small town of the Canadian West, one woman who grew up in a very traditional family was often entirely responsible for making sure that modern movie magic was available to the women, men and children of the area where she lived. As years passed, movies became more popular everywhere in the world, and increasingly, women would play roles in technical and production aspects of the industry.

Lena's Story

Lena Yacyshyn (nee Marchuk) was born in Saskatchewan in 1929, at the outset of the Depression, and married in 1949. First the couple operated a garage, but finally, they sold it. They decided to go into the entertainment business, and the couple had a theatre built. By then, they had three young children. Nevertheless, Lena was the projectionist.

To make extra income, Lena's husband would go for one or two months north to Thompson, Manitoba, to work. While looking after the children, Lena shouldered the entire responsibility for their movie theatre when he was away. Even in the winter, she would pack up the children and off they would go to the theatre each night.

Circumstances meant she had left school in grade nine, but she had to take a correspondence-style course. An examiner came to Pelly so she could write the exam to qualify to run the complicated movie equipment of the time. In doing so, the people of Pelly, Saskatchewan, a community of only about 350 people at the time, and of the entire surrounding farm communities could continue to escape into worlds of fantasy when a movie was at the top of their entertainment lists. They got movies from

Winnipeg or from MGM, Columbia, all those that you see now, we would get movies from them. They would come in great big reels in a container and there used to be about four big reels in each container. And you usually got about two [containers] so the show would be about two hours long....There was *Lassie*. We played Elvis Presley, *Then in Time*, his first show to come out....The rest were mostly cowboy shows and musicals. We had [the theatre] for at least twelve years....The reels shipped from Toronto cost about $18. Some were $21. It depended on the length of the show. The salesman used to come to the house, and I would order...from them and put [down] the dates so when one show finished, I received the other one on the train....[Once a year] Salesmen used to come from each company and show the whole set, and you picked out....which ones you want. You have to pick so many for a whole year, so you would have two shows a week. Each company had their own salesman.

It was 50 cents for adults, 35 cents for teenagers and the little ones were free. [The theatre] held 250 seats, and if it was a good show, it was pretty well full and if not it would be half full. [Each] show ran for three days. [We sold] chips, pop, chocolate bars [but no popcorn].

I liked the job. I don't know about the training [that] I took. It was pretty hard because we ran it by arc [similar to the welding process], not by power. There were two arcs, the negative and the positive, and you would have to move it until it connected and made a flame to [project] the show out on the screen. It was not run by bulbs. Then, there were no machines run by electricity, at least that we had [available]....[5]

V. Women's Culture, Women's Lives

As well as being part of the general community, women of the prairie provinces had a culture that was quite uniquely their own. They loved clubs and causes, and both offered times of exhilaration for hard-won victories and times focusing on entertainment. Traditional crafts were also very important to large numbers of women, and through those crafts, they shared aspects of female culture and ways of working together that were different from the male-dominated culture around them.

While doing dishes in the kitchen after a community event or party, women caught up on each others' families and the local gossip. Sometimes, a joke or true story about men brought gales of laughter, and sometimes women planned how they might help a neighbor in need. By 1953, for a cattle auction in Pincher Creek, Alberta, these women assumed traditional roles, but smiles and laughter were still in order.
Glenbow-Alberta Institute, NA 4510-114

Women's culture meant other things, too. Occasionally, women laughed at men's jokes, but jokes told at showers and meetings about men and menopause were more likely to tickle their fancies. When women's groups catered an event, men had their assigned tasks of bringing in wood or coal or cream-cans of water, but once muscle wasn't required, often women shooed men from the community kitchen areas. The message was "Get out from under our feet," or "No men allowed." Once they were gone, women shared work, worries and their sense of humor. They washed and dried mounds of dishes and heaps of pots and pans. But, time and again, a positive women's culture unfolded. Acquaintances became friends; remedies for health problems were shared; hints regarding child rearing and housekeeping were exchanged; love, sex and survival became topics of conversation, and women's laughter filled many kitchens.

Just Another Agenda

At one time or another, likely, the majority of prairie women became involved in clubs or loose associations of women with specific objectives. They shared ideas and agreed upon the kinds of communities women wanted to foster. Often, they had to raise money to achieve those ends, and some of their methods worked better for women than for men. They had kissing booths at fairs; they sold baked goods and lemonade at events; they made and raffled quilts and other crafts; and they catered weddings, anniversaries and special events. Their methods often involved work, but just as often, women had a good time while they were at it.

At many gatherings, the groups' business was followed by recitations, songs, skits or games. Having provided food for the mind and soul, the gatherings concluded with sandwiches, cakes, squares, cookies, tea, coffee and more time to talk.

With women coming from different cultures and countries, the types of clubs organized early in the 1900s reflected a range of interests and values. Soon clubs included: Imperial Order of the Daughters of the Empire, Women's Institute, Women's Christian Temperance Union, Local Council of Women, Westward Ho, Red Cross, Women's Free Employment Bureau, Equal Franchise League and dozens and dozens of other women's clubs geared towards almost every imaginable interest.

The Women's Section of the Saskatchewan Grain Growers' Association was just one such club. The group was definitely political and had many political and economic goals. Some considered it Canada's most radical women's group. Two hundred women attended the 1915 convention. These and other women's groups were largely responsible for legislation that alleviated serious problems for women, and having adequate medical services was one important cause.

However, such organizations often had other, less critical objectives, too, ones that addressed the lighter side of women's lives and stressed cultural values. Despite being an organization of serious women, at the time concerned with prohibition, votes for women, world peace, education and laws related to women, cultural and social activities were not such frivolous matters that they were taken for granted or dismissed. For example, in the constitution for the Women Grain Growers, cultural goals included:

To establish libraries, literary societies, reading rooms, arrange lectures and to further extend the knowledge of the members and their families....

To encourage members to provide suitable halls and meeting places and properly equip and furnish same for the social and educational benefit of the members.

To make farm life more attractive thereby keeping the young people on the farm.

To beautify the home, the home surroundings and the school.

To foster and develop local taste for literature, music and the finer things of life.[1]

No matter what the form of transportation, going to a meeting mattered. In the early 1920s, these members of the Rinard Club in Alberta set out in a horse-drawn wagon to attend a meeting. Sir Alexander Galt Museum and Archives, P19841071009-GP

Politics, Theatre and Laughter

Early in western history, professional theatre and drama had a foothold, but impromptu theatre with political goals also did well. One particular performance would long be remembered as the best satire and parody ever performed. Laughter could be a fine tool in achieving women's political ends, and no one was more aware of or better able to use that tool than Nellie McClung. She was a teacher, a writer, a lecturer and a women's rights activist. In debate, she was a fearsome opponent. The serious messages in her writing and speeches were always clear, and her arguments were forceful. Yet humor was part of some of her greatest successes. She could take the barbs and jokes made about her by political opponents and newspaper cartoonists. But she could always give as good as she got. Her sense of irony and comic timing meant she could have an audience in stitches, and she did in 1914. A mock parliament by women in Vancouver got good reviews as part of the campaign for women's suffrage, and the Political Equality League in Manitoba decided to stage a similar parliament. Members sold tickets to the event at the Walker Theatre, scheduled for the evening of January 27. The League made its serious plea to the premier and the Legislature on the afternoon of the same day. For it, Nellie made an eloquent speech on behalf of women's suffrage. Premier Roblin's actual reply became part of the *script* for that evening. The cast had been prepared to improvise, depending on what reply the delegation received. Nellie was cast as Premier Roblin, and by her evening performance, Roblin's response to the women's delegation seemed as ludicrous as his reasoning had been. For his speech, Nellie substituted a male reference for every female one, and the evening was a hit. Many women in the audience laughed so hard that tears streamed from their eyes.

The Sweetest Story of the Year

Sowing Seeds in Danny

By NELLIE L. McCLUNG

A Book that Gives Pleasure to all who Read It

CLOTH, WITH FRONTISPIECE, $1.00; LIMP LEATHER, BOXED, $1.50.

NELLIE L. McCLUNG.

Nellie McClung was a successful writer, public speaker and women's rights activist. Her speeches set out challenges and verbalized goals for women, but Nellie knew how to entertain, impress and fascinate. Her stories were well-loved, but her speeches made many a woman hoot with laughter. British Columbia Archives and Record Service, E-06027

Nellie recreated the event in her novel *Purple Springs*. One of her characters sup-posedly attended the event, and she responded in the same way as the hundreds of women in the real-life audience. The young woman wipes her eyes and claims, "I shouldn't laugh...for my husband has a Government job and he may lose it if the Government members see me, but if I don't laugh, I'll choke. Better lose a job than choke."[2]

The play, known as *The Women's Parliament*, did more than strike a blow for the cause; it also applied a humorous female perspective to serious issues. Whether that mock parliament was most remembered as an enjoyable passage in Nellie's book, as wonderful theatre or brilliant politics, the play would remain one of the most humorous memories prairie women shared in terms of their popular culture. The *Winnipeg Tribune* carried the story. According to the paper, for the performance, there was "deafening applause and laughter of the audience."

How the Vote Was Not Won – Burlesqued in Women's Parliament

29 January 1914

Smiles of anticipation[,] ripples of merriment, gales of laughter and storms of applause punctuated every point and paragraph of what is unanimously conceded to be the best burlesque ever staged in Winnipeg when the Political Equality League presented last night at the Walker Theater a suffrage playlet showing "How the Vote Was Won," and a woman's parliament showing how the vote was not won.

The audience, which filled the house to the roof, were held up in the foyer and asked to sign a suffrage petition to the government, which many of them did. Men were actively engaged throughout the house in selling a pamphlet on "The Legal Status of Women in Manitoba," by Dr. Mary Crawford, in which they seemed to be very successful judging by the number of those seen in the hands of the audi-ence as they left the theatre chattering or laughing uproariously over some choice bit of sarcasm which had particularly delighted them....

Mrs. Nellie McClung's appearance before the curtain was the signal for a burst of applause from the audience who instantly recognized the woman whom many of them had heard make such an eloquent speech on the floor of the Legislature last Tuesday morning. She explained that they would have to use their imagination as political conditions were reversed and women were in power....In fact, had she been a star comedian her every sentence could not have brought forth more continuous applause.

The curtain rose revealing the women legislators, all with their evening gowns covered with black cloaks, seated at desks in readiness for the first session....

Petitions were first received and read. The first was a protest against men's clothes, saying that men wearing scarlet ties, six inch collars and squeaky shoes should not be allowed in public. A second petition asked for labor saving devices for men. A third prayed that alkali and all injurious substances be prohibited in the manufacture of laundry soap as it ruined the men's delicate hands....

Votes for Women was one of many gender issues that united most prairie women. They staged drama productions on their themes, often using humor to convey the message. For this performance, women equated their lot with slavery in a minstrel show presented in Winnipeg in about 1915. Today, minstrel shows might not be well received, but they were popular and common at the time. Provincial Archives of Manitoba, Foote 1640, N 2721

The pinnacle of absurdity was reached when a deputation of men, lead by Mr. R. C. Skinner, arrived at the Legislature with a wheelbarrow full of petitions for votes for men. Mr. Skinner said the women were afraid that if the men were given the vote that [they] would neglect their business to talk politics when they ought to be putting wildcat subdivisions on the market. In spite of his eloquent appeal he could not touch the heart of the premier.

The premier (Mrs. McClung) then rose and launched her reply to the deputation, almost every sentence of which was interrupted by gales of laughter… [from] the audience which was quick to appreciate her mimicry.…

"I must congratulate the members of this delegation on their splendid appearance. Any civilization which can produce as splendid a type of manhood as my friend, Mr. Skinner, should not be interfered with…But I cannot do what you ask me to do – for the facts are all against you.…

"If all men were as intelligent and as good as Mr. Skinner and his worthy though misguided followers we might consider this matter, but they are not. Seven-eighths of the police court offenders are men, and only one-third of the church membership. You ask me to enfranchise all these.…

"O no, man is made for something higher and better than voting. Men were made to support families. What is home without a bank account? The man who pays the grocer rules the world. In this agricultural province, the man's place is the farm.…Politics unsettle men, and unsettled men means unsettled bills – broken furniture, and broken vows – and divorce.…When you ask for the vote you are asking me to break up peaceful, happy homes – to wreck innocent lives.…"

"It may be that I am old-fashioned. I may be wrong. After all, men may be human. Perhaps the time will come when men may vote with women – but in the meantime, be of good cheer. Advocate and educate.…"[3]

Always Something to Share

Club work and social reform were enormously rewarding for many women. Yet so often, for early women, when they became deeply involved in club work and social reform, detractors criticized them for failing at family life. Much of the club work was actually directed at improving the lives of women and children, but even at a personal level, club work was often something shared between generations of women within a family. Many of these women made conscientious efforts to remain close to their children, long after the years of being physically responsible for their children had ended. Mother-daughter relationships had always been a very special aspect of female culture, and the sharing between adult women within a family would always be one of the most interesting, wonderful and challenging of relationships.

There would always be issues. Most mothers and daughters lovingly offered help and advice to each other whether the help or advice was wanted or needed. Sometimes, the relationship had to be carried on through the mail, but when week after week, letters were written and the ups and downs of life were shared, there could be no clearer example of love.

A Mother-Daughter Story

Henrietta Muir Edwards is known for her leadership in the early women's movement. Her childhood was a privileged one. As an adult, she worked tirelessly on the executive of the National Council of Women, especially in her role of convenor of laws on the rights of women and children. In doing so, she studied legislation regarding women, and she wrote "The Legal Status of Women in Alberta" in 1916 and revised it in 1920. She lobbied for the provincial and national franchise for women, and she was one of the five co-signatories of the Person's Case, spear-headed by Emily Murphy. In winning their case, this Famous Five established the legal and political right of women to sit in the Senate, and the implication meant equality for Canadian women and men, at least in theory and law.

In 1931, two years after the success of the Famous Five with the Person's Case, Henrietta was invited to write an article for a column entitled "Looking Back on Life," in the May issue of *Canadian Home Journal*, which had a circulation of 150 000. She called the article "Motherhood, God's Greatest Gift." She concluded "The most precious thing I have learnt is that Motherhood is one of the greatest of God's

Telephones meant ease in communicating with family and friends. They also facilitated organizing meetings and planning special events. With the first phones, even the operator, sometimes called the Hello Girl, relieved feelings of loneliness. Rural, party lines made it possible to listen in or rubberneck on neighbors' conversations. Once the telephone rang, without saying a word, a lonely, rural woman might learn all the important and frivolous goings-on of the community. Saskatchewan Archives Board, S-B 7234

gifts. A mother is a co-worker with God, in a way that no man can ever be, in the building of a temple for a human soul...." For the period and for the season, the sentiment was nothing new. It was May, and near Mother's Day.

But conveyed in Henrietta's weekly letters to her daughter was the personal truth of Henrietta's life, family and political work, the truth of her words about motherhood and the depth of her sentiment. Each year Henrietta sent a Happy Birthday letter. Again, congratulatory words were expected, but even this sampling of letters revealed the connection between mother and daughter.

Blood Reserve, August 31, 1912, My dearest Alice

Very many happy returns of the 6th. I am sending by this post a few "hankies," some for every day use and some of Irish linen [that] I sent to Robinson and Cleaver for. I hope the receiving them will add a little to the pleasure of the day.

Father and I are going in to Macleod today to take the early train Sunday morning up to Calgary....I am feeling much stronger and hope to enjoy the Stampede next week....I wish dear Alice words [could] convey to you how precious you are to take Father and myself and how thankful we are that we have such a daughter. You will never have anything to regret when we are gone in your conduct to us. Neither Father nor I can recall a rude word or a disobedient action and that is saying a great deal I think....

University Campus, March 8, 1916

I am so pleased at the prospect of seeing you all next week....Last week was a busy week – Wednesday was the great day for the women at the Legislature [Edmonton, Alberta, franchise bill]. Thursday I was up at Government House in the afternoon and had a delightful time....There was a big reception of women delegates being held when I came in. Mrs. Brett [wife of lieutenant governor] asked me to stay after the delegates left as a few of the Calgary ladies were staying. Mrs. Sifton [wife of Alberta premier] and a few others, only two of them, so I stayed until six o'clock when Mrs. Sifton drove me home in her car or rather to cousin Frances where I was due for supper. After supper I went to a meeting called at Mrs. McClung's to consider the new franchise which has been granted us – Friday. I called on Mrs. Jamieson at the MacDonald [Hotel] and seemed to spend most of the rest of the day at the telephone....

Monday I spent all day writing letters in connection with Council work. Tuesday is trying to get something in shape for an address I have to give to the W.A. of the University...Saturday afternoon – I feel quite nervous about this address as I know I cannot come up to what is expected of me. The association has

In the early days, when horses were needed in fields, even if a farm woman could drive them, she was stuck at home. The presence of tractors for fields and family cars for transportation changed their lives and offered freedom. In 1906, Saskatchewan had 22 motor vehicles. By 1923, there were 60 931 cars, plus other motorized vehicles. Stettler Town and Country Museum.

made quite a feature of my address and have invited between 2 and 3 hundred guests. The meeting is to be held in the Convocation Hall of the University and refreshments served at the close of my address – I feel like an imbecile in only [getting] three pages written yesterday although I worked at it all day. The thought of Saturday makes me hot and cold. I think the little brains I had, have been muddled by the different bumps [ups and downs] I have had, at least I do not seem to be able to think accurately or consecutively....

Macleod, Sept 12th 1926, My dear Daughter

Fifty years ago this evening I was married. If Oliver had been here we would have been celebrating our golden wedding. It seems impossible that that day which does not seem so far back was fifty years ago. In looking back the way seems strewn with blessings, hard places that were sometimes in the road but what happy companionship! What a son! What two dear daughters – What a husband!! I think few women are so blessed as I. I feel very grateful to God for I do not deserve what He has given me – My husband and I walked together in perfect accord for 39 years. My children have never given me any anxiety. It is true. I sit alone here tonight, but Aunt [Min] is with me, in looking backward from childhood my path has been strewn with love and care, in looking forward there is the joyful day of reunion – a little while between – I cannot tell you how my thoughts and heart turns toward you and how grateful I am that I have you – such a dear daughter you have always been. I think it is wonderful that I cannot recall a single incident when you and I disagreed.

I have been reading over your letter of the 5th. I think it is very probable that your feeling of depression is due to the physical change. In my last letter I said you would have to have patience with Oliver [likely Alice's son]. You will also have to have patience with yourself and when feeling depressed remember you have no cause from out side circumstances but remember the depression is purely physical and have patience for time to cure.

Three letters from you this week! How lovely! You are so good in writing such long letters with the details of each day – the letters span the distance we are apart....[4]

Needles and Crafts

From the earliest days on the prairie, women have enjoyed their handicrafts. First Nations women decorated clothing and pouches with dyed and intricately woven porcupine quill work and fringes. Fur traders brought manufactured beads, and beadwork became the popular and beautiful decorative art of Métis and Aboriginal women.

With settlers came other traditional arts that had been a part of women's culture in their earlier homes. Some of those arts, such as quilting and knitting, served very practical functions. Quilting meant cosy beds in winter, and knitting meant warm socks, sweaters, mittens, scarves, tuques and even coats. Other handicrafts had more strictly decorative functions, but all of the handicrafts served the important function of passing the hours pleasurably. That was especially important on long, winter nights when people were in the house. For many women, necessity was part of the reason for needlework. Yet the fact that some work was entirely decorative, and other work was both practical as well as beautifully designed and made, means functionality was not the only reason for handicrafts. Fairs and exhibitions allowed opportunities for women to display their crafts, and in many instances, prizes were awarded in a wide range of categories.

Handicraft enthusiasts still work, meet and share knowledge all over the country. They never have been limited to a particular geographical area, but

In 1906, this woman at the sod home of Edward Moorhouse spends time sewing. Interior decorating was also important to quality of life and of interest to some women. Here the sod walls have been lined with building paper. Hanging pictures also made the home more welcoming. Saskatchewan Archives, R-A 3483

for women on the early prairies, crafts were a way of life, and for the most part, the types of handicrafts pursued by women related to clothing, household necessities and home decoration.

Even getting craft supplies could be a joy for a would-be crafter. Sewing, knitting, crocheting, tatting and embroidery were the most popular and common forms of needlework. For every one of those crafts, women could ponder the value and price of endless notions and supplies. Something as simple as needles and pins was worthy of attention. There were sewing needles, scientific needles, darning needles, glove needles, between needles for tailors, chenille needles, straw needles for milliners, packing needles, self-treating needles, upholsterers' needles, machine needles, netting needles, steel or rubber or bone knitting needles, embroidery needles and carpet needles, and many came in a range of sizes.

The pin department of catalogs at the turn of the century offered a variety of types of pins in various sizes and sold on sheets or pincushions or in pin cubes. Although 1¢ for an aluminum thimble might signal that the 5¢ steel thimble offered more protection, there were thimbles sized for misses, small women, women and large women. Most crafters had some kind of thimble, and most also had crochet hooks, but other notions were intended for the crafter who knew exactly what she needed. For some a tatting shuttle would be essential. Others would know how to use a plaiter, pinking iron, Swiss darner or tracer. Some notions would go out of favor. Others would be as essential, for those making a particular craft, a century later as they were in the late 1800s and early 1900s.

Spinning was also both useful and a pleasure for some. A few women did spin their own wool for knitting, especially if they lived on a farm where there were sheep. But wool could be purchased in all the basic colors, plus shades of pink and mauve, from catalogs and general stores. Many women learned to knit while they were still girls. Most learned to knit from mothers and grandmothers, some of whom were early settlers to the prairie provinces. They started with simple knit and pearl garments such as scarves.

Girls even had knitting clubs at school, and occasionally, grown women had knitting clubs. Especially during the two great wars, women gathered in groups to knit socks for the men overseas, or the women knit socks at home and then gathered for sock showers, where they brought as many pairs of socks at they had knit to the "shower," so the pairs could be packaged together to be sent overseas.

Crocheting was equally popular, and many girls did learn the art, but being finer work and taking a great deal of time and patience, it was most often the craft of the older set. Commonly, the edges of handkerchiefs, pillow cases and tablecloths were crocheted, but those with the time and money might even crochet trim on aprons and tea towels. Chair back or arm covers and doilies did have practical uses, protecting furniture from wear, but they were equally important as decorative pieces, and patterns were widely advertised.

Two Generations Good with Needles

Many women were competent at a variety of needlework crafts. Gladys Hanna Hurl and her mother, Annie Louise Hanna (nee Close) were two such women. Oldest in the family, Gladys was born in in 1909 at Yellow Grass, Saskatchewan, about 70 miles south of Moose Jaw. Growing up, Gladys learned some of her needle craft skills from her mother, but she also learned and improved her skills through her own independent efforts. She liked pretty clothes, and when knitting, she was able to combine her fashion sense with her skills, creating entire outfits to enjoy wearing for years. Annie had been a tailor before her marriage, a skill she had learned in Ontario.

As someone with excellent sewing skills, Annie made many of the children's clothes. "She made some dresses for me for school....They were really nice, and she put a little bit of embroidery work on them....[Also] she crocheted and knit." Both women learned to play the piano, as well as enjoying photography. But needle crafts

Born in 1901, Marie Randon was a very sophisticated rural woman. She and her sister, Claire, never married. They spent two years in France in the 1920s, but returned to the family ranch near Fenn, Alberta, where they resided throughout their lives. Interested in fashion, they made many of their own clothes and hats. Stettler Town and Country Museum.

were the everyday means of passing time pleasurably for Gladys. To her and thousands of other girls and women, needle crafts became an creative outlet, and finished works could become gifts or valued clothing and household decorations for the family. As well as making clothes, Gladys tatted; she crocheted tablecloths, bedspreads and doilies, and she knit Afghans. She even won prizes at the Calgary Stampede for socks that she had knit.

I learned to crochet before I started school. And then I learned to knit shortly afterwards. That was a struggle…but I mastered it. Then when we went to school, there was an hour and a half for the noon period. We pupils from the country had to stay on the grounds so there were five or six of the girls [who] would knit…and we made sweaters. I think I made my dad a sweater, a sleeveless sweater, [when I was] about twelve. Then, there was a variegated yarn, so we got some of that, and we knit just the band, and then we got real big needles to poof it [the sweaters for the girls] way out, and made the yoke smaller. Oh my, they were wonderful.…

After we [the Hurls] were married, and we had the family, it was hard times. In the Dirty Thirties, I made all the boys' pants – we didn't have zippers then either – and coats. I had a White treadle-type sewing machine. [As a girl, I] went to CGIT [Canadian Girls in Training] and took some lessons.…[For my sons], I knit their sweaters and socks, their toques. The only thing I had to buy for them was their overshoes and their underwear....For gifts, we used to get white linen handkerchiefs, and I would crochet the edges in coloured thread for my friends....

I've knit hundreds of pounds of yarn. We got it from Regina, a yarn shop in Regina. Once I got yarn for 25 cents a ball, a wine colour, and I did myself a...short sleeved sweater and long coat...about in 1934 or 35. Then I got tired of it and I ripped it [out] and I...washed it, and I rolled it up in balls again, and I knit a different pattern...a two piece outfit....Anyway the end of the story is during the war, the priest who lived quite close to us got a letter from his sister at home saying that things were so hard....so I had started to knit this yarn again [a third time], and I thought "Oh, I can't do it. It was too much." So, I bundled it all up and gave it to him and he mailed it to his sister...Oh, she was just so thrilled. I still have the letter she sent me. She was in Germany....

[I made thirteen crocheted tablecloths]....that was in the war, the Forties, and my daughter is still using [one]...It was 25 cents a ball...For this one [made in 1998], it was $6.99 a ball.[5]

More Than Just for Bedding

Quilting bees meant company, conversation and the warmth of friendship, but quilting was also a pastime that filled countless evenings for women who worked alone, enjoying the artistry and skill of the craft. In many families, it was a valued aspect of women's culture handed from one generation to the next. There were as many designs as there were people and groups that worked on quilts. Signature and patchwork quilts enjoyed decades of popularity with women, and they too had special stories.

There was always a story behind the names on signature quilts. Sometimes made as wedding or anniversary presents, the quilts might have the names of family and friends. The patches indicated the names of women in a club or class. Some quilts named the women who were raising money for a special cause. Something might be needed for the community hall or church, so women worked together, sold tickets and raffled a quilt. Usually, signature quilts were of two colors, with red and white cottons working well as colors that would readily show the letters of names embroidered on the squares. For the same reason, signature quilts were seldom made of the irregular shapes of other patch work quilts. More often than not, they were group efforts. Patches would be embroidered with names, whenever convenient, by the individual women at home. The quilts were usually long term projects that stretched over a few months, and the group would meet as needed for quilting bees during afternoons or evenings so that the squares of the cover could be sewn together.

Quilts were community projects, but handmade quilts were certainly associated with family and loving care. In fact, newborn babies were the reason that one group of women made their signature quilt. In the late 1880s, after giving birth to her sixth child alone, before the doctor could arrive to help her, Lily Young of Springbank, Alberta, made a vow. She would be there as a midwife to help other women in her district, and she was. According to Nellie Hutchinson-Taylor, Lily was "like a ministering angel to any in need."[6] She expected nothing in return and accepted no rewards, with the exception of one very special gift lovingly made for her and presented to her by the South (Union) Church of Springbank in about 1917. The patches of the red and white comforter had been embroidered, and on it were the names of 80 families of the community, whose children she had helped deliver.

Patchwork quilts were particularly practical but could also be a marvel of artistry and a history of sorts. What had been the *life* of each patch before it found its way into the quilt?

One quilt to survive the ups and downs of prairie life was even filled with more mystery. In the 1990s, a few years after her mother had died, Lillian Rediger had a quilt she knew to have been in her mother's possession in the early 1950s. Since it had faded, Lillian decided to restore it, or at least recover it. To hold the feathers, similar quilts often had a large bag, sometimes made of gunny sacking, sometimes of new cotton, but just as often of cotton flour and sugar sacks. Lillian opened one seam. Inside was an unexpected treasure and a mystery.

An even earlier quilt had been hidden by the cover. What was its story? Had it been made by her grandmother, Jane Graham (nee Jones), who as a girl of 12 had moved from Ontario to Saskatchewan in 1914? Lillian's grandmother had quilted and had once tried to teach her young granddaughter the art. She had brought a crazy quilt cushion as a gift to Lillian and wanted the young girl to try the feather-stitch around its patches.

The quilt that Lillian discovered so many years later was an heirloom of many colors and fabrics, including satin and brocade, velveteen and velvet. Embroidery stitches were varied and delicate, outlining each patch and decorating some with flower designs. Then each patch had been knotted with yarn in aqua or rose. Exactly when the old quilt was made will remain a mystery. The comforter itself would become a family heirloom, and the joy of its discovery decades after it had been made would be shared with others when Lillian Rediger wrote of "Grandmother's Heirloom Quilt," for the Winter, 1991-1992 issue of *Folklore* magazine. While treasuring the folk art of her family, she would continue the tradition by pursuing her own interest in quilting.[7]

Quilting bees meant friendship and socializing. At the same time, women made much-needed bedding or created practical, yet decorative handicrafts for fundraisers. The women who made this quilt in 1907 were from the Balmoral area near Red Deer, Alberta. Red Deer and District Museum and Archives, P125-c-5-4

Jane's Story

Born in about 1900, Jane Aberson and her husband came to western Canada from the Netherlands in 1924. Jane wrote home about what was good and what was difficult for her living on the prairies. By 1929, when financial conditions worsened and other Dutch people were interested in emigrating to Canada, Jane began to submit articles to Dutch newspapers. She covered topics as far ranging as cooking for threshers to social life and handicrafts. Years later, her articles were compiled for her book, *From the Prairies With Hope*. In it, she recounts bits about the life of prairie women, including the experience of going to a quilting bee.

Quilting Bee in a Very Cold Winter

March 1933

My second outing was to the home of one of our neighbours for a quilting bee. A group of people [had] come together to make a quilt cooperatively. This quilting bee was organized by the same ladies' club that had made the cushions I wrote about a bit ago. This quilt will be auctioned off and the proceeds used to help the needy.

With my closest neighbour, Mabel Timm, I hit the road at half past eight on a bright, sunny morning in our toboggan. I sat in front, driving the horse, and Mabel sat in the back, keeping an eye on the things we were carrying. It had been agreed that each of the ladies would contribute one item for a potluck dinner. We soon saw sleighs coming from different directions on the lonesome, sparsely travelled country roads. One would have a loaf of bread, another butter or a bowl of applesauce, another vegetables, and so on. We looked forward to a regular feast.

The work on the quilt was divided up among the various ladies. A few started to pin the quilt blocks together. Another sewed them together on the sewing machine, and others put up the wooden frames on which the quilt had to be stretched. Several women went into the kitchen to prepare dinner, which was most festive.

After the dinner a layer of cotton batting was stretched over the quilt lining on which the neatly stitched blocks were stretched. Then a design was drawn by hand, which we had to follow with neat little stitches. Those without work on the quilt entertained us on the piano and sang songs. All of us who were stitching joined in the singing. The coal oil lamps were lit, and I felt as though we had gone back a hundred years to an earlier time in history....[8]

Lover's Hankie

Many craft items did double duty. They brought hours of enjoyment to the women who crafted them. They also served an important purpose in the home: they made homes more comfortable or beautiful, or they became items of clothing. Hankies were one of these craft items. They were essentials, and every man and woman had many. Some were purchased and made of fine linen; some were made from flour sacks. Often women's handkerchiefs had beautifully hand crocheted or tatted edges; but men's were usually plain, white for good and colored for work days.

One type of handkerchief had a very special purpose. The women of the Hutterite Brethren enjoyed making a variety of textile arts, which also doubled as practical and useable items. Though clothing and other textiles for personal use were usually of dark colors and might feature simple, lighter-colored designs, such as tiny florals or polka dots, the designs were conservative and not intended to draw attention to an individual. The sweetheart handkerchief was an exception. Hutterite women made handkerchiefs as gifts for family members. But the sweetheart hankie was a courting gift. It drew attention to a young woman, and it was her unique way of saying "I'm interested" to the man of her dreams.

The custom of making such a gift dated back to the seventeenth century, and the young woman who made it even dated and initialed or signed her handkerchief so her potential suitor would get the intended message. As English became important to the colonies' survival, increasingly over the years the messages were embroidered in English rather than German, the Hutterites' first language.

On squares of linen or cotton, young women embroidered romantic messages, or if they were quite shy, they would use words and symbols with a more religious tone. By the time the young women were old enough to be thinking of marriage, they had already completed hand-stitched samplers and mastered spinning, weaving and sewing. Samplers were common in households and schools with various ethnic backgrounds, but the sweetheart handkerchief was a special project for Hutterite women.

As part of their design, the handkerchiefs commonly displayed two birds or hearts, but flowers might also speak of love. In 1935, Rachel Hofer, of the Pincher Creek Colony in Alberta, bordered her handkerchief with "You are only kind and true. My heart is full of love for you." At the centre, she wrote "Happy thoughts 1935" while her name was designed into the mid-ground.

On the Cameron colony at Turin, Alberta, George Hofer received a sweetheart hankie. Katie Wurz had hand-crafted her gift to show the depths of her feelings, and her cross-stitched message read, "True Love This Gift Is Small But Love Is All, 1935, To My Love."

The custom of creating the special gifts was slowly dying out, but in 1943, living at the Cayley Colony, also in Alberta, Maggie Stahl made a handkerchief for John Wurz. Though including both their names on the hanky and using an attractive rose motif, she was less forward in her words, and her cross-stitched message was simply, "Many Joys to You 1943."

A man was not obliged to pay special attention to the woman who gave him such a gift. Some hankies ended in happy marriages; some did not, but by the 1960s, modern Hutterite women had stopped creating the special little gifts. A few of the sweetheart handkerchiefs remained as treasures from other times, as reminders of romances decades ago, but the custom had disappeared.[9]

New times and new technologies brought change in every sphere. Much has been gained and diversified in terms of women's culture, but some things have, at least to a large extent, disappeared. Not only did cloth hankies fall into disuse, many of the traditional arts that interested women for generations are no longer learned by young girls. Male and female cultures have much more in common; most clubs are open to both men and women, and today's women laugh and tell jokes in the company of men, jokes their foremothers would have whispered and laughed at only in the company of other women.

Many women had china. Tea cup collections were fairly common, but some also collected ornaments or salt and pepper shakers. On the early prairies, a very few women actually made porcelain items. One woman learned the very special technique of porcelain draping for female figurines; she was not only a craftsman but an artist. In this 1912 photo, a woman shops at Revellon Freres in Edmonton. Provincial Archives of Alberta, Ernest Brown, B 4152

VI. What About the Outer Me?

A woman's real worth has never been rooted in things, in superficial or worldly considerations such as fashion, hairstyle or physical appearance. Still, for most women – though definitely not all – fashion and beauty-related items were a pleasure. When a woman had time and could afford to dream of what she might like, just for herself, sometimes it was a new dress or coat or silk stock-ings. Other times, it was related to more important issues – the dream of a holi-day from work or of having some sort of birth control.

However, the joy that a mail order cata-log brought to wo-men was not simply because they could plan Christmas pres-ents for others or order some type of gadget for the kitchen. The arrival of the catalog meant dreams of a new hat,

T. Eaton's Fall and Winter Catalogue, Number 21, 1909-1910, Glenbow-Alberta Institute Library

shoes, night gown or handbag. It meant hours happily deliberating over what lace would look best on the new blouse a woman intended to sew for herself. Newspapers and magazines brought the same pleasure to women. Most had one or more women's columns in which the newest styles were discussed, and some even offered knitting patterns free of charge.

A related pleasure for many women was shopping. Undoubtedly, those who lived in towns or cities shopped whenever they wished. For rural women, especially those a half day's travel or more away, going to town and having a few hours to wander in and out of stores, to discover what they might buy or make for themselves or their families was a fine and wonderful experience. Even going grocery shopping was a treat, but it seldom compared with the pleasure a woman knew when she went to a beauty parlor for a hair cut or when she spent an hour with a dressmaker, being measured for new clothes.

Looking one's best was one way to attract a potential suitor. It was also part of keeping the romance alive in marriage. It meant keeping up appearances, and a new dress said, "Things could be worse, or life is getting better." There was more to real friendship or a loving family than appearance, but being fashionable or appropriately dressed helped create self-confidence. A new hat couldn't permanently change one's feelings of self worth, but it could mean a small glow inside, at least for a few moments.

Fashion Politics

Did an interest in fashion or wearing a corset reduce a woman's ability to play a role in the sporting, cultural, intellectual or political life of her community? In fact, many of the women who actively lobbied and won political rights for women, supported education for women, or became leaders and forerunners in

Although born in 1906, three years before Bob Edwards poked fun at women's clothing and linked it to the subject of voting, by the early 1940s, this prairie woman does not let her slim and stylish skirt or fancy shoes limit her risk-taking when on a mountain vacation with her husband and friends. Walt and Faye Holt collection.

politics and professions did care about their appearance. Women's interest in fashion certainly resulted in jokes by men. But with most women, the interest was not a controlling element of their lives. When no one was around or when they just felt like it, sensible women wore what they wanted. They didn't wear corsets, or they wore the pants that belonged to the men of the family, when pants made more sense for outdoor work. Sporting women made adjustments, wearing their skirts a little shorter, and they quickly took to less restrictive styles such as riding skirts and breeches. If they wanted to swim rather than sit in the sun, they purchased slimmer-fitting bathing suits.

Not surprisingly, newspaper man Bob Edwards, who made fun of almost everything, made fun of women who cared about fashion and beauty.

Women should vote. Certainly she should....She says she has as much practical sense as a man has. Then she starts out to prove it in public. Watch her get ready to go out to prove it. She adds to the few strands of hair adhering to her scalp...

Then she hermetically seals herself with a time lock into a hipless corset and a strap contrivance to keep her stomach flat. Afterwards she uses a shoe-horn and forces herself into a one-piece dress. She then gets in front of a mirror and reaches for a hat that looks like the roof of a merry-go-round, covered with feathers and fruit and flowers and birds and buckles and long stick pins and starts out to prove her common sense.

In that set of snaffles and martingales and hobbles which would make a man scream for the bartender and bite himself in a dozen places, she sallies forth and immediately remembers that it is Mrs. Winkle's receiving day. Into Mrs. Winkle's she accordingly drops and helps to 'pour tea'....Of course woman should vote, whenever she pleases. Anyway, she will some day.[1]

The Early Fashion Scene on the Prairies

In the days of fur traders and early missionaries, NWMP and settlers, women had few options for finery. Now and again, the lucky ones travelled to big cities with large clothing stores. Also, friends and family living elsewhere sent packages and gifts of clothes or accessories, which were usually treasured. For women whose spouses or fathers were employed by the Hudson's Bay Company, once a year it was possible to order finery from England. Other women also ordered what they needed or wanted, or they depended on travelling peddlers, who usually had only a very limited selection of women's clothing.

By 1856, in the Red River area, John Higgins carried a good stock and variety of dry goods for both men and women in the long wagon he had adapted for sales. Rather than going door to door, he made regular stops on his route around the region. Once word spread that Higgins had arrived, crowds gathered. He stayed some days, showing his wares and the latest fashions. He carried a few ready-made items and shoes, but since most women sewed the family's clothing, or seamstresses in the area did the sewing for them, he had a good stock of calico and gingham, as well as some silks. Thread and needles were necessities. Zippers didn't exist, so hundreds of buttons were also essential.

Higgins sold what he could and moved on. However, by 1865, he had opened a small store on Main Street in Winnipeg, and the range of goods he carried expanded. In 1873, he built an even larger store, beautifully fitted with chandeliers and multi-drawer mahogany cases. His old building still housed the groceries, various household goods, crockery and locally made pottery, but on the second floor of the new Mercantile Palace, women could purchase almost any current fashion their hearts desired in the clothing and tailoring departments.

By the time the West experienced even the first wave of settlement, for the most part, the hooped skirt was out of fashion. However, dresses were long and skirts were full, requiring yards and yards of material. Sometimes, if a travelling salesman had little material to choose from, women purchased entire bolts of cloth. As a result, members of the same family had very similar clothes, with only the pattern or type and color of trim being different. By the early 1900s, dresses were slightly shorter, a blessing to prairie women who faced dust or mud daily throughout the summer, even in the towns and cities where boardwalks were still a luxury.

All the same, many western women were determined to be fashionable, and some did have gowns from Europe. Others had ones made in North America, sometimes by prestigious houses. Lillian Young of Calgary, Alberta, was socially active and enjoyed attending balls and theatre. Of her beautiful and fashionable evening dresses, at least one was sewn by the dressmaker of a local firm, based on the pattern of a Paris designer. Made in about 1913, it was blue-green with a sheer cotton layer over an underdress. Flowing from the neckline of the high-waisted gown were panels rich with embroidery work. Another evening gown was deep purple with tiny white dots. Made of satin, it had an overdress of black net.

Information about fashion trends around the world may have been limited, but word did get around. Books and periodicals with sketches of popular fashions were available, though not necessarily at the local general store. Sometimes family or friends residing far away sent the books or magazines. New settlers brought them, especially if the settlers were from eastern Canada or the United States, who were able to load the few luxuries they already owned onto railway cars provided to settlers free of charge within Canada. American and eastern Canadian settlers visited relatives, and they returned with fashion ideas and magazines. Even after the clothing styles became a little dated, one woman might pass her magazines on to a neighbor who was hungry for any glimpses from the world of fashion.

One periodical that made its way from Britain into western Canadian homes was *The Woman at Home*. Included were fiction, biography and travel pieces, and articles on cooking, courtship and fashion, including dressmaking and millinery.

Coats were essential in the Canadian west, where every day in winter was cold and many summer days and evenings required coats. However, they were expensive to buy. For the lucky few with copies of *The Woman at Home*, the January 1905 issue tackled the topic. The article, "Home Dress-making" by A.F.M., acknowledged the financial constraints many women faced, but the writer had a suggestion. The beautifully sketched, reversible wrap with its high collar and large sleeves flaring at the wrist did not seem too difficult to sew, and certainly had an air of elegance.

If statistics were taken as to feminine requirements, I am certain it would be found that a large majority of women existed to whom necessity was not only the mother of invention, but likewise an arbitrary ruler of fate in the matter of clothes, and that to make one garment meet many needs was a problem that hundreds of women were bent on solving everyday.

Now one of these needs is undoubtedly the long winter wrap. If this can be made [so] that it serves as an evening cloak as well as a day one, a considerable expense is saved, and there is no need why this desirable end should not be achieved. It can only be so, however, when the purse is a limited one, by the exertions of the home dressmaker, for the good reason that the "ready made" coat is for day wear invariably of tweed, for evening wear of cashmere, and fashioned moreover in a manner not at all calculated to fit…it for street wear.

For this reason I have this month selected a design which, with minor variations, is finding favour amongst the best tailors of the day. Its *construction is simplicity* itself, and its seams few.…

As sketched, the cloak is fashioned of one of those warm reversible tartan cloths which have a plain cloth surface upon the upper side, and a rather fleecy plaid woven upon the under one.…The fur edging also adds that touch which brings the wrap within the realm of evening cloaks.…[2]

Hats, Gloves and Other Accessories

Of course, there was more to fashion than dresses, blouses, skirts and coats. Hats were a must and were worn to town, meetings, church and every other occasion, event or celebration. For settlers from Eastern Europe, kerchiefs played much the same role, though wedding hats took the places of veils. For other women, especially those in towns and cities, going without a hat was unthinkable, and an entire service industry was dedicated to hats. Many women found employment in millinery shops, and others started or dreamed of starting their own businesses. Especially for women good at needle crafts, making hats was a desirable job that allowed them to use the practical skills they possessed, and to be creative with designs. Also, for the hat maker at home, millinery supplies were reasonable in price, varied and readily available, including by mail order.

No shape seemed to be unsuitable as the base of a hat. Then what might be piled on top of that base depended only on the imagination of the creator. The home crafter or milliner could purchase fancy hat ornaments. Beautiful hats might feature ribbons, bows and lace, in any of the latest shades, and all three could somehow be assembled on the same hat. Even more spectacular effects

Fur was popular for collars, stoles and muffs in the early 1900s. At the time of this photo, a muff cost about $50 for Persian Lamb, $10 for seal, muskrat or raccoon, and $20 for Australian opossum. A few women, such as Miss Armstrong of Botha, Alberta, wore long or hip-length fur coats, which ranged in price from $80 to over $375. Patricia Lyster Fenske collection.

were created with ostrich feathers, but full pairs of bird's wings were also popular around the turn of the century. Hat veils came in many forms and went in and out of style. Some were attached to hats; others were scarf-like and loose, placed over or around the hat. Some tied under a woman's chin or at the back of her hat, creating an air of mystery. The newest or best of women's hats were often worn to church as Easter bonnets, a custom in even small communities such as Paradise Hill in Saskatchewan.

Along with the hats went gloves, and even if a woman's only major outing for the week was church, a well-dressed woman of British or American background wouldn't be seen without them. Prior to the 1950s, there was an outstanding range of gloves available, too. Generally speaking, with the exception of some women who were desperately poor in the 1930s, there was something to fit every pocketbook. If the price for ready-made was simply too high, patterns were available for sewing gloves.

Featured in the 1897 spring and summer catalog from Eatons were kid gloves of various weights, including French, Derby and Czarina styles. There were silk, taffeta and lace gloves, gloves with five buttons or without buttons. Driving gloves were popular, but they were for holding the reins of horses rather than for the wheel of a car. And of course, for the truly practical at heart and those who couldn't knit gloves, there were mitts.

For most women, stockings were also treasured accessories. Women often knit their own long wool stockings for winter warmth, but those who had silk, rayon and eventually nylon stockings would wash them with great care, hoping the costly luxuries would last. When they didn't, many women sewed the runs so as to wear them a little longer. Like other things, the range of available stockings styles increased, and in the 1920s a woman could buy them in a variety of shades, with fancy ribs above or below the knee, or with embroidered designs on them.

Hemlines continued to go up, until the twenties brought radically different dress styles that were almost knee length and very loose fitting. Some had a belted effect around the thighs, but at the time, fringes of every rippling and glimmering sort were more fashionable than belts, since tiny waists were no longer the desired look.

Like hemlines, neck lines went up and down. Bows came and went, and generally, young women were most interested in the fashion shifts and were the first to embrace the new fads.

Unisex Clothes

Unisex styles and work clothes were other surprisingly early, practical options. In contrast to the very feminine hats and dresses of early times, some women were choosing the practicality of trousers even by the end of the nineteenth and first decade of the twentieth century. At first, trousers were the choice of outdoor types of women and those who enjoyed *physical culture*, but only for activities such as riding, hiking and cycling. By 1898, a few of the women who were adapting to the environment and everyday life in the prairie provinces of western Canada saw the sense of fashion styles designed for men.

Women solved problems created by long skirts in ingenious ways. Here, women at York Lake, Saskatchewan, fish from a buggy backed into the water. Sometimes the wagons were driven into even deeper water. Glenbow-Alberta Institute, NA 2878

Full skirts and the long bloomers that were part of the well-dressed woman's underwear meant women could ride horses comfortably, though most middle- and upper-class women rode sidesaddle. The divided riding skirt of the early 1900s was an even better solution, but women who moved to the sparsely populated areas of the West were often less conscious or amenable to the fashion restrictions that ruled elsewhere.

Western style leather skirts and jackets were popular with some. Métis and First Nations women crafted beautiful, soft leather clothing, and they were often happy to sell items for ready cash. Better yet, the jackets, gloves and moccasins seemed to wear forever, and it was possible for any woman who knew how to tan and sew hide to make the items for very little cost if someone in the family hunted.

Mrs. Mary Amelia Magrath Simpson of Crescent Lake, Saskatchewan, would often wear a long skirt and fringed leather jacket while packing a gun at her side. By 1918, many women who chose western wear had taken the fashion a step further. They wore men's pants or riding breeches for work and added chaps for riding. Alta Hirsche, a cowgirl on the R6 Ranch at Stirling, Alberta, had a holstered pistol at her side, but for women who actually rode the range checking or moving cattle, a gun might be considered essential if an animal was hurt and must be put down or if bears, coyotes or wolves were real or perceived threats.

Many ranch and farm women were early converts to the uniquely western styles. They spent time outdoors, working with livestock and sometimes helping with field work. Few people were around to notice, let alone comment, so for many prairie women, men's clothing styles were a reasonable and practical alternative to skirt hems that became muddied. One of the best known early converts to trousers was Cora Hind. Breeches – in three different styles and similar to the ones worn by Cora, women riders and hikers – were available in the mid-1920s from the catalog at a price of $4-5. The styles were wide from waist to knee and tight-fitting from knee to ankle.

As an editor and columnist for the *Winnipeg Free Press*, she was well known, and her field of expertise was agriculture. Since she toured farms and worked closely with farmers, she chose practical clothing, wearing knee-high boots, trousers, a leather fringed jacket and the fedora-style hat popular with men. As opposed to the more feminine dresses of other women, her clothes encouraged men to talk to her in the fashion they would talk to another farm man. Whether that was the reason for her choices could only be surmised, but she got the information she wanted, and as a result, she was a well-respected spokesperson for prairie agriculture.

With the First World War, overalls designed for women also became available. As they did during the Second World War, on the home front, women worked at jobs formerly filled by men. For some jobs, overalls were the most appropriate style of clothing, and by the late teens, women's styles

In the late 1920s, pictures such as this of women were fairly rare. Cameras were not commonplace, photos were expensive and women didn't want to be shown in work clothes. Here Eva Moyer, whose family farmed near Fort Saskatchewan, Alberta, is working at the woodpile. Walt and Faye Holt collection.

came in bib and full shirt styles, at a cost of $2.50-3.75. Long-wearing and serviceable, they were roomy everywhere except at the tight ankle band.

By the 1930s, being cash poor became the major influence on what women were wearing. Many who would have otherwise enjoyed shopping for clothes had no option except to make them. When it was no longer suitable or didn't fit, the material was reused for patches, quilts or another style of garment. However, those without money to buy new materials could still enjoy looking at the range of fabric and cloth designs available. Even the pleasure of feeling the various fabrics, as women balanced cost against how well the material might wear and how good the finished product would look, could be a pleasurable part of planning.

All Done Up

Women of the prairies were not without other aids to beauty. Some needed help with their hair; others wanted help with their faces, and others were happy just to smell good. Hairdressers were available, at least to a limited extent, in many communities. Perfumes were widely available, and popular fragrances at the turn of the century were carnation, rose, violet and lily, but there were also aloe, briar, honeysuckle, wallflower and crab apple scents. They came in cut-glass bottles often packed in elegant little boxes. For those who couldn't afford the real thing, eau de toilette was less expensive, and perfumed sachets or even real rose petals in little packages were placed in dresser drawers and left a very light, lingering fragrance.

A problem with one's face was more difficult. Two difficulties plagued the woman who wanted to hide wrinkles, narrow the appearance of her nose, change the shape of her lips or highlight her natural gifts, be they her eyes or her cheek bones. First, she faced the problem of availability of products, and then there was the risk of being the target of whispered gossip. A woman could always pinch her cheeks to give them color, but most women wanted more substantial and dependable help with their facial beauty. Often, except for those women whose religions forbade use of make-up, even women who others considered beautiful wanted more help. By the turn of the century, a variety of creams could be purchased. Face powders, bath powders, tooth powders and even foot powders were widely available, but for the most part, lipstick, rouge and eye make-up were the stuff of dreams.

When it came to hair, most women pioneers were left to their own devices, but increasingly, prairie communities attracted women who ran their own beauty parlor businesses. In families a long distance from town and where little money was available for extras, women learned to trim the hair of everyone in their families. In those homes, hair was washed in a basin of water once a week, though sometimes more often.

Doing each other's hair became a bonding time for mothers, daughters, sisters, grandmothers and aunts, any of whom might live in the same house or live nearby. It was acceptable for young girls to wear their hair long and loose, but in the late 1800s and first decades of the 1900s, when a young woman married, she was expected to wear her hair up.

Various kinds of hairpins, barrettes and combs that held the hair in place were essential. The combs could be simple or beautifully designed, the ordinary black combs selling for 17¢ and those with complex designs costing as much as 40¢. Bejewelled combs were an even greater luxury.

Not all of the beautiful hair on a woman's head was necessarily natural. For the woman whose hair was fine or thin, there were a wide variety of hairpieces and wigs available from catalogs. The Eaton's fall and winter catalog of 1909-1910 had a full wig with a middle part and hair swept up for $25. There was also the pompadour, circular padding which extended around the head, and which came already covered with hair or might be covered over by the woman's own hair. Also available were wavy switches, straight switches, coronet curls and "the Marie, a Grecian head dress consisting of three 5½-inch puffs." The Evaline Hair Wave had three large puffs in the centre and two 4 ½-inch ones on the ends, which made a "splendid dressing" for only $3.75. To get the right color for the mail order hairpiece, all a woman had to do was send a sample of her

The artistic photograph of multiple images of Mrs. A.C. Ross and daughters in 1917 shows a range of styles where the hair is worn "up" or off the shoulders. Although most women of the time had very long hair, such styles often incorporated hair pieces made from human hair. Provincial Archives of Manitoba, Foote 475, N2075

hair, one that showed the full length from scalp to tip, but the experts' advice was that the artificial hair should always be a shade darker than a woman's natural color, just in case the hairpiece faded.

When it came to getting a hairdo, rags were the name of the game in thousands of homes. The art of *tying* the rags was not terribly difficult. Strands of hair were selected and positioned on a long strip of cloth. The hair and cloth were rolled up, and once close to the head, the ends of the rag were tied. In fact, as well as ordinary rags, there were fancy hair *rags* that served the same purpose and were set in the same manner. For them, thick but bendable wires were covered with cloth, and the long end

In about 1915, these Manitoba hairdressers are using electric curling irons. Prior to the availability of electricity, curling irons were heated by placing the curling iron in the lamp hood and leaving it until it was hot. The hairdresser's experience was the only control over the temperature of the hot iron.
Provincial Archives of Manitoba, Industry, Commerce, Hairdresser 1, N 231

pieces were sewn so as not to fray. The curling technique worked, especially to make ringlets, but wonderful curls of other types were also possible, depending on the length of hair and how it was combed. Combing the ringlets or curls to become the fashionable hairdo the woman wanted might be a greater challenge. As effective as the rags were, usually, metal hair clips and curlers were high on a woman's list of desirable beauty aids once they were available or a woman could afford them.

The boyish bob became the fashion in the 1920s. Young women flocked to hairdressers to get the new cuts, or they had their mothers and sisters cut their long locks for them. Some older women chose the popular style, but until the 1930s, one sort of bun or another was still popular with them. Beauty parlors and hairdressers could offer women many options, and women with hairdressing skills were in enormous demand.

Dorothy's Story

Dorothy Clark moved to Lethbridge, Alberta, in 1924 when she was 24 years old. She had just completed her training in beauty culture in Minneapolis at the Academy of Beauty. To pass her exams, she had studied hair care, scalp and skin care, beauty culture equipment and nutrition. She had learned to give facials with mud packs. There had been no course on make-up, but she learned how to massage necks and shoulders. She learned techniques for giving manicures, though there was no nail polish, and she had learned about haircuts, dyes and hair styling techniques such as the marcel.

Responding to an ad that she had seen on the blackboard at the beauty school, she contacted Mrs. McKinnon, who owned and operated the Florentine Beauty Parlour in Lethbridge. With Mrs. McKinnon expecting her, Dorothy purchased a train ticket and set out for a new job and life in a new country.

She and Mrs. McKinnon were the only hairdressers in town, and everyone needed hairdos. Society women wanted her services, but to her surprise, so did the young ladies from the red light district. Once a week, they took taxis to the beauty parlor and sat in her chair waiting to be made more beautiful. Dorothy was uncomfortable and never totally became used to the idea, but as she got to know the girls, she felt for them. Most were in their early twenties, were very quiet, wore little or no make-up and were surprisingly plain-looking to her.

At the time, permanent waves were just becoming popular. Not having taken the course and uncomfortable with the electric contraptions that were used, Dorothy left perms to Mrs. McKinnon, who wrapped her client's hair around metal curlers. Each was attached by wire to the post that fed into an electric outlet, and the perms did work, but most clients went out with some raw burn spots around their necks. Mrs. McKinnon also did facials, shampoos and booked appointments, but for her $35 wage, Dorothy was responsible for all other types of hairdressing. Bobbi haircuts were popular, considered somewhat risqué but simple to do. She started with her scissors just below the ear at one side and cut straight around the head to the other side. She also did a great deal of marcelling, which meant heating a special curling iron over a gas flame. There was always the danger of burning someone's hair, so she would hold the hot iron close to her nose to test the heat. Usually, she finished in half an hour, and occasionally, when the iron had been too hot, she didn't charge her customers, who usually paid a dollar for the hairdo.

Short hair and waves were popular in the 1920s and early 1930s. The hairstyle was created with a marcelling iron, which was either electric or heated in a lamp. The end of the iron had a rectangular shape, forming a three dimensional wave. The special iron left these tidy waves when it was removed from the hair. Walt and Faye Holt collection.

Dorothy also did some bleaching and colors, but women did not want it known that they had dyed their hair. The shop had a small curtained area for privacy, and the process began. For blonde, hair was bleached with hydrogen peroxide. For color, a henna powder was mixed into a gooey paste and dabbed on the hair. Black was not possible but the henna gave a rich brown highlight, though the temporary color eventually washed out. Then as now, hairdressing took imagination as well as skill. Women walked in the door with pictures cut from magazines, and they wanted to walk out looking like the picture.[3]

Body Awareness and Body Beautiful

Rich and poor, fashionably or plainly dressed, women possessed different kinds of beauty. The stereotypical type of beauty was only skin deep and such a beauty was usually youthful. Nevertheless, older women and those prairie women who faced the elements and whose roles made being body beautiful a difficult challenge could also be beautiful – if they had the right advice and remedies.

In the Palliser Triangle of southern Alberta and Saskatchewan, even the air attacked beauty. Dry winds made a woman's skin age. Winter and summer, chapped hands were common problems. There were partial and temporary solutions suggested in newspaper columns. Usually, a neighbor knew of a remedy or household hint for every situation. Books offered advice, too.

Mary Melendy's book *The Perfect Woman* was published in the United States in 1901, but found its way to the Canadian west. At a time when most women had little or no information about love and sex, it was very informative. For the most part, it supported the status quo, but its treatment of men, women and their bodies left little to the imagination. It also gave the home remedies women craved as they tried to keep or achieve their ideal of beauty. With all the available contemporary potions and creams, some of the remedies were long ago abandoned, but a few of the passages remain as true today as when a prairie woman read them long ago.

For Chapped Hands: Tie a teacupful of bran in a muslin bag, and put over night into a large water can or jug of rain water. Use this water to wash with on the following morning, and every morning until the chaps are cured. As often as water is withdrawn from the water can or jug, refill with fresh rain water, in order that the bran may be constantly soaking in it. The bran in the bag should be renewed about twice a week.

Take particular care to dry the skin well every time it is washed: then, as well as every night at bedtime, rub a piece of deer's suet over the parts affected; a few dressings will perform a cure. The deer's suet may be bought at any of the shops where venison is sold. Another excellent remedy is glycerine, which should be smeared, by means of the finger or a camel's hair brush two or three times a day to the parts affected.[4]

Air Baths Beneficial to The Skin: Stimulating the little nerves that lie upon the surface of the body tends to stimulate the healthy action of the skin, the circulation of the blood, and, finally the operations of all the organs. To do this successfully completely disrobe, go into a room filled with fresh air, and rub down. This is particularly gratifying after a long day of hard work or shopping or visiting. If you feel nervous or irritable try this simple method of opening the pores. It will make you doubt if you were in a bad humor after all, so pleasing will be the change.[5]

A Great Beautifier: There are few things more conducive to health than walking exercise. Walking – I mean a walk, not a stroll – is a glorious exercise; it expands the chest and throws back the shoulders; it strengthens the muscles; it promotes digestion; it tends to open the bowels, and is better than any aperient pill ever invented; it clears the complexion, giving roses to the cheeks and brilliancy to the eye, and, in point of fact, is one…of the greatest beautifiers in the world.

The early morning is the most desirable time for a walk.…

We also wish to impress upon your minds that you can be as healthy at fifty as at fifteen years of age, with an improved mental education, experience and culture, which should add to your attractions.[6]

Beach Fashion, Beach Life

Not surprisingly, fashions and conventions of the towns and cities were a little more relaxed when women were on holidays or at the beach. Over time, bathing suits and beach wear changed dramatically. One area where beach life reflected the increasingly informal expectations of society regarding fashion and behavior was at a lake near Edmonton. First named the Wabamun town site, renamed Kapasiwin in 1918, the village became a place of summer fun for thousands of vacationers. On weekends, people from all walks of life, rich and poor, went to the beaches there. The first to have cabins in the area tended to be financially comfortable and of Canadian, American or British heritage. When they went to the lake, they took with them the general attitudes about what was appropriate or risqué. From the time she was a girl, Queenie Palmer spent time at Wabamun and saw enormous change in bathing fashions and social conventions.

Queenie's Story

Queenie Watson's parents, Fred Watson and Rilla [Hannah] Watson (nee Barker) purchased a lot at the new town site, sight unseen. Soon the family's newly built cottage became the centre of family fun.

For more than 80 years, Queenie Watson Palmer, her children and then her grandchildren spent part of every summer at the lake. Life there had its unique attractions. Swimming, canoeing and sports competitions were part of summer fun. Queenie's father sold life insurance and was also an instructor at the Morris School of Physical Culture, a gym and training facility sometimes used by Edmonton's great women's basketball team, the Edmonton Grads. So, Queenie was raised to respect society's conventions, but also to value physical activity such as swimming. Years later, Queenie's husband, Miles Palmer, himself an Edmonton sports hero, organized sports days at the beach, once again emphasizing the value of physical culture, including for girls and women. Queenie not only witnessed the changes in bathing suits, beach wear and beach activities, she experienced them.

Hazy Recollections

In later years, the big social event of the week was to meet all the fathers, husbands, and house guests who arrived on board the Campers' Special [train] on Saturdays at 3:00 p.m. It was quite fun to watch as all the passengers stepped down from the train, and we could see which cottagers were having guests for the weekend. Some would have as many as twenty! Imagine cooking for so many on a wood stove in a hot, dark kitchen.

Everyone dressed for this occasion. The ladies were immaculate in either voile or dimity dresses with white kid or canvas boots, kept spotless by rubbing Bon Ami on them. The girls had wash [cotton] dresses and proper summer sandals. I remember one special dress I wore which was a lovely pink and green small-check gingham with a huge bertha collar of white organdy and a gorgeous white sash that tied in a large bow.

All the fancy food for weekend entertaining would have to come out on the train. Fathers would be encumbered with at least two enormous valises full of supplies. Those clothes which had been taken into town on the previous Monday would be returned all starched and ironed, perhaps from Lee Kee's Laundry on 108 Street, south of Jasper Avenue.

Besides meeting the train on Saturdays, we really stayed properly dressed all week. We did not have easy lounge wear which is available now. Ladies wore cotton print dresses and laced canvas boots. What else would we wear out at the lake? Nothing else had been invented yet.

As for bathing suits, the first ones I can remember were made of a lustre fabric in red or navy blue. These were two-piece outfits. The top, resembling a dress which extended to the knees, had a fairly full, gored skirt, in a princess style, and was quite ripply and full around the hem. The gored line continued to the shoulders while the sleeves were elbow-length, puffy, and complete with a frill. The necklines were usually V-shaped with a sailor collar and a tie at the front. They looked much like miniature sailor suits only with full skirts and decorated with a white soutache braid. Several rows of this braid were stitched around the edge of the skirt, the sleeves and the collar.

With this costume, a matching lustre bathing cap with a full crown and frill was worn. An elastic band under the chin held the cap in place. The second part of this costume was a pair of bloomers which tied around the waist and extended to a frill at the knees. Some women wore stockings with all this, and bathing shoes, too! An essential item if the beach was stony, but not necessary at Kapasiwin.

The costume wasn't meant for swimming so much as for paddling around the edge of the water. It definitely was not very practical for much swimming as the full skirt would float in the water to around the waist, and, of course, the cap didn't keep hair dry. The lustre material, too, became quite heavy when wet, so serious activity of any kind was greatly restricted. When we went down for a swim we did just that as sitting around in a lustre bathing suit was not comfortable — they were very scratchy when wet. Besides, our housekeeping was suspect if we loafed around the beach too long....

The men's knit bathing suits were complete with tops, a button at one shoulder, and round necklines, both front and back. They were shorter in length than the ladies' extending to mid-thigh with a straight skirt at the front and back.

About 1919, some of the women discovered that the men's bathing suits were much more practical for swimming than their own lustre ones. So the daring ones would show up for their swims in their husbands' bathing suits, but only during the week when no one was around. Some were criticized; indeed, criticized most severely for wearing them. Visits were received from neighbours, expressing

In 1915, women enjoyed the many lakes of the West. The increasingly skimpy bathing suits offered freedom, but most women still just paddled around or swam, as opposed to diving from a high board or towering rock.
Provincial Archives of Manitoba, Foote 1206, N 2182

their disapproval. I remember my mother went down for a swim once in my father's suit. One of the neighbours...spoke to her stating that she thought my mother was rather depraved to be wearing such an outfit. From then on, comfortable swimming had to be stealthily done!

Gradually, the lustre suits went out of fashion, and more practical bathing suits came into vogue after Annette Kellerman, a famous Channel swimmer, introduced the first knit suits which women could wear for real swimming. These suits left little exposure for suntans as the back and front came to within a few inches of the n[e]ck, had short sleeves, and knit skirts.

In 1922, I remember someone, probably a pretty girl, walking on the beach with a suit that showed the middle of her back. It was remarked that there was "rather too much skin showing." But in another summer or two, everyone was wearing much the same style. Gradually, the suits became tighter, shorter, and much smarter-looking. Then rubber bathing caps came into use. Bobbed hair, in fashion at the time, went well under one of those....

As to bathing habits, we very seldom swam in the morning, although a pre-breakfast swim was compulsory for many of the children. Certainly, the mothers never got away for a swim until afternoon. There was too much housework to be done. No one ever dawdled around at the beach in a bathing suit just to sit in the sun! That was just too informal!...

One social event worth mentioning was the afternoon teas. Children would be included in these occasions when a group of ladies would meet at about three o'clock in the hostess' cottage for gentle conversation, freshly-baked biscuits, home-made cake, and cups of hot tea. Guests came attired in crisp summer dress-

Competing during a Loyal Order of Moose picnic at Victoria Park in Edmonton, these women don't seem inhibited by either their dresses or their shoes.
City of Edmonton Archives, EA 160-1420

es, white shoes and stockings, and proper hair-pinned hairdos. So long ago that it now seems quaint. These pleasant but rather stylized gatherings gradually became fewer when afternoon sun-bathing on the beach became popular, and housewives, mothers, and grandmothers became "emancipated."...

The sports days were not organized until about 1925....The first were held only on the beach, and strangely enough, did not include any events in the water, but only running races on the sand, and of course, a grand tug-of-war.[7]

VII. Exploring Other Landscapes

Some of life's greatest pleasures came from setting aside time – time for a vacation or to explore new places, whether they were geographical landscapes or places of the heart and mind. Renewal also came from trying new artistic endeavors, hobbies or activities. Even spending time alone, quietly contemplating feelings and ideas, or reading was as important to some prairie women of yesteryear as it is today. Just stepping out of or away from everyday responsibilities for hours or days to read, write or paint brought the revitalization that busy and tired women needed.

What was intrinsically pleasurable and relaxing would always be unique for each woman. One woman's passionate hobby would be another's idea of utter boredom. Gardening was a hobby to some, a gruelling toil to others. A holiday outing for one was just something added to the workload in another woman's eyes.

Still, there were days of leisure and pleasure, and people on the early prairies did take holidays. Sometimes they did not travel far; sometimes they travelled the world. Many women had only a weekend or few days at a beach or by a mountain stream. Others had months in which to relax.

Some fortunate women did travel the world. Accompanying her husband, Alberta's premier, Mary Sifton and her daughter Nell travelled to Egypt in the early 1900s. National Archives of Canada, PA 127251

Communing with nature was a tonic for some women's souls, but going to the lakeshore or to the mountains could bring joy or discomfort in equal measure, depending on the individual woman. To the naturalist, they were places to discover new birds and stones and flowers. For artists and photographers, they were subjects for paintings and photos. To the women who liked to write, everything that they saw or experienced was worthy of documenting in journals, stories, poems or letters. The key was taking time to explore whatever landscape, real or imagined, created moments of pleasure.

Lakeside Life

Areas in and around Edmonton, Alberta, had been settled since the days of the fur trade. By late 1800s, groups and families would go off for a few days of camping or shooting in the wilds. The Cooking Lake area was close to the town, and by 1894, wanting a permanent site for setting up their tents, a few families of camping and holiday enthusiasts purchased Pine Island. They would set out by buggy from Edmonton between five and six in the morning but not arrive at the lake until after seven in the evening, having endured a long, bumpy and often muddy trip. However, once at their destination, which they renamed Koney Island, the fun seekers had access to the toys water-lovers have long valued. In fact, they needed them to get back and forth from the mainland. So, there were rowboats, canoes, sail boats, dinghies and in 1899, the club could brag of having the first motor launch in the West.

Another popular lake near Edmonton was Wabamun, which developed two popular beach communities. One was Kapasiwin, where Queenie Palmer and her family spent their summers. The other was Seba, and there, lake-life was similar to that in summer vacation communities at regional lakes throughout the prairies.

From Seba to the Mountain Top

The women of the Lockhart, Douglas and Duggan families handed the ability to enjoy themselves from one generation to the next. The three families dated their arrival in the West to the first decade of the 1900s. Eventually, they were living in Edmonton, related by marriage and sharing good times at Seba Beach on Lake Wabamun.

The Lockharts were in Edmonton by 1908, and pioneer William Lockhart built a vacation cottage at Lake Wabamun, likely one of the first four cottages in the wilderness area that would become the village of Seba. Originally, it was named Alderwood, and the family enjoyed time there. Daughter Marion married Henry

On July 12, 1914, this group visits a quiet beach near Wynyard, Saskatchewan. Water sports don't seem to be planned since one woman reads; the others likely enjoyed the view, the breeze and the sound of the waves. University of Alberta Archives, 77-193-35

Ward Beecher Douglas in 1906, and their first baby, Jean, was born the next year. Over the following 20 years, five other children arrived. They eventually owned the cottage, which they renamed the Doug-Inn.

From the time of Jean's birth, her mother and father vacationed at the lake. Although very early trips to the cabin may have meant taking the train to Fallis and then a ferry across to the beach, from early on, the Douglas family owned a car. Henry Douglas would drive his wife and children to the lake at the beginning of summer. The cottage had a beach front and was surrounded by trees. Over the decades, the original building was enlarged and became more comfortable. But the people and the joy of physical activities around the scenic and ever-fascinating lake were central to the good times.

Marion had a very optimistic personality, and her attitudes seemed to rub off on her first-born daughter, Jean, who loved the lake. There, adults and children enjoyed canoeing, by themselves and with friends. The children became good swimmers, and young Jean could swim as far as the YWCA camp about 16 kilometres (10 miles) away, on the other side of the lake. The family grew to young adulthood.

By the time Jean was a teenager, summer dances were held in various locations at Seba until, in the 1920s, a pavilion was built. A fiddler played for the very early dances, but by the late twenties, whenever there was no band, a piano might roll out the tunes. With the music of a four-piece band, dancers paid 5¢ or 10¢ for each dance at what were called Jitney Dances.

By the 1930s, the family hosted the Douglas Printing Company annual picnic at the lake for employees and their families. "During the day, the men would have on some kind of top hat, and they would even have them on when they went swimming. And the women, of course, were in dresses."[1] But their clothing didn't inhibit the fun. The day-long picnic featured games of horseshoes and baseball. People swam, competed in tug-of-wars and ate huge amounts of food. The long board sidewalk, about a foot off the ground from the cabin to the water, was covered with tablecloths and piled with food. Men, women and children sat on the ground beside it, and the feast began.

When they hosted the annual picnic for Douglas Printing Company employees, this raised boardwalk was covered with tablecloths and used as a picnic buffet table. Nancy Allison collection.

In 1931, Jean married Ken Duggan. Ken's parents, Welsh-born David and Hannah (known as Marian), had arrived in southern Alberta in about 1905. After Ken's marriage to Jean, the entire extended family would find that Seba Beach was the place to spend the summer.

Like their parents, Ken and Jean Duggan had an active social life, and soon they also had two daughters, Sally in 1934 and Nancy in 1941. Summer was spent at the cottage, and the cabin was busiest during the summer months. However, as roads improved, sometimes in the winter the Douglas and Duggan families skated at the lake, and they even supplied their own music by taking the gramophone outdoors with them.

Yet, summer fun provided the most vivid memories. During the day, the women painted the deck chairs and picked berries. But according to Nancy Allison (nee Duggan) they didn't can the berries. They just ate them that day or in jams, jellies and pies.

There were games with others on or near the beach. Adults started many of the games, including hide and seek, run sheep run, or kick the can, and the children were happy to join in. Evenings meant campfire time and stories, especially ghost stories.

The vacation home saw endless happy occasions and family gatherings for children, grandchildren and great-grandchildren. At the cottage, all discovered the value of relaxation, fun, family and friends. Not surprisingly, those good times would become very much a part of who they were and perhaps even shaped their attitudes towards life.

"With six...Douglas children in the family, there were always lots of relatives around." According to granddaughter Nancy, there were clear signs that they enjoyed being there, enjoyed each other's company and that of lake friends. "Just hearing them talk was fun for me and my cousins. My grandmother, who I remember and adored, loved to tell stories about the early days at the lake. She had a great laugh and told about some hilarious parents [of other children at the lake]."

In about 1940, before Nancy was born, the cabin became home to a Peterborough canoe, tippy but renowned for its speed, whether manoeuvred by its owners or by someone from Seba Beach who had asked to use it in the races during the August Annual Regatta. At the regatta, women as well as men entered canoe races, swimming and other water competitions.

Eventually, the Douglas cottage was sold. Nancy took her own children camping, and that was the beginning of good times in the wilderness and a love of the outdoors for her own daughter, Leanne. She developed a pioneering spirit and style of her own. In May, 1993, Leanne Allison – great granddaughter of Marion Lochart

Canoeing was one of the many favorite pastimes of the Douglas family, whose cabin was at Seba Beach on Lake Wabamun, Alberta. Nancy Allison collection.

Douglas and Hannah [Marian] Duggan – was a member of the first all-women's team to climb Mount Logan. Situated in the Yukon, the mountain is the largest in Canada, and it is snow-covered all year around.[2]

Mountain Times

By the end of the 1900s, women had been enjoying the mountains of western Canada for more than a hundred years. Some were fortunate enough to live where foothills, mountains or lakes created dramatic vistas, and where they could hike on virgin ground or along well-worn paths. In other instances, families made holiday trips to these awe-inspiring areas. The sports and recreational endeavors of these holiday playgrounds were seldom limited to males, even in the early days, and women trod where some would have perceived the landscape too wild and dangerous for the fairer sex.

Soon after the railway made travel to the mountains more realistic, increasing numbers of women stopped at the mountain hotels. They wore long skirts or long, divided riding skirts and bowler-style hats out for an adventuresome day of hiking or climbing. For the outings, most went with guides, such as those of the CPR, or with male family members or friends.

For those with less money, camping was a popular mode of holiday travel. Whether holiday-hunters travelled to provincial and national parks, or to nearby lakes, women enjoyed the buggy or car ride or rail travel. Seeing new countryside,

Women alpinists from around the world helped to make hiking and climbing popular along Alberta's western mountain border. Here, in 1903, Beatrice Longstaff Lance tackes the rock, despite the inconvenience of her clothing. Whyte Museum of the Canadian Rockies, NA 30-50

water sports, fishing, hiking and camping could be adapted to whatever degree of risk and discomfort women and their families preferred.

There were many popular places for camping and outdoor holidays, but some were ideal destinations. The Rockies attracted vacationers who spent a few weeks sightseeing and camping, and the mountains attracted those who wanted to be active and adventuresome.

Given the opportunity, numerous women became serious mountain enthusiasts. In 1906, the Alpine Club of Canada was officially organized, and its members were serious hikers and climbers, including women, who were not welcome in some of the American clubs. In Canada, of particular interest to the ACC were the Banff, Lake Louise and Jasper areas, but members of the club climbed and hiked throughout the Rockies, not only hiking readily accessible trails but also crossing glaciers and climbing.

By August of 1933, some of those enthusiasts organized the Skyline Hikers of the Canadian Rockies. As a qualification to join the group, the man or woman had to have completed "certified" hikes of at least 25 miles (40 km) in the Canadian Rockies, none of which could have been hiked before August 4, 1933. On the very first hike, both men and women were from far-off places like Philadelphia, New York, Chicago and England. Some were renowned in their fields, such as Carl Runguis, Georgina Englehard and Byron Harmon. Women from the Banff area attended the first Skyline Hikers camp, but so did at least two women from the flatland prairies, Miss Martha Houston of Lethbridge and Miss Margaret Moorehead of Bassano.

For most women hikers, the physical effort, the beautiful landscape and spending time with like-minded people were all part of the pleasure. Such people could be found in Alberta along the eastern edge of the Rockies, or like Mary Schaeffer, they moved to the mountains. However, they might also live a long distance away, and year after year, they made the holiday trip to their beloved mountains.

Mary Schaeffer first arrived in Banff as a tourist, but she became an avid hiker and explorer and moved to the area. For her, camping was one of life's finer pleasures. Whyte Museum of the Canadian Rockies, V439/PS-1

Elizabeth's Story

One of the driving forces behind the Alpine Club of Canada was Elizabeth Parker from Winnipeg, but both she and her daughter Jean played an active part in the organization for many years. Elizabeth became the club's first secretary, and Jean became librarian. For volume one of the *Canadian Alpine Journal*, in recording the objectives of the club, Elizabeth noted, "It is the [Club's] business to support the picturesque and wholly enjoyable transit to the mountain-places by pack-horse and saddle, and to promote the too much neglected exercise of walking. Your true lover of Nature is also a man of the unfamiliar roads and forest trails...."[3] The club was to further scientific knowledge of the mountains, to cultivate interest in art and photography related to the mountains and to publish a guidebook.

Elizabeth had first visited Banff and the Rockies in the 1880s. With the organization of Canadian Alpine Club summer camps, she spent many seasons exploring. The second annual camp of the club, held in 1907, meant hiking at Paradise Valley. Other female hikers and climbers were once again in attendance. For comfort, they opted for short, mid-calf length skirts or pantaloon-type britches. But the actual joy and experience of early mountaineering for prairie women was captured for others in Elizabeth's writing. For some of her articles published in the *Canadian Alpine Journal,* she wrote under the pseudonym A.L.O.W.

My first visit to the Rockies was a summer in Banff in the late eighties before it began to be a popular watering place. There were good roads to the Cave and Basin, to the Hot Springs and to the Spray River below the Falls; but enough of the mountain wilderness remained to give our holiday an aspect of remoteness. The next visit covered all the seasons and included a climb through the snow to the top of the hill called Tunnel; also a guideless rock-climb with five other unequipped innocents up the long ridge of Cascade Mountain to within 200 feet of the summit, on a glorious day in September. We saw Mount Assiniboine, a white pyramid south, piercing the blue above, and wondered if it had a name. I forget the year, but by that time the village had two wooden churches, a good school-house and several attractive residences. The C.P.R. hotel had many guest[s], and one of the serious sights at the Hot Springs was an array of crutches and staffs hanging on nearby trees. You were liable to meet distinguished persons almost any day....

Winter was a continual joy by day and night. Every snowfall was windless and snow mushrooms were everywhere; the "gathered intensity" brought to the blue and purple in the recesses of the mountains westward, and all the changing colors were a daily wonder....

The annual Banff Winter Carnival did draw some for winter holidays. Attending in 1930, Mary Cross (Dover), left, and friends went cross-country skiing. Festivities usually included women's hockey and figure skating. Glenbow-Alberta Institute, ND 8-506

There were other visits to Banff, in summer or in autumn. I remember a borrowed fishing basket and a climb down the steep bank of the river to the pool below the Bow Falls one fine sunset. When I reached the angler's recess, there I found a workman named Hughie, who generously helped with hook and fly and gentle instruction. I caught nothing and Hughie gallantly helped me up the long steep bank. Then I said "It's a beautiful evening." He straightened himself, looked toward the west and said "It's a *beautiful world.*" Wordsworth would have made a poem out of that incident....

[She set off alone for the Upper Lakes, Mirror and Agnes, and had an exhilarating day. Then back at Lake Louise]....I followed the damp trail under the trees, noticing the wild flowers on [the] way, and before coming to the Beehive, I scrambled up that most lovely inclined meadow where velvety forget-me-nots grew. The tourists have destroyed all that bloom; – miserable vandals!...

I wonder if any accustomed visitor ever has recaptured the surprised delight of his first view of Lake Louise. Certainly he never forgot. One summer, when the chalet had grown to a charming hotel, whose rates were within the limits of a very modest competence, my climber spent nine hours on the summit ridge of Mount Victoria. She started from the Chalet by starlight and went through the Death Trap to Abbot's Pass before the avalanches were loosened, and so up to the ridge, where a bitter wind was blowing. Guests watched the

Smaller and less expensive cameras made photography an increasingly popular hobby. Here, near Borden, Saskatchewan, in about 1910, Helen Mallory Schrader takes snapshots outside her farm home. Saskatoon Public Library, LHD 5258

white Mountain through a telescope all that day in some anxiety; for a slip of a girl [Jean] was in the small climbing company. By night they returned, worn out with all the arduous ascent but thankful for one more summit attained.[4]

Worlds and Words

Words were the stuff of magic to countless prairie women. Whether a book offered much-needed medical information, directions on how to develop photographs or insights into nature or love, through the words of writers like Pauline Johnson and George Elliot, books allowed women to travel at will to other worlds and also to acquire the knowledge they needed or valued.

Early school libraries were very small, sometimes comprised only of books owned and brought to the community by the teacher. Some children took out books that their parents enjoyed reading; but the catalog carried pages of book titles. Many homestead families brought about 20 or more books, so books written in various languages were available. Neighbors shared books, but there were simply never enough. Lady Aberdeen, whose husband became governor general of Canada, visited the West in 1890, became aware of the problem and began a campaign to make more books and magazines available to settlers. She encouraged women in Winnipeg to get names from the immigration agent, put together packages of reading material and perhaps add in some other useful item that might lift the spirits of homestead women. Organizing a society for the purpose, women were able to send the packages free of charge on C.P. rail.

With the war and other priorities, 1914 brought an end to the service initiated by Lady Aberdeen, but by then, books had become more available, and local book groups and literary societies were fairly common in communities across the prairies. Based on a shared interest in reading, the groups often included both men and women. Despite the social pleasures that came with an evening devoted to talking about books, the creation of public libraries, which could serve the many families in communities, was considered the best way to encourage and support reading. Both sexes forwarded the cause, but significant support came from individual women and women's groups. Education was high on their agenda. The cause was a worthy one, and for those in isolated areas or very small communities, travelling libraries evolved into the popular alternative.

The creation of open shelf and travelling libraries brought books to the general population. Part of the push for these libraries and the extension of them throughout the province came from Saskatchewan's first female M.L.A., Sarah McEwan Ramsland.

During her two terms, Sarah Ramsland was concerned with providing adequate libraries, among other issues. By 1924, just before her defeat in the 1925 provincial election, the province had about 800 travelling libraries that served rural districts. After leaving politics, Ramsland administered the travelling library system for the provincial Library Service. In doing so, she helped to bring pleasure and knowledge to thousands of women in isolated areas or communities that had not yet been able to finance a library.

At the same time, towns were also building their own public libraries, and women were often involved on the library boards. To raise money for books, they held tag days, and some women's groups even had book showers for their local libraries.

Ina's Story

In Alberta, Ina Scanlan (nee Greene) was an early librarian with a vision and a world view. For her, books and travel brought much pleasure. Ina grew up and attended school in Red Deer, and by 1914, when the town opened its library, the third public one in the province, Ina became its first librarian. The job paid 25¢ an hour, but it was only part time, so by 1916, when her family moved to Medicine Hat, she went, too.

After Ina spent a short stint working at a local law office, she set out for new horizons. She stayed with her sister in Montreal, and then she and some other Medicine Hat girls lived for a time in Toronto where Ina attended a ladies' college and won a medal in her business course. While in the East, she took art from Arthur Lismer of the Group of Seven, but by 1930, she decided to return home.

Soon, she was off on a cruise with her father, a journey that began in Victoria, continued through the Panama Canal and ended in Halifax. During the thirties, she married and moved to the Athabasca region of Alberta. In 1948, after her husband's death, she returned to Medicine Hat and was instrumental in building a strong and varied library program there.

After taking courses at the Calgary Public Library, she set up a children's program in Medicine Hat. Ina had story time at the library, and it became so popular, her readings grew to include as many as 500 children and had to be held at the theatre. She organized a reading club, and each week, she broadcast on the radio a 15-minute story time for children.

Not only did she enjoy the worlds created in books, she saw more of the world while she learned about libraries. Along with other Canadian librarians, she toured libraries in Sweden, completing much of the land travel by bookmobile. The group crossed the Arctic Circle and departed for home via Denmark. Other years in her life

While dealing with issues of the larger world during the Second World War, these Alberta service women escaped the seriousness of life through reading, fun and friendship. However, the gas mask – which they had been trained to use – suggests the importance of their military duties. Dunny Hanna collection.

were also filled with travel, and as a result, she had a great deal of knowledge and understanding of the world to offer while serving book lovers.

In many ways, her work at the library served children. However, by making children enthusiastic about stories and books, not only did she broaden their worlds, she gave their moms one more reason to go to the library. She gave them quiet time, too, when the children were immersed in the imaginary worlds of the books they loved.

Rediscovering Our Own Landscapes

Writing would bring pleasure to many women. Sometimes the pleasure came from writing a letter; sometimes it was from picking up a pen simply for the joy of exploring ideas and putting words to paper. Some western women would become famous for their novels, poetry, journals, reports or letters. Others would remain entirely unknown, but their pleasure in working with words would be no less.

Winnifred's Story

Like famous and unknown writers across the prairies, one day Winnifred Lois Kloster (nee Gallop) picked up the pen. In sitting down and putting her perceptions on paper, she acknowledged she had a story to tell; she and that story mattered; and her choices in how to tell it were part of who she was. It meant struggling with how to understand the past and its meaning in the present.

Born in Battleford, Saskatchewan, in 1928, Winnifred was raised on a farm in the Eagle Hills area. She loved the beauty of her natural surroundings. Not surprisingly, given her ancestry, a second interest became western Canadian history. Her earliest ancestors in Canada were English and Scots fur traders and surveyors who found wives among the indigenous women. Winnifred became interested in poetry as an adult, when she discovered the work of Robert Service. "I thought if Robert Service could tell a story in poem form, why can't I?" Having learned the history of her country and her mixed-blood roots, she, like many other women, discovered that writing could be a wonderful pleasure.

"Poetry was my way of expressing this love and documenting some of the stories of my family and friends for my children. I have no formal education in this area, just a love of rhyme." Like others who pursued a hobby, she started in a small way. The more she wrote, the more she wanted to write, and her narrative poems became longer and longer as she explored her feelings about her heritage.

Writing poetry has provided hours of quiet, introspective pleasure to her, but to some extent, she also writes so that her children and grandchildren will know about her past. One of her poems, a very long one, tackles the history of the west. In 1955, with the fiftieth anniversary of the province of Saskatchewan, the community picked the poem to represent them in a book telling the stories of early life in various school districts. The poem on the next page reflects on the past and tells her feelings about her heritage and the landscape. She has chosen to feel positive about the past, but her words don't deny other realities, too.

Far Away and At Home

Without telephones and e-mail, communication with those far away meant the written word. Letters conveyed to distant relatives and friends what mattered at home and far away. They recorded the small events in people's lives, and they recorded the important events that unfolded in western Canada.

For many, simply writing a letter brought pleasure, and letters brought pleasure to the recipient. They were awaited with great anticipation. Then, people read and reread them. The letters that have survived suggest the many landscapes that were part of the lives of prairie women, and like life, they mingle joys with sorrows.

Letter writing did not end with early telephones. In the 1940s and 50s, long distance calls were still expensive, so the children of those early pioneers who moved

The Eagle Hills

As you travel on the Highway
    Just south of Battleford town,
Look at the view in front of you
    And you will be spell bound.

Look there, across the horizon
    Kept in a purple haze,
The mystery that enthrals you
    Will set your heart ablaze.

Look there, against the skyline
    As far as the eye can see,
Patches of hills and valleys
    With all shades of greenery.

Look at the beauty to behold there
    Think of the price that was paid,
For the privilege we enjoy here,
    Because of the will that stayed

Think of the lives that were taken,
    A price that would give one a chill
Read your history and learn
    Of the battle of Cutknife Hill

How the Redcoats surprised the Indian
    In their ti-pi'd town.
How the Indian fought to preserve his freedom
    And tried to drive the white-man down.

How the ravines echoed the war cries
    Of the white-man and Indian, alike.
How the eagle mounting the skies
    Screamed in confusion and fright.

Where are those eagles
    For which these hills were named?
Where are the Indian tents
    That dotted connecting plains?

Where are the buffalo,
    Which roamed at will?
What the Natives used and ate
    They planned to kill.

Where are the noble chiefs
    Who hunted with pride?
Decorating their costumes
    With eagle plumes and buffalo hide.

What are the possible memories
    That could be etched in those hills?
What are the possible stories
    That even the eagles could quill?

Are they all hidden
    In the splendor of the hue,
Protected by the Majesty
    That enthrals you?

Stretching from Cutknife passed Baljenne,
    Their beauty did not remain
Keeping their tales of many
    From generations who made new claims

So we drive along in silence
    As the sun sinks in the west
For a moment I think, what if...
    But I am sure it all worked out
    For the best.[5]

away, often at retirement, passed along news from the family and community. Such letters revealed the ways life had changed for women and the ways it had remained the same.

The letters suggest individual perceptions and interests, too. Some writers seemed to have optimistic spirits and mental landscapes that allowed for joyfulness, despite the ups and downs as one year followed another. Often they showed that even in the midst of work, there were small joys worthy of note right in women's own backyards.

Evelyn's Story

As a girl in the late 1920s, Evelyn Stiller lived near Botha, Alberta. Her first jobs on graduation from Normal School were at one-room schools in rural Alberta, and she found herself desperately lonely. So, she began two pursuits that would bring her pleasure over a lifetime. She became more serious about art, and, in a small scribbler, she wrote a story about a young woman teaching in a rural school.

By 1947, Evelyn married Verle Lyster. During the years that followed, Evelyn pursued her passion for drawing and painting, among many other arts, but her writing would become more practical. On a trip to Montana and North Dakota with her husband, Evelyn wrote the first of the surviving letters to her mother-in-law, who was living on the farm with them at the time. For almost 40 years, she and her husband corresponded weekly with Verle's widowed mother, who later moved to California. Sometimes, each wrote a separate letter; sometimes one started the letter and the other added a section. Often the letters were a blend of personal and community life, joys and hardships. In a 27 August 1956 letter, one paragraph told of their tenth anniversary celebration. The next gave haunting news about a woman who had been driving a tractor and ran over her 2-year-old son, killing him.

Over the years, letters would reveal problems. Friends became ill. Polio threatened local communities. Her children, Pat and Norman, contracted the normal childhood diseases.

In November of 1952, Evelyn mentioned reports that an H-bomb had exploded. That month, Verle's letter explained the health problem Evelyn had experienced beginning in September. Doctors weren't able to readily diagnose her problem. Few would have suspected heart trouble in a young woman of only 28.

At age 42, Evelyn suffered a stroke that changed her life. She became partially paralyzed and struggled to recover as much of her former abilities as possible. She wrote only the shortest of notes to her mother-in-law during this period, and they were efforts of time, labor and love.

Art remained one of the few pleasures she was able to pursue until her death in 1991. It had been a part of Evelyn's life in large and small ways. After the stroke, it was a sustaining joy when her health meant life was truly challenging. Strangely enough, this passion was not discussed in the letters to her mother-in-law. Most recorded the everyday pleasures enjoyed by many farm women. All but the first of those that follow are written while she was on the farm at the outskirts of Stettler.

August 23, 1947, From Medicine Lake, Montana: Last Sunday we were over to see Clarence and Gerald to find out how they were making out. They were in a fashion. Saturday Gerald had every stitch of clothing ripped off him in the combine....Lucky he wasn't hurt. Thursday [Verle] and I celebrated our first anniversary – remember – by taking the day off and going to Williston. Shopped and went to a show "Buck Pirates Come Home," starring Abbot and Costello – if you ever get a chance to see it please do. I laughed till my sides ached. We got a cabin for the night & came back here in time to get dinner Friday. All in all a wonderful time.[6]

July 9, 1948, Lysterville: It's a gorgeous, splendiferous, amazingly lovely evening – hope you know how really nice it is from all those adjectives. Anyway its sunshiny & warm, and although we need rain everything seems to look lovely and green. Potatoes, peas, beans all in bloom – & oh yes the lilies are simply an orange mass. Wilma and I have decided we've never seen them so thick before. Seven & eight blooms on one stock....

Aunt Edna has been picking pounds 'n' pounds of gooseberries. Fern Holmes has oceans of strawberries. Sent us up a quart of fresh ones one day. You can imagine how we ate.

Tuesday Noon [ca. Feb 26, 1951]: Made Pat [daughter] 2 cute dresses this week. Wish you could see them. One is white eyelet, made on same pattern as ones you made. Am getting pink lingerie sewed for a slip which should look nice. For the other you'll be interested as I made [it] of that print you brought up & some of that print material I had. Made a full flared skirt from print & a ruffled pink blouse. Making ruffles from pieces of print. It fits her perfectly & does look sweet if I do say so. Will send a snap of it sometime....

[Of photos included] How do you like her [Pat's] curls? I was putting it up in pin curls every day for a while but got tired of that so we (Verle cut, I held & Pat squirmed) cut it straight with bangs again. She is really quite cute with curls & we are going to give her a home permanent on her 2nd birthday.

December 14, 1952: You'd never guess what we did today. Oh yes we went to Sunday School & this afternoon Don picked us up & we drove out to a coulee near Hutterites & cut ourselves lovely Christmas trees. Did we ever have fun & why not with the super weather we're having. It was 55 above today & the little snow we did have was almost all gone.

[Date unclear]: All week she [daughter Pat] has been having tea parties for she and Mummy. Very delectable affairs, she goes to the sand pile and fills two cans with sand, takes two old spoons and some empty paint jars, puts them all on the basement door outside and then calls Din, din Mummy. Of course I have to oblige by pretending to eat. You'd laugh to see her rocking her dolly to sleep. She gets up on the kitchen chairs after wrapping dolly up in a blanket and holding her cradled in her arms she sways back and forth. One day she went forward too far and chair and Pat toppled over much to her surprise and my wasn't she disgusted. Of course, had to laugh.

August 14, 1956: Last week each day from 9 to 12 the children & I went to Vacation Bible School. I and a Mrs. Anderson (Audrey) taught the big girls & boys (10, 11 & 12 yr-olds). We had an average of 82 boys & girls for the week. And oh Mother what a wonderful time we had. We had 23 decisions for Christ. I had 5 in my class....we're so hoping they will go on now to grow & live in the word. I never experienced anything like it. At last I've done something worthwhile – if I've been responsible in a small way for even one soul finding life.

November 2, 1969: I went to Edmonton to take treatments for the "change of life." X-ray treatments. Now I'm all finished...I'm free....Thursday night Verle & I went to Don & Marilyn's to a masquerade party. It was fun....We are hoping to go to California but you are not to count on it!

January 18, 1970 [Letter by Verle]: Evelyn is at my elbow. She has been trying to write thank-you notes but can't manage it alone. So she will be expressing herself in this letter. But she won't be copying it.

Thanks so much for keeping us. [They had spent Christmas in California]....Do you remember the black slacks Evelyn wore so much there. They hid the brace, they didn't crease and can be washed without ironing. Yesterday Evelyn got a new identical pair except that they are blue. Evelyn is telling everyone about how wonderful the trip was.[7]

VIII. Out to Win

Women of the prairies played countless sports. Some sports were life-long pursuits that were easy to enjoy in their own backyards. All of the prairies had snow at least part of the winter, so non-competitive activities such as skating, sledding and cross-country skiing were popular even from the very early days. In the summer, there was boating, fishing and swimming, but women also played tennis, badminton and golf. They went horse-back riding and hiking along rivers or beside lakes as well. Of course, there were more dramatic ideas of fun and sport, such as ice boating in the winter. In addition, women riders competed successfully in horse shows and horse races from the very early days.

However, in those days, lack of readily available transportation did limit the ability of many women to compete in arenas beyond their local communities. Love of sport sometimes had little opportunity to bloom in one generation, but was encouraged in the next, and being able to offer that support brought pleasure. Work loads and physical health issues, sometimes related to large families and nutrition, may have affected the opportunities for sporting successes. Undoubtedly, as women aged, their changing values and physical prowess affected choices related to sports.

Basketball would become one of many sports where women of the prairies excelled. In about 1910, these women played on a makeshift court of very dry and hard-packed soil in order to dribble the ball. Provincial Archives of Alberta, A 6094

In the late 1930s and early 1940s, many competitive sports were open to women. Boxing was not one of them, but this young woman seems successful with the gloves in this playful bout. Walt and Faye Holt collection.

Not surprisingly, particular games or activities which appealed to women of one age did not appeal to an older generation. Swimming, boating, curling, skating, fishing, badminton or lawn games such as croquet did not require youth. On the other hand, basketball, hockey and baseball were games in which speed and agility mattered, especially when the game was being played competitively for a title. Older women enjoyed watching such games or listening to them broadcast on radio. They were enthusiastic supporters, but they left the playing to younger people.

Memoirs, histories and newspaper reports do reveal that women were interested in sports and were not always inactive. Although some stood firm on ideas of Victorian restraint as a model for women, by 1901, another point of view was being heard. Books like Mary Melendy's *The Perfect Woman* claimed exercise was good. "Do you desire to be strong? Then take exercise. Do you hope to retain your bloom and youthful appearance and still look charming in the eyes of your husband? Then take exercise. Do you wish to banish nervousness and low spirits? Then take exercise."[1]

As years passed, women of Alberta, Saskatchewan and Manitoba excelled at team and individual competitive sports. During the 1920s, women's sports were more varied than ever before, and sporting women were sometimes the brunt of jokes in which they were labelled "Amazons." However, with most people, successful women's hockey, baseball and basketball teams were the source of phenomenal pride. Over the years, in many different women's sports, there were provincial, national and international successes for prairie women. Sometimes, these became common knowledge and were heralded. Sometimes, they went virtually unnoticed.

L is for Ladies' League

Women of western Canada were not laggards in forming associations which would allow them to take their love of sport to higher levels of competition. The means to that end was organizing league play. For young women increasingly in attendance at educational institutions such as high schools and normal schools, house leagues offered competition, but not surprisingly, there was interest in competing with others in larger and larger geographical areas. Women who attended college and university programs in western Canada as early as the first decade of the twentieth century got at least some support for their involvement in physical culture. As a result, varsity league play opened to young women. League competition was available to them for basketball, baseball and hockey in the teens and twenties, but one of the earliest of the organized team sports for women in the West was curling.

Fastest Brooms in the West

Curling was popular in western Canada for good reason. Often, a frozen lake and stream was just out the door, and there was nothing too difficult about cleaning snow from a curling lane. Both women's and mixed teams could play, and for casual fun, they needed no special equipment. A jam or lard can filled with water and frozen became a rock. Household brooms were readily available, and no skates were required.

The team sport of curling was played outdoors, often using household brooms and jam cans, weighted by ice inside. However, by about 1906, these women had ice time for curling at the Winnipeg Board of Trade building. Provincial Archives of Manitoba, Foote 1075, N1875

As a result, interest was widespread, and women of all three prairie provinces established curling associations early in the 1900s. The Alberta Ladies' Curling Association was only one such organization formed to facilitate competition. Although first playing informal curling games with family and friends on a patch of natural ice, Edmonton area women became more serious about regular play. In the downtown area, the Capital City Club originated around 1903. The club offered women an opportunity to compete for the Scona Cup. How many clubs and competitions existed, as well as who played in them between then and 1912, is not clear. However, by 1915, the Royal Victoria Club was one of the active clubs, and bonspiel play became an annual event. In 1924, when serious steps were being taken to form a provincial association, local women's clubs included the Granite, Thistle and Edmonton clubs, each with a number of rinks.

For a fee of $4 per rink, 21 rinks entered the 1924 bonspiel, and 25 rinks paid fees for the January 1925 spiel. Of course, the women enjoyed more than the competition. At the end of the bonspiel, they celebrated the winners with a luncheon at the MacDonald Hotel, and at the banquet, ladies supported the formation of an official association to organize a big bonspiel each year. By March of 1926, the secretary of the newly formed Alberta Ladies' Curling Association wrote the various clubs. "To carry on this work we must have funds therefore it was decided to ask each club for an affiliation fee of two dollars to be paid when joining the Association. An Annual fee of two dollars to be paid each year, and a per capita of twenty-five cents per member in each club, to be paid by the club."[2]

That year the name was changed to the Northern Alberta Ladies' Curling Association, an organization that sponsored successful bonspiels, year after year. During the war years of 1943 and 1944, bonspiels were cancelled, but by 1963, the association could boast of sponsoring one of the largest ladies' bonspiels in the entire country.

Glory of Golf

Golf was not every woman's sport. Like today, women who golfed tended to be more economically prosperous, but the sport had a surprisingly early history for women of the prairie provinces. The Winnipeg golf courses were first in the West, but in Alberta, by 1895, Fort Macleod had a nine hole course. In 1896, Edmonton built a private golf course, and in less than 20 years, it had its first public course. Even small towns began building courses. Most players were male, but before the turn of the century, the West had women golf enthusiasts.

Calgarians, like Edmontonians, organized a golf club, which opened in 1896. The next year women golfed regularly on Saturdays. For a fee of $1, ladies became associate members, and by 1898, there were 15 female associate members. Within three years, fees dropped to 50¢ for them, but they weren't eligible as full shareholders, and an associate had to be related to a male shareholder. However, for the woman who wanted to golf, there were other means of joining the ladies' golf groups at the club. Without having an associate membership, a woman might become elected to the Board of Management, thereby gaining most of the privileges of associate members.

Soon, women also played in mixed foursomes, and they organized specific women's competitions for best drive, approach shot and putt. By 1908, under the auspices of the newly formed Alberta Golf Association, women were competing in provincial tournament play. That year Miss Brown won the provincial ladies' tournament. She was from Edmonton, where the number of women golfers had increased dramatically.

However, to many of the female golfers, more than sporting competition was important. At the Calgary club, afternoon tea followed the Saturday games. Many golf enthusiasts had other avid interests related to community service, and their sporting association extended or complemented social and community ties. For instance, Jean Pinkham, who was wife of the Anglican Bishop of Calgary, not only presided over the Anglican Women's Auxiliary and the Local Council of Women, she organized the Hospital Aid Society and was also involved in the Victorian Order of Nurses. One of her golfing partners was Mrs. Lougheed (later Lady Lougheed), who was also involved in a wide variety of community work and who hosted countless social events in the city.

Competition in ladies' golf became increasingly important and commonplace in the entire province, as elsewhere on the prairies. In the early part of the 1900s, Alberta women played for a variety of championship cups. In 1908, the ladies' provincial championships were held in Calgary. Whether changing styles of dress or attitudes about physical culture for women were the reason, women golfers just got better and better. By the end of the 1900s, the longest drive for women in local competitions had been 111 yards. During the 18 holes of the provincial championship in 1908, one woman drove the ball 160 yards. By 1914, the longest drive for an Alberta woman in championship play was 215 yards.[3]

Paddy's Story

It was the late 1930s before local golfing enthusiasts would be truly thrilled with the almost unbelievable golf successes of Paddy Arnold, a member of the Calgary Golf and Country Club. To her golf teacher, Jack Cuthbert, the young woman did not appear to be someone who would excel at the sport. Despite having problems with sight, she was a hard-working and conscientious student of the game. She practised, and she progressed at lightning speed. In 1938, she won her Calgary club championships, the Calgary City Championship, the Alberta Provincial

Championships and the Dominion Finals. In 1939, she repeated those accomplishments and added the Banff Springs Hotel Golf Club Brewster Cup. She continued to hold the Calgary club championship title until 1950. Over the next two years, she faltered but held the Brewster Cup. By 1946, she was once more winning all her previous titles except the Dominion Finals. Then in 1947, '48 and '49, she again captured the Canadian championship titles. There were other wins during those years too, but in 1950, a detached retina was to end her competitive career in golf. All the same, she had been a credit to herself and her club.

In the Medals

Conditions were right for the West to develop many fine female track and field stars in the 1900s. Little equipment was needed. The need for social events and simple entertainments meant that picnics and sports days held races for young girls, as well as for adult women. The growth of this

In the 1930s, Robina Higgins Haight shone as one of Canada's outstanding women athletes. From Winnipeg, she set a national ball throw record in 1935 and a javelin record in 1938. Both records stood for more than 12 years. Competing in Sydney, Australia, she won the javelin title at the British Empire Games, and over the years, she won titles in shotput and discus. For a winter sport, she played basketball, helping her team win provincial and city championships over five consecutive years. Higgins retired from competition in 1940. She shifted to golf and curling after her retirement. Manitoba Sports Hall of Fame.

sport at competetive levels was a natural extension of these ordinary pleasures open to many girls.

By the teens, some schools offered physical culture and team sports to female students. For many of the young women who eventually competed at provincial, national and international levels, competition began during their early schooling. They had parents who encouraged and supported their involvement, and sometimes their parents – especially fathers – had achieved success in sports. Often, both or one of their parents were prepared to make sacrifices or adjustments in family life to help their daughters succeed in sports. In addition, the girls who became truly renowned athletes as young women usually had attended some educational institution where their talents were recognized and the coaching and success of young women in sports was considered important. Those prerequisites were generally the same for women in team and individual sports as for men.

The Story of Saskatoon's Lily

Track and field has had few stars like "the lily." Her real name was Ethel Catherwood, and she was one of the first women, along with five other Canadian women, to compete in the Olympics. Her major event was high jump, and she could jump better than any other woman in Canada, in fact in the world. Ethel was 20 at the time of the Amsterdam Olympics in 1928, but already, she had demonstrated her phenomenal abilities to her Canadian fans.

The Catherwood family had immigrated to Saskatchewan from North Dakota, where Ethel was born on 28 April 1908. The family first settled in Scott, which was about 180 kilometers west of Saskatoon. As a young man, her father had been a sprinter, but he was also a talented roller-skater, and he had competed professionally – and won cups – in numerous American communities. Ethel's mother was also an enthusiastic and competent curler, and the two parents passed on their love of sports to their children. One of Ethel's brothers was a sprinter, and her two sisters played hockey, one with a collegiate team and the other with the University of Saskatchewan women's team.

When Ethel was still a young girl, family entertainment included backyard jumping. Ethel's father *coached* his children in baseball and developed their skills more indirectly by making a game of catching fly balls to determine who would do dishes. Not surprisingly, Ethel became good at baseball, and also at hockey and basketball. At annual school fairs in nearby Wilkie, Ethel competed in races, skipping, ball throw, broad jump and high jump. She was a shy, almost withdrawn girl at times, but always pleasant.

After a growth spurt of six inches in 1924, when she was 16, Ethel became a young beauty, who wore her dark hair in a short bob, a style popular at the time. What mattered most to her athletic father was that she could clear 1.62 metres (5' 4") in the high jump. Performing in the cramped conditions of the backyard and without any official measurement, Ethel had jumped so high to prove that she could do it and to please her father. If the measurement was accurate, in formal competition, she would have set the Canadian and world record for a woman.

The next year, the family moved to Saskatoon. There, Ethel and her sister Gwen enrolled in the Bedford Collegiate program, and in basketball during the following years, Ethel and her team won three provincial championships. Learning of her potential, E.W. "Joe" Griffith of the University of Saskatchewan became her track coach, and his objective was to get her on the Canadian Olympic team for the 1928 Games.

In the 1920s, Ethel Catherwood thrilled audiences with her high jumping and athletic excellence. This photo, taken prior to her success in the 1928 Olympics in Amsterdam, Holland, show the Saskatoon team logo on her shirt. Canada Sports Hall of Fame.

During 1926, Ethel wowed her audiences at track meets in Saskatoon and at the provincials in Regina. With the events under the sanction of the Amateur Athletic Union of Canada, Ethel set a Canadian high jump record of over 1.57 metres [5.151'] at the Regina meet, but the record was not officially recognized on a national level until December 1927. The jump not only thrilled the 1500 who attended the event, it inspired countless athletics and sports fans, both male and female, around the country. Ethel loved jumping, and she felt that she performed best during competition. In the summer of 1927, fans cheered wildly for her when she competed in running high jump at the University of Toronto in the first Canadian Women's Track and Field Championships. But surprisingly, high jump was not her only record-breaking event during the meet. She also set a women's record of 34.9 metres (114'7") in javelin.[4]

For the meet, she wore a white uniform with the name of her sponsor, Saskatoon Elks, across the front. She also had a long purple cloak as a warm-up wrap, and at just over 5'10½", with her regal-looking image, poise and championship performances, the *Toronto Globe* named her "Queen of the Women's National Meet." Other sports reporters called her the "western gazelle," a "morning glory" and the "Saskatoon Lily." She was "Toronto's Sweetheart," especially once she moved to Toronto in 1928 to train for the Olympics. Still, to those who knew her, despite her beauty and athletic excellence, she was unaffected and modest, a soft-spoken and friendly Saskatchewan girl.

While training in Toronto, she took business courses and worked at a brokerage firm, finally travelling to a Halifax meet to qualify for the Olympics on July 2, 1928. After a javelin throw that surpassed Canadian records, Ethel cleared 1.6 metres [5.25'] in running high jump. She was off to Amsterdam on July 10, and she carried with her the well-wishes and devotion of fans all across Canada.

Women's high jump was on the last day of track at the Olympics, and it was three hours before the field of 23 had been narrowed to Ethel, a competitor from the United States and one from Holland, who was favored to win. Doing her first jumps in her track suit in order to keep her muscles warm on the cool and drizzling day, she became serious enough to remove the suit at 1.5 metres [4.9']. Between jumps, she wrapped herself in a red wool blanket. Her winning jump was 5'3" (1.59 metres), and with it Ethel won a gold metal. Her Canadian fans were ecstatic. On their return to Canada, the victories of the Canadian team were celebrated with parades, banquets and endless news coverage. Some reporters raved about her as not only the world's greatest woman high jumper, but as "the prettiest girl at the Olympics."

Saskatoon was particularly jubilant, and huge crowds welcomed her back on 5 September. On 26 September 1928, her local fans celebrated Ethel Catherwood Day, and no one could have been prouder of their hometown girl.

In the following month, Ethel returned to Toronto, where she intended to continue her education, train and compete. Within two years, however, her life turned around. Life was complicated with physical injuries, athletic expectations, educational opportunities, dreams that didn't work and a job. Then it was further complicated by an early marriage, divorce and remarriage. Once her competitive years had past, she lost interest in sports, and her impressions of everyone and everything changed.

Yet no matter how she changed, she had brought a kind of joy and pride to western Canadian men and women. She would have no equal in terms of individual women's competitive sport in the prairie provinces, and her Canadian record in javelin was not broken until 1936. In high jump her record stood until 1954.[5]

Team Spirit

The Edmonton Grads became the best known women's team on the prairies. Their game was basketball, and they played it better than any other women's team in the world. They drew huge local crowds when they played; newspapers covered their games in depth; and many of their games were broadcast on radio in Alberta. The team, coached by Percy Page, started with a group of high school girls called the Commercial Grads. After graduation, they stayed together, convinced their coach to continue working with them and played as a women's team. Since members of the team changed over the 25 years the team played, no one or two outstanding player could be given all the credit. Instead, it was teamwork that made them famous, and the record of their wins would be one of which they and other prairie people were proud for decades to follow.

In total, the team played 522 games and won 96 percent of them. One winning streak ran for 147 games. After losing one game, they continued with another 78 consecutive wins. They held the North American women's basketball title in all but one year between 1923 and 1940. Going on three European tours, the team claimed numerous European titles. In 1924 they competed in France, playing some games in Paris, for what was called the "Women's Olympics," international competitions at the world level. They played 27 exhibition games in four different Olympics, including in the Berlin Olympics in 1936. Winning, they were declared world champions. Although their travelling expenses were funded, the players competed as amateurs and received no pay.[6]

Over the years, there were many high scorers. At various times, Abbie Scott was one of them. She played in Paris in 1924, and not only did the trip mean success on the court for her, it meant a wonderful time travelling and exploring Europe with her good friends and teammates. When the team returned home to Edmonton, they were given a homecoming parade down Jasper Avenue that attracted hundreds of enthusiastic and cheering fans.

In 1925, after watching the Grads play a championship game at Guthrie, Oklahoma, James Naismith, who invented basketball, praised the team members both for their outstanding play on the court and for their poise and courtesy off the court. In fact, they were continuing a long-standing tradition of being outstanding sportswomen and informal ambassadors for their country. For generations of young

Having just won their final game to become world champs for women's basketball, the
Edmonton Grads pose for a formal photograph with the championship banner.
Lois Forsyth collection.

women, the Grads set an example of strong, competitive women, out to win, yet all
the while valuing teamwork and team spirit, enjoying good times and being respect-
ful of others.

Abbie Scott and the Grads by Jill Forsyth

Abbie Kennedy (nee Scott) was my husband's grandmother, my grand-
mother-in-law. While I only met her three or four times before she died, I have
grown to have a sense of the accomplishment of the Grads and the part the basketball team played in her life. Abbie's daughter, Lois, describes her mother's involvement with the Grads as "the time of her life."

Abbie played for the Grads from 1922-1924. The uniqueness of their
situation — an all-female basketball team in the 1920s — was only made more
unique by virtue of their incredible talent and success.

"The Grads were taught that, above all, they were ladies," said Lois, "If they lost, they did it like ladies. But, especially if they won, they did it like ladies." The demand for the lady-like behavior was placed upon the team by Percy Page, the only coach the Grads knew over the 25-year span of the team. Abbie spoke affectionately of Mr. Page and said that, when she finished her time with the team, he had become like a second father to her.

In June, 1924 the Grads left Edmonton for a journey that took them across Canada, and then to Europe. London, Liverpool, Luxembourg, Strasbourg, Brussels, Ypres, Vimy, Edinburgh and Glasgow were just some of the spots the team visited. The highlight was playing an exhibition game at the Paris Olympics. Back in North America, the team set off for New York and Chicago, before returning to Toronto for the train ride home. Abbie and her teammates were entertained at yacht clubs, country clubs and various forms of athletic clubs, and the team toured cathedrals, museums and cultural monuments in vehicles ranging from passenger trains to a *char-le-banc* in Paris.

Abbie kept a diary of the trip that has become a family treasure. In one entry, she revealed a drive to test herself. She wrote of going to the Strasbourg Cathedral on July 10, 1924. There were three of them and they went to climb the tower.

> *There are eight flights of stone stairs up to the top, so we each chose a different one. Occasionally we would meet on some landing and talk things over. One place near the top was only 4 inches wide, and had no protection in front. It was very scary, but we all felt we had accomplished something.*

On July 18, Abbie wrote that she bought herself a Paris gown, "…made of georgette in a Nile green shade, with silver lace petals on the skirt, and is made by hand – every stitch." It was in this gown that she attended the Embassy Ball in 1928, held at the largest hotel in Paris, the Continental.

On the way back home, the team was held up between Edmonton and Unity, Saskatchewan, because of an earlier train wreck. They were all disappointed because of the homecoming awaiting them. On August 30, in her diary, Abbie wrote of making the most of it. Some girls golfed; some went for a walk around the town. They "…also discovered that among the passengers was a girl who used to teach in Unity, and she said she felt sure she could arrange to have a dance for us in the fire hall, which she did, and the whole town turned out to give us a good time. We are all very grateful to the townspeople for helping us put in the time in such an enjoyable manner."

The Grad team took these young women from Edmonton beyond the lives they had known, and through the experiences with the team, transformed them and the lives they came back to. Abbie remained in Edmonton for the rest of her life and attended the Grads Reunion every year. I have been inspired by the sense of team that these women defined. They found a way to create a community — their team — and then they thrived in the community they created.[7]

Hockey Stars

Already, in the 1890s, women were playing hockey with brothers and male friends on frozen sloughs, lakes and streams, and by 1896, there was an official ladies' team in the North-West Territories, today's prairie provinces. That first club, comprised of Regina women, practised for an hour twice a week, on Wednesday afternoons and Sunday evenings. By 1900, a number of Saskatchewan communities, including Prince Albert, had women's hockey teams. Similarly, at the time, Manitoba women began organizing teams. Uniforms for team members were not always identical. Most teams wore long skirts, sweaters or coats, and tuques, but the Brandon ladies team of 1898 was striking with long, dark outfits, and light colored tuques and sashes. Still, could the ladies play hockey? Some scoffed.

They could and they did. If there wasn't a women's team in a nearby communi-ty, occasionally ladies' teams played against men's teams. Although not a common

In 1916, these young women enjoy hockey practice at Diamond Park in Edmonton, Alberta. Provincial Archives of Alberta, A 2972

practice elsewhere, the Saskatchewan Co-operative Ladies Team was in regular competition against the married men's team. With rules against body checking for those games, the women were as likely to win as the men.

In the late 1800s and early 1900s, even small towns such as Red Deer, Alberta, and Hartney, Manitoba, organized teams. Schools such as Mount Royal College in Calgary and universities such as the University of Saskatchewan had teams. Women with various backgrounds enjoyed playing, and by the mid-teens and early twenties, ladies' hockey was receiving serious attention.

City of Champions

From early in the 1900s, not only was Edmonton a basketball town, it was a hockey town, and the women there loved hockey – playing it, that is. The first of their teams were competing by 1899, and "Some hectic battles were witnessed, according to old-timers, and at times tempers flared a little, adding a dash of paprika to the contests."[8] At the time, at least two teams had been organized, one from Edmonton and another from Strathcona, then a small town on the south side of the river. During the first seasons, the north side won the local championship cup, but finally, in a rough game, the Strathcona team wrestled the cup from them. By the 1916-1917 season, numerous local teams were stick handling down the ice. Goalie and manager Isabel Coffey was the guiding light for the Edmonton Victorias, formed in 1915 by members of the First Presbyterian Church. In the Alberta championship, one of their scheduled games was with the Calgary Regents, but the two playoff games were against the Calgary Crescents. Both were so tight that no goals were scored, despite ten minutes overtime in each game. That year, the Victorias amalgamated with the Nationals, another Edmonton team, and became the Monarchs – one of the most impressive women's teams to play the game. In 1926, the team captured the Misner Cup of the Alberta championships and went on to win the Alpine Trophy in the Western Canada championships against teams from Calgary, Vancouver, Vulcan, Fernie and Manitoba. According to the *Edmonton Journal*, again in 1929, the team won the Alberta and Western Canada championships.

During the 1920s and early 1930s, a fierce rivalry developed between the Monarchs and another city team, the Jasper Place Rustlers. The Rustlers' team was first formed in 1928 with girls who attended school together. Many continued with the team after finishing their education, and in 1931, the team was reorganized as senior women's team and renamed the Edmonton Rustlers. They won numerous titles, including at the city, northern and provincial championships. One of the Rustlers' best players and all-round athletes was Hazel Jamison (nee Case), who also curled in winter and played golf and swam in summer.

By the early thirties the show-down in Alberta women's hockey was staged at Banff during the Winter Carnival, where the competition continued off the ice. Queen of the 1932 carnival was Miss Margaret Stevenson of the Monarchs, taking over the crown from a young Vancouver woman. Hockey was the big draw, and women's teams from throughout the West attended, but there were other types of fun, too. In 1933, Violet Davis, also of the Monarchs and an all-round sports woman who enjoyed speed skating, skiing, swimming, tennis and riding, reigned over the carnival.

City Girl Queen Winter Carnival Banff Next Year

Edmonton Journal, [ca. Feb, 1932]

This is the third carnival in Banff Miss Stevenson has attended, always taking part in the hockey and various novelty events....Born in Montreal, Miss Stevenson came to Alberta when she was a very little girl. She lived for five years in Slave Lake before the family moved to Edmonton about twelve years ago [1920]. It was here that she first took up winter sports – "and summer sports, too,['] she added. "I love to swim."

A beautiful blanket coat and the regal diadem which she will wear as queen of next year's carnival are Miss Stevenson's mementos of this happy occasion.

Had Glorious Time

The weather was beautiful for the carnival, she said, and while there was no snow for tobogganing and skiing on the mountains, the ice was hard enough for hockey, skating and skiing on the river, so that every person present had a glorious time.

The queen laughed merrily, remembering the dog race she won against Ike Mills, Banff's famous professional dog musher. "I mean the race the dogs won for me," she amended. "All I did was get on the sled and shout...."

For the first time in the...15 year history of the Banff winter carnival an Edmonton girl has been elected to reign over the festivities. The slim, fair little sportswoman who represents her city, the provincial capital, is a fitting monarch to make such history.[9]

Edmonton Rustlers Win

Edmonton Journal, 10 March 1934

Today the Edmonton Rustlers wear the western Canada senior women's hockey championship crown and are awaiting the completion of the eastern

In a country where ice was inevitable for much of the year, figure skating was popular with women. However, there was also early interest in speed skating. Anna Gibson School in Winnipeg had its own speed skating team, seen above in 1933. Manitoba Provincial Archives, Sport, Skating, Speed 1

Canada playoff to enter the final for the dominion championship which they won last year.

Last night out at the Arena[,] Coach Tufford's Rustlers wound up their two game, total goal series with Winnipeg Eaton girls with a 4-0 shutout – and they were full value for it. As a result of their 4-1 victory over the Manitoba champions in the first game, the Rustlers take the series by an impressive score of 8-1.[10]

Title-Seekers End Training With Impressive Practice

Edmonton Journal, March 17, 1933

Running through a sparkling work out at the arena last night, the Rustlers, western Canada champions of women's senior hockey[,] put the finishing touches to their training for their Saturday game here with the Preston[,] Ontario, Rivulettes for the dominion championship.

With all their plays clicking smartly and every girl in perfect condition, the Edmonton stars are awaiting the eastern Canadian champions without any fears. It will be a two-game, total goal series with the second game on Monday night and the recently presented Lady Bessborough trophy going to the winners.

During the visit of the Rivulettes to Edmonton the Canadian Amateur Hockey association will be formed, the first dominion-wide organization for women's hockey....[11]

Ladies and Their Gloves

Western women didn't just like pulling on their gloves, they liked picking up bats, too. When they didn't have gloves, balls or bats in hand, there was always the thrill of running the bases, and scouts soon noticed just how good they were at baseball. At picnics and sports days, women were playing the game long before the All-American Girls' Professional Baseball League was formed for women. There were many successful teams in the twenties and thirties, including the Ramblers Girls' Softball Team of Winnipeg playing in the twenties, the Drewry's Dry Ladies' Softball team, who were Saskatchewan Provincial Champions in 1932, and the Quaker Oats Ladies' Softball Club, who were Northern Saskatchewan Champions in 1934. In the forties, successful teams included the Aces, a women's softball team that played at Cairn's Field and won titles in 1939, 1940, 1941; and the Saskatoon Pats, who wore uniforms very much like the men's and who thrilled their home province with trophies in 1944, 1945 and 1946.

There were dozens of other teams that had strong winning streaks, but the most international acclaim came to Canadian women ball players as a result of their playing in the American league.

Canadians Go Stateside

The All-American Girls' Professional Baseball League was the brainchild of P. K. Wrigley, and women's competitive baseball was intended to temporarily fill the gap while male players were serving in the Second World War. The two-week spring training camp was held at the Wrigley Field in Chicago, and for a small number of Canadian women, making one of the six teams meant the opportunity of a lifetime.

The American players were widely known, not only in the late 1940s but when the movie *A League of Their Own* dramatized the stories of the women. Years later, at home, Canadian women players who were part of the league were made members of the Sports Hall of Fame in their home provinces, but they remained less well-known and received less fanfare.

Over the years of the league, a number of prairie women played in America. Whether baseman, fielder, pitcher or big hitter, each had a story to tell. Four

Saskatchewan girls, Muriel, Mary, Daisy and Arlene, set out with very different strengths, but all returned with memories from the big leagues to cherish for a lifetime.

Muriel Coben was a pitcher. In the mid-1930s, she pitched wins for the Tessier Millionaires, and then in 1938, she joined the Saskatoon Pats. For the 1943 season, she played with the South Bend White Sox, but afterwards she returned to Saskatchewan. A great player, she didn't quit ball and helped win numerous Saskatchewan and Western Canadian championships for the Saskatoon Grey Cab Ramblers.

Regina-born Mary Baker became one of the South Bend Blue Sox and, during three seasons, she was an all-star catcher. Called "Pretty Bonnie Baker" by the

A Manitoba ball player, Olive Bend Little thrilled audiences in both Canada and the United States with her pitching. In 1940, she moved to Saskatchewan, and played in both provinces during their provincial championships, leading her teams to victory. Recruited by the Rockford Peaches (Illinois) during World War II, she also played in Wrigley Field as part of the American all-star team. These games inspired the movie, <u>A League of Their Own</u>. Olive never forgot her Canadian roots, and returned to Manitoba, where she was inducted into the Sports Hall of Fame in 1985. Manitoba Sports Hall of Fame.

press, she worked part time as a model. As a result, the "special" training for the girls in etiquette, in walking and talking like "ladies," and even in how to get in and out of a car, was not exactly a challenge for her. However, being a great ball player was a worthy challenge, and she was very serious about ball. When the League play ended, Mary returned to Saskatchewan leagues and played with the Regina Legion team. With many titles to their credit, the team players ultimately won the World Ladies Softball Championship game played in Toronto. She became a full-time manager for a ladies' ball club, and at the age of 45, she rated another first – first female sportscaster in Canada.

While playing for the Regina Caps in 1945, Daisy Junor was scouted and asked to attend tryouts in Chicago. She did, and from 1946-1949, she played in Indiana for the South Bend Blue Sox. An all-star fielder, she was also a power hitter. But Daisy did not end her sports involvement after her baseball days were over. Other types of ball-related games interested her, and she took up bowling, becoming Saskatchewan's representative to the Western Canadian 5 Pin Bowling Championships. Golf became her game too, and she repeatedly won club and city championships and won the Provincial Senior Ladies' Championship.

A farm girl raised near Ogema, at 20 years of age, Arleene Noga (nee Johnson) had been working in a Regina office and playing ball for the Meadow Diamonds. In 1945, when Hub Bishop asked her to try out for the All-American Girls League, she was one of only 16 Canadians hopefuls, six from Saskatchewan, some of whom had already been playing in the league. Arlene won a place on the Fort Wayne Daisies, where she played for a year before being transferred to the Muskegon Lassies for the next three years. As third baseman, she played all 112 league games in one year, and in doing so set the record for a third base player. Over the three years with the Lassies, she played 300 consecutive games, earning the nickname "The Iron Woman of Baseball" from reporters; her team won the pennant for the league in 1947. Although she was offered a contract for the 1949 season, Arlene left the league. At home in Saskatchewan, she married, but she didn't give up her glove, and she was on a winning team for nine provincial championships. Her team came out winners for five Western Canada championships, and as well, Arlene played in the 1953 World Championships in Toronto. During the 1990 production of the movie based on the women's league, Arlene played the role of the third base coach for the Peaches.

Snowshoeing is generally an individual sport. However, in 1925, for their snowshoe outing at Kildonan Park (Winnipeg), the women employed by the Jerry Robinson Company appear to be a team – given the similar styles of their coats and tuques and the logo on the left arm of the coats. #125, Public Archives of Manitoba, Foote 1193, N 2776

The Builders

Successful women in various fields of sports went on to build interests, skills and opportunities for other younger women. Each province had such women, some of whom worked with school and university sports programs, some of whom went into administration for various associations. Long before health clubs became popular for women, the YMCA, and later its sister organization the YWCA, were encouraging and supporting the development of female athletes. The range of sporting events would also broaden for successive generations of women. By the 1980s, about one hundred years after some of the first western Canadian women's sports associations were being initiated, many of the outstanding early female sports figures were being appointed to provincial and national sports halls of fame. They were models for young sports women; their accomplishments created pride in fans and family members, and their talents had brought many moments of joy to those fortunate enough to be present for highlights in their careers.

IX. Sisterhood

Many circumstances meant that women had to support each other and discover good times amongst themselves. Shared experiences and moral support meant a great deal to the huge numbers of women left when husbands and fathers went to war. Many of these women worked together on volunteer projects to support the war effort. When possible, they created something positive – even found moments of joyfulness in the midst of challenges. Countless women shared the memorable, and often the most joyful experience of their lives – the return of those fathers, brothers, husbands and sons.

In about 1910, these ladies from Red Deer, Alberta, tried a variety of poses for the camera. Informal poses, such as those where their faces are turned from the camera, were unusual. Generally, a formal pose was chosen to be made into prints, and these were included in letters as gifts. Red Deer and District Museum and Archives, P180-469.

Although the majority of women raising families were not employed outside the home prior to the First World War, many a young, unmarried woman left home at an early age to take a job. These young adults joined the workforce as domestics, store clerks, clerical workers, teachers and nurses, often remaining at those jobs until marriage. For some employees, the opportunity to be independent from family brought happiness; in other cases, the jobs were intrinsically rewarding. The first women employed in a particular field and those employed at less-than-desirable jobs valued the support of other women who understood or shared the experience.

Happiness and well-being also came from the opportunity to develop talents and skills and to gain knowledge. The first female students to attend postsecondary educational programs shared many good times together. In the first decade of the 1900s, postsecondary education was open to women at western Canadian institutions. That opportunity was available to very small numbers, but to most who attended, the experience was a good one.

Teamwork, leadership, friendship, shared ideas and time spent enjoying each other's company created a strong sense of sisterhood among such groups of women. They did face challenges, but a sense of humor, tackling things in creative new ways and standing beside each other whatever the circumstances helped to create good times.

A University Experience

According to Marjory MacMurchy, in her book *The Woman – Bless Her: Not as Amiable a Book as It Sounds*, the universities in the prairie provinces all had women students enrolled by 1916. Most already had women graduates. That year, at the University of Alberta, there were 55 women students. Saskatchewan had 53 females university students, and Manitoba could boast of 153 women in programs at the university.[1] There were also many women's college programs in the West, and still other women from the prairies were enrolled at distant universities and colleges.

On the prairies, political resistance to women postsecondary students was neither strong nor sustained, though many of the programs were geared towards men or had only men enrolled. The cultural and economic circumstances for settlers and new immigrants, plus a general lack of family and societal support for education for females, did mean that few women enrolled in the available programs. However, for those who did, the achievement and experience was rewarding. Academic success was most important, but socializing brought pleasure, too.

Story of the Wauneitas

The University of Alberta opened its doors to students for the 1908-1909 school year with Dr. Henry Marshall Tory as the university's first president. All students were part of the Faculty of Arts and Science, and instruction was offered by four male professors. Located in Edmonton but still without a permanent campus, the university enrolled seven women among the 45 students admitted in its inaugural year.

These girls, who attended the University of Alberta between 1916 and 1919, gathered in the dormitory room of Hazel (Tillie) Tillotson at the Pembina Residence on campus. U. of A. 73-18-18

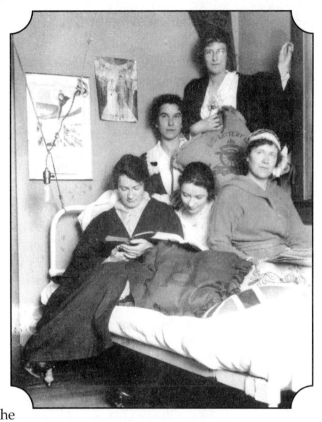

The very first woman to complete her enrolment forms was Winnifred Hyssop of Lethbridge, and she became one of the five women in the first graduating class in 1912. M. E. [Libby] Loyd was the youngest woman to attend that year and to graduate. A third in the initial graduating class was Stella Ruttan, who had already completed two years at Queen's University when she came west because of her health. The first group also included Agnes Wilson, who had the reputation for being the "jolliest" girl in the class. Also, she was the first white child born in Strathcona (later Edmonton, south side), and she was talented with a fiddle and a bow.

With seven in the supposedly secret society, the women students called themselves the SIS, Society of Independent Spinsters. By the next fall of 1909, they formalized their goals and chose a new name. The club's goal was to promote friendship among all the female students at the university, and it would meet every second Tuesday. In the second meeting that year, SIS was dropped as a name, and the group became the Wauneita Club, a name meaning *kind-hearted* in Cree. For each meeting, two members were to organize a social program, and at the end of the year, there would be a prize to the two who had offered the best entertainment. Membership was 75¢.

The young women were also active in other ways on campus. With the organization in 1908 of a Students' Union, and in 1910, with the launching of a university newspaper and annual yearbook, the *Gateway*, women served on executives and as writers and editors with male students. Until her graduation in 1912, Ethel Anderson was student leader of the women's athletic program.

In 1911-1912, a new source of assistance became available to women students. Mrs. Helen McHugh Sheldon was appointed the first Advisor to Women Students. Others followed in her footsteps, supervising the conduct and welfare of female students, and eventually, the position officially became Dean of Women. By the early 1930s, Mrs. Sheldon participated in yet another development affecting women associated with the university. She was a charter member of the Faculty Women's Club. It did have serious goals, but was primarily social in nature, sponsoring the Convocation Tea and a wide range of other events and activities, which were popular and fun for students and faculty.

In the meantime, the Wauneita Club evolved, too. In 1917-1918, residence rooms were provided for women on the north side of Athabasca Hall. The girls called the third floor Angels' Retreat; the middle floor was Broadway. The main floor was Happy Hades, and one of the women drew a picture of seven little devils for the corridor door. In 1929, Wauneita became the official women students' society of the university. By then, it sponsored dances, including masquerades and formals.

Minutes and Meetings, 1909-1910

Third Meeting

[A]fternoon very pleasantly spent in an interesting plant contest, a delightful supper and a walk. The winner of the contest, Miss Millar was awarded a bunch of choice cut flowers, jonquils. After supper, cameras and Kodaks took a part and several unique "snaps" of the members present were taken.

Fourth Meeting Social

A sewing contest stirred everyone to activity and much fun was had when the prize, a card of darning yarn, was awarded to Bessie Brickman. Speech making followed on certain fixed topics but the short orations were each and all composed and delivered with such eloquence and mastery of detail that no conclusion could be arrived at as to who should be awarded the palm, or olive wreath. A very enjoyable supper closed the proceedings....

Fifth Meeting

Conducted by Ethel Anderson and Dot Hissop and Ada Johnstone in Indian attire. Fortunes were told....[predicting] future hopes and blights with much truth and forethought. Time letters which were to be opened at some future date were written and all adjourned to the wigwam for the sumptuous repast....

Sixth Meeting

A flower search was entered upon and a huge bonfire lit....The bean supper was much enjoyed and there was nothing to mar the pleasure of the evening except the presence of some very naughty boys who hurled stones and little rocks after the departing host. The evening was brought to a close by the giving of the Club yell, originated by Ames Wilson and Kathleen Lavell: Dippy, Dippy Dee, Who are we? We are the guests of Doc Toree, Hoopra! Hoopra! Gee![2]

In 1940, these university students were part of an October 12th parade along Jasper Avenue in Edmonton, Alberta. The rest of the year would mean serious work, but for the moment, there was time for a smile. University of Alberta Archives, 72-58-323

Technician or Artisan?

Other educational programs also opened to women of the prairie provinces. In particular, art and fashion became the serious business of education programs. At technical institutions, education was geared to job training. In Calgary, the MacDonald Manual Training School was launched under the auspices of the Calgary School Board. At first, training was for boys, but by 1902, women teachers offered courses in sewing for girls. Within eight years, food preparation, nutrition and home economics were added to the domestic science program.

At about the same time, during large fairs, departments of agriculture on the prairies provided demonstrations in tents to help men and women learn important practical skills. The departments also sponsored better-farming trains that stopped in rural communities, where various skills were demonstrated. Learning how to churn butter, can, take care of infants and sew were all useful skills for interested women who lacked experience.

Courses were a time to share interest in art or writing. By the 1920s, some institutions offered off-campus workshops and evening programs as part of continuing education initiatives. This group enjoys art classes at beautiful Emma Lake, Saskatchewan.
Saskatchewan Archives Board, S-B 5593

Sewing was considered women's work, though many men worked as tailors. Women had also been independent seamstresses and had worked in tailoring shops or clothing factories since the late 1800s. For many a woman, having a tailoring business of her own was the dream. Some learned their trade within family businesses; others learned it by apprenticing in shops and factories; and courses were available in the East and the United States.

By 1923, Calgary's Provincial Institute of Technology and Art (later Southern Alberta Institute of Technology, S.A.I.T.) became serious about teaching women. With the Calgary Normal School becoming part of the institute, and other programs for women being launched on campus, female students were outnumbered, but they did have a presence. The three major programs to attract women were art, teachers' education, and dressmaking and millinery, often referred to as D and M. Eventually, a very few young women also registered in the station agents and telegraphy program. Both art and education programs included male and female students. Large numbers of women were on campus for teacher training courses during summer school. However, dressmaking and millinery was the only all-female, full-time program.

Academic and shop requirements were demanding, but the program also meant good times for most. Vastly outnumbered by male students, the women enjoyed enormous popularity, and they seldom needed to attend an event unescorted – unless by preference. They also became a close-knit sisterhood.

Story of a Fashion Program

The courses in dressmaking and millinery allowed a select number of young women to combine their love of fashion with practical experience and workplace skills. Acting as a course catalog for potential students, the *Third Annual [Tech] Announcement*, 1922-1923, described the program.

> The up-to-date dressmaker or milliner requires to be more than an expert needlewoman. She must have a trained sense of artistic values, a knowledge of color and design, an acquaintance with all the materials of her trade and a considerable amount of business acumen.

> The object of this course is to train girls not only for the occupations of dressmaking and millinery, but also to act as capable sales-ladies, who would be able to give sound advice regarding the compositions and wearing values of various materials. These girls would command good positions in the larger stores of our cities, and would also be qualified to take charge of the ladies' department of a general store in any of the towns throughout the province. This training, coupled with trade experience, should qualify them to become capable buyers.[3]

In the first year, shop work for dressmaking included "practice in various methods of sewing different material; machine sewing; cutting and making various garments, simple at the beginning but progressing to more difficult ones and better materials." For millinery, students would "practice in stitches used in millinery; pattern drafting for adults' hats; trimming and lining a regular shape."

Textiles was a lecture course covering the characteristics and uses of various fabrics, some history on the manufacturing of textiles, aspects of the dying process and of preparing materials for the marketplace. During the color and design course, students addressed practical problems related to color schemes and designs for both clothes and decorative arts. They worked with fabrics and paints, and their projects ranged from fancy work, interior design, window trimmings, stencilling and block printing to various aspects of clothing. Under the tutelage of their instructors, the D and M students had mentors and models for success in a field that was both practical and artistic.

During the initial years, students came from all over Alberta. Some years, young women from Saskatchewan enrolled in the program. The athletes among them played for the Tech's girls' basketball team, and D and M students were on student council.

Not surprisingly, romance became part of the good times. According to the yearbook, one student made her "sentence at Tech a cheerful one by using her big blue eyes on boys." One girl was talented at playing the piano, singing, dancing and "sewing up the buttonholes and sleeves of boys' coats." Ambitions varied from those who wanted to design Paris fashions to one who admitted she wanted to be "a dressmaker, housekeeper, saleslady, or somebody's wife" and another who "hopes to be a great saleslady before somebody gets her."[4]

The popularity of the students with their male counterparts was reiterated in issue after issue of the student newspaper, *The Emery Weal*. In it were jokes about the challenges and pleasures of courting the D and M girls. The paper reported on dances and on the Tech girls forming the Skookum Tillieum club. Also covered were

On stage and at school, many social and political views concerning women were presented at postsecondary institutions. Some were serious, others more lighthearted. In about 1913, these girls from the Alberta Ladies College in Red Deer, Alberta, danced in a production of Gypsy. Red Deer and District Museum and Archives, P48-18

the dressmakers' annual pageants and fashion shows, all part of the good times for the women students.

For a pageant in November of 1929, the theme was costumes worn by women throughout the ages. Applause greeted the student who modelled the dress of "primitive woman." The young women appeared as Egyptians, Grecians, Romans and Anglo-Saxons. Representing the fourteenth century, one student "in her trailing gown and gorget and whimple on her head acted the part of a lady of the Middle Ages to perfection." The pageant ended with two of the young women dancing the "Charleston Toddy" and with "the entire company parading around the stage being well applauded...."[5]

Rewarding Employment

The most common jobs for women in the early days were as domestics, clerical workers, store clerks, teachers and nurses. Although employed women worked very hard for very little money, the lucky ones found jobs they liked, and they had warm relationships with employers. Often, it was the first time they had money in their pockets and could afford small luxuries. Some women discovered their work was valued. They shouldered significant responsibilities; and their successes were considered important to individuals and the greater community.

Teaching offered employment to many prairie women. As communities were settled,

These nurses at the Calgary Hospital enjoy a tea break at their workplace in the early 1900s. As more and more women, both single and married, became employed outside their homes, the collegial time together during such breaks would become a valued part of their social lives. Glenbow-Alberta Institute, NA 2600-3

At the Normal School for teacher training in Dauphin, Manitoba, out-of-class fun included this baseball game in 1912. Provincial Archives of Manitoba, Dauphin, Schools, Normal 2, N5245

families wanted basic education for their children. In the earliest settlement times, many of those children sat at ordinary tables in someone's home or at the church while they learned to read and write from parents, neighbors and ministers. Usually, as soon as possible, communities built one-room buildings for schools. Such schools remained in use until the late 1940s and early fifties.

In about 1890, male teachers had to be at least 17 years old, but female teachers could be as young as 15. The earliest programs for teachers in the West were offered at normal schools. In 1882, Manitoba drafted legislation that allowed both Protestant and Catholic school boards to create normal schools for teacher training. The earliest programs were offered at St. Boniface and Winnipeg. However, Portage la Prairie, Manitou and Dauphin also had programs before the end of the first decade of the 1900s. In 1912, the Brandon Normal School opened. At the same time, programs were becoming available in Saskatchewan and Alberta.

Teachers for rural areas were in the most demand. There, one teacher assumed the entire role of educating children of all ages, abilities and grades, many of whom did not have English as their first language. Despite the challenges, some teachers were outstanding and loved their jobs.

Many rural educators lived in small homes, either attached to the schools or built next to them. Where communities were very new or financially pressed, teachers stayed in the homes of local people. In terms of sticking with the job, those living conditions also became positive or negative for the young teacher.

Eva's Story

Eva J. Bond was recruited from England to teach in western Canada, where teachers were desperately needed in the 1920s. Educated at a teacher training college in London, England, and moving to some very isolated communities, the conditions she found were rough, but she loved her job.

Her first school was a one-room school house near Waterfield, where she moved in with a family. Despite discovering there were fleas in her bed and mice in the house, she was undaunted. "Of course, that wouldn't scare me but it was a bit odd. Then the coyotes that I had never heard before were howling outside the window – that I thought was rather nice," she remembered years later. She liked her students, and was happy, but the water from the well was not suitable for drinking, and no one had told her. She broke out in boils, became so very sick that eventually she had to be hospitalized and her first job ended.

The Canadian Teachers' Agency found her another job, this time 75 miles north and west of Prince Albert at Camp Lake. Once again, she stayed with a family whose two children would be her students. For about two or three weeks, like the children, she slept on the floor while the family built a room for her. Because her new room was under the stairs, the only place the 5'8" woman could stand up was at the room's centre. In her room, she had an iron bed, upturned apple box and a small basin, but she was happy, and she taught at Camp Lake for two years.

Well, I suppose teaching at Camp Lake were practically the happiest days of my life. It was just exactly what I wanted. [The newly built school] was hewn logs; it was beautifully built; it was one room, no porch or anything. It had a beautiful hardwood floor. It had the best desks I have ever seen before or since; individual desks with the tops that adjusted for art work and that sort of thing; a nice little drawer underneath....There was no equipment whatsoever, except a box of chalk; six beautifully tipped rubber pointers...a register and that was it....the readers – that seemed a great word in the West – were on order....

I can't remember exactly, but I had about 30 students. When I got to the register...pretty well all the surnames, the last names were Isbister, but they were not all the same family. I have since learned that a certain Scotch Isbister rambled through the West one day years ago and I suppose these were some of his offspring. They looked exactly like Indians to me but they were really what in those days were called halfbreeds or Metis and nicer wonderful people you would never meet.... There were some Icelanders; there were the two Bird children who were Canadian, the mother from Ontario, the father from England. That was about it....

[W]hen I was training in London the great thing in those days was individual work . We had to do everything individually with large classes. But in the West it seemed to be a smear over Grade 1, Grade 2 and Grade 3....

Now, I had a boy called Adam....He was 17 and I was now 20. He was as nice as he could be....I had to teach Adam to read because he had never had the opportunity. So teaching wasn't anything like I had expected....This I thought was a wonderful opportunity....

There was another Indian boy who was quite brilliant in his way. He had a wonderful flair for English Literature....He really was outstanding....They were all teachable but they hadn't had a chance....

I had specialized in physical education and advanced English. There was no apparatus for physical education but we had this beautiful floor which reminded me of a gymnasium floor in England. We had individual desks. So, everyday we would push the desks aside and we had good old phys ed lessons, and country dancing. It was good. They really enjoyed it.

I just loved those rural schools. To me they were much better education in many ways than a town school, simply because in a rural school it was a family. You knew the community well; you knew the children. The older children helped the younger children naturally....I don't know whether I was a mother figure, I didn't exactly feel it but it was a nice little family.[6]

Wartime Family Album

For women with families, who were left behind during the various wars to affect western Canadians, war meant hardship, loneliness and sometimes feeling overwhelmed by the responsibilities. They might be in happy marriages, but war made them single parents. Worry for their loved ones became a fact of life. It was a circumstance shared by many, and sometimes that fact and those friends who understood the stress did make life easier. Not only did women look after their families, they also organized fundraisers for the war effort, packed Red Cross parcels for the servicemen and sewed vests and knit hundreds of pairs of socks.

Mike's Story

Elga Muriel Hegan (nee Stayner) was nicknamed Mike. The history of her family's involvement in the service of her country and their history in western Canada is a distinguished one. Her father, one brother and husband were all lieutenant-colonels in the armed forces. Another brother was a flight lieutenant who flew Spitfires, and all had impressive service records. Her father was given the prestigious honor of Commander of the British Empire. He received the Distinguished Conduct medal and the Military Cross. For his service, her husband was made a Member of the British Empire, and her brother received the Distinguished Flying Cross.

Not surprisingly, Mike and her mother's lives were deeply affected by that military service. Worry was a natural response for such women, who had relatives in the wars, but the reunions with those in the armed forces were joyous times. Born in 1913, Mike would also be affected by the changing attitudes that became prevalent from the teens to the 1940s about women, education for women and women's work.

While the family lived in Saskatoon, with the university located close to home, Mike was able to attend the University of Saskatchewan between 1930 and 1933. At a university dance, she met Robert (nicknamed Larry) Hegan, who was also attending U. of S. There was "chemistry" at first sight, but Mike admits playing hard to get. One afternoon, when she was hosting bridge club, the phone rang. Larry Hegan asked her to the formal banquet and dance celebrating the opening of the CN's Bessborough Hotel. She already had tickets, but the thrill of the phone call meant she hardly saw any of her cards during bridge that afternoon.

To her, the opening of the grand hotel was like a Hollywood première. There were lights, and crowds watched as she and others stepped out of cars. Many of those watchers had wanted to attend but simply couldn't get tickets to the posh affair.

Other events also brought the young couple together, and during a six year courtship, like many others during the Depression, they enjoyed less spectacular outings. They skated and went to shows and dances. By 1939, they married, and they enjoyed the luxury of honeymooning in Winnipeg. On one street, a blaring radio hinted of things to come as it broadcast a German-language speech by Hitler, but the honeymooning couple thought little of it.

Mike moved to Regina, where her husband was working. Then, with the onset of the Second World War, the young couple was separated. Like her mother, Mike was faced with the hardships and loneliness of having a husband at war.

In the meantime, like countless other women helping the war effort from the home front, Mike went to the local Red Cross rooms. There, she and other women volunteered time knitting and sewing to make uniforms for the armed forces. They cut leather for seamen's vests. The yarn sent to them to be knit into vests and socks often had a greasy film on it, so the women washed the wool. Then, they knit socks

Posed here with her husband, Mike (Elga) Hegan (nee Stayner) was about to join the ranks of women whose husbands were off to war. At the time, she was expecting her first child. Mike Hegan collection.

and vests, all according to the patterns and colors required for the army, navy or air force. Mike's fondest memories were related to her university experience, her few years at an office job and her husband's homecoming after the war.

All of a sudden I just felt like I spread my wings....I started [at the University of Saskatchewan] in 1930 and graduated in 1933 at nineteen....I took general arts and I minored in French and majored in history. I got an A, and that was...so hard to get in those days. I got it in English....The social part was great....In those days, it was fun being a girl....[When] a boy had asked you out to a dance...everything was paid for, and it cost a quarter, too...At the university, they had a dance every Saturday night at the common room. That was informal, and then each college had a formal dance every year. The boys — if they had them but very few had them — wore dinner jackets, and the girls had evening gowns. And we had a new one every year. You had to get asked [to the dance], and I guess some girls didn't have a very good time, but most of them did. Then you could check in the girls room and watch them smoke, and talk about how many bids you got for a dance....It was so much fun....

They didn't have sororities. They had Pente Kai Deka, which was the women's organization, but Saskatchewan didn't have sororities....As a matter-of-fact, I was president in my last year....

I [was friends] with a bunch of gals whose fathers were doctors and lawyers, but a lot of them couldn't afford to go to the universities....When I graduated,

In 1933, Mike (Elga) Stayner and her friend graduated from the University of Saskatchewan. From its 1907 beginnings, the prairie university determined there would be no discrimination based on gender. The only faculty violating that precept was agriculture, which finally changed its men-only policy in 1915. Mike Hegan collection.

nobody could find a job...I got a job [since a family friend needed help]....It was a great job, because there were two girls – well the other girl was sixty years old. She was Daisy – and there was me. Then there were twenty-two men....I just was general steno and gopher gal. It was a stocks and bonds department...I just worked there two years before I was married, so that would be about 1937-38. I always enjoyed it....I [had gone] to business courses first...Mrs. Roberts was *the* business college in Saskatoon....Typing and shorthand was all you were good for [as a steno]....but I was very good at writing letters....

Then [after I got married and] the war came, and everything was so muddled up....I was married in 1939, but I came back to Saskatoon for six years during the war....

Larry was a colonel, and he was coming back to New York on the Queen Mary. He was to be in Winnipeg....It was better than being married. Really! It was so exciting....I made a reservation at the Fort Garry [Hotel] where we spent our honeymoon....I was so excited, and I went down on the train. I went into the Fort Garry to ask them about our reservation, for Larry was arriving that day or the next....There wasn't [one]...I said that I made this reservation and it was for a colonel. That still counted. No!...They said, well, they would let me know later. But the big moment was all planned, and the train was getting in the next day. There was a big potted palm in the rotunda, and I was absolutely overcome. I sat down behind that palm tree and I burst into tears....I was heartbroken. And all of a sudden it was [good friends from Regina and their friend, a railway official]....."Well, just a minute," the other friend said. She went off and she was back in about ten minutes, and I had a room....They came rapping on the door bright and early next morning....and they took me down to the station. It was crowded because this troop train was coming in....They lead me up as close as they could...and then they tactfully withdrew....I'll never forget it....[7]

Brotherhood or Sisterhood?

War meant positive and negative experiences for women on the home front. It meant the same for those women serving in the military at home or abroad. When the wars were over, the women who had served their country were often given good or important jobs at home, and some did move into previously male-only domains. In the First World War, Canadian women's military participation was as clerical support and nursing sisters. Roberta MacAdams was a nursing sister with a speciality as a dietician. In 1916, MacAdams became one of the first two women elected as members of the legislature in Alberta. She was put forward as a soldiers' candidate, and the soldiers from Alberta united behind her.

In most areas, the police force was another all-male profession. Edmonton had had women serving in various ways with its police force as early as 1913, but Calgary had been a holdout. A woman's service in the military made her more credible as a police officer, and by the end of the Second World War, women were confident they could serve in such capacities and more were interested in joining the police force. In many cases, police women were assigned to cases involving women and families. For some, working with many different kinds of women in the military also helped them to be more understanding of the women in trouble. One such police officer was Marg Gilkes.

Marg's Story

Marg Gilkes was daring as a young woman and she enjoyed being daring. The work she would do later in life was difficult, but Marg Gilkes loved it. She managed to keep a sense of humor, made good friends within that *brotherhood* of police officers and even fell in love with a fellow officer. Through that work, she came to know how things that seemed negative could become all right. In the strangest way, when circumstances were dire, police intervention could provide a day or two of better times.

In 1941, Marg enlisted in the Canadian Women's Army Corps. She trained other women army recruits, and eventually, she was assigned to the Motor Transport Pool in London, where she lived during the worst of the bombing.

After the Second World War, she returned to Alberta, and in 1946, as a 29-year-old woman with a military background, Marg was welcomed into the City of Calgary Police Force. For 15 years, she worked as one of the first and the few women police officers in Calgary. She was part of the police brotherhood, and the male officers never let her down, dropping everything to come to her assistance if she was in trouble. As police officers do in order to deal with the human tragedies they witnessed, it was also a brotherhood that laughed together – often and loudly. In contrast, her charges included women with every imaginable problem. Instead of making her hard and disillusioned, the job made Marg sensitive to the plight of others and it made her grateful for the experience of working with the women. Years later, it would give her stories to tell, and she wrote compassionately and lovingly about troubled women.

After getting married and raising her children, Marg wrote *Soldier Girl*, her first book. Then, she recounted the history of the Calgary police force in *Calgary's Finest*. She gave her readers a less formal picture of life as a pioneer police woman in *Ladies of the Night*, in which street women come to life. Marg was part of a sisterhood that, from personal experience, understood the plight of women down on their luck or trapped in self-destructive behavior. Her professional work wasn't what other people would have considered a positive experience, but on a personal level, for Marg, it was an experience and time of her life for which she was truly grateful.

"**A** police woman!" my refined, cultured, convent educated mother moaned when I told her about my new job. "I shall never sleep at night now. Your grandmother would leave Heaven if she knew."

"She made you refer to legs as 'limbs', too, didn't she?" I teased, "that is if you must mention that part of your anatomy. What's wrong with being a police-woman[?] It's better than being a lady bronc-rider, isn't it?"

"Why must you be so untamed?" mother lamented. "First it was those awful bucking horses you insisted on riding, then the army and now this!"

"Now mum," I said, tickling her under the chin, "just because I don't think babies burst from your navel after miraculously getting in there doesn't mean I am untamed."

In spite of her misgivings, mother laughed....I knew I had won her over. Anyway, she was so glad to have her baby safely home from overseas that if I'd said I intended to rustle cattle, she couldn't have stayed upset too long....[8]

[Her introduction to the "bullpen," the women's cells and the problems was a shock and distressing. Eventually, Marg recognized that they too had a part to play.]

I had no way of knowing that, to the hopeless winos and worn out old prostitutes on skid row, she [the jailhouse] was an old mother of the night, grimly welcoming her derelict children home to the warmth of her embrace. In the shelter of her arms they met old friends travelling the same road. For a short interval, they had full stomachs....Although they cursed her [the cell],...they gave her back a bitter kind of love. She was all they had. Later, I was to come to know her lost children; Old Mary....had been a respectable young school teacher once, until she met a fellow....[9]

Maybe there are things a person is best not knowing. But....I was grateful – NEVER WRITE ANYONE OFF. Under the ugliness and the evil, there is a warm human heart beating. We are all part of a whole. As old Mary used to quote in her drunken, gravelly voice: "There's a destiny that makes us brothers. No one goes his way alone."[10]

An Army Education

Serving in the military brought prairie women other opportunities and interesting experiences. Whether they served overseas or in Canada during the Second World War, the women in the Canadian Women's Army Corps belonged to a sisterhood that played an important part in the war effort. In a world filled with tragedy, hard times and bad times, still there were movies, dances, good professional entertainers, jokes and general silliness to lighten the days and nights. After the war, Canada's financial support package to those who had served in the military was available to both men and women through the Department of Veteran Affairs. The money could be used to buy property, start a business or to further one's education.

Dunny's Story

Dunny Hanna (nee Robertson) enlisted in 1942 before she really knew what was happening, because the military wanted women like her. Dunny's sister, Peggy, became the second woman to enlist in the Canadian Women's Army Corps (CWAC) for Military District 13, with headquarters in Calgary. About twenty-five and having learned to drive at home, after basic training she became the driver for a brigadier, the D.O.C. (District Officer Commanding) of M.D. 13. Later, after officers' training, Peggy was posted to Woodstock, Ontario, where she was in charge of training CWAC drivers. In fact, it was a great joy for her to control the convoys of military trucks from her motorcycle.

With the beginning of the war, Peggy thought her younger sister should join the army, too. She and the brigadier believed that Dunny was the kind of woman the army needed. As a teacher, she had the background to be a training officer and recruiter, and both were desperately needed.

Captain Margaret (Peggy) Robertson of the C.W.A.C., and in charge of drivers at Woodstock, was from the ranching province of Alberta. She was a stenographer at Calgary in civilian life. Dunny Hanna collection.

With the end of her second year of teaching, Dunny looked forward to her summer holiday. She was happy at the thought of relaxing for a while, and she had to consider a new teaching post that she had been offered. When she returned to Calgary, she discovered that a captain in recruiting had booked an appointment for Dunny. Just to see if she would pass the physical, the captain said.

Not wanting to disappoint her, Dunny went to the appointment. The doctor declared her fit; the recruiter said, "Sign these papers."

"But I need a holiday first," Dunny had said.

"Well, just sign, so you are ready to go in the army."

Dunny signed.

"You report for duty tomorrow," declared the recruiter.

"But…."

"You're in the army now, Robertson, and you report tomorrow."

After the fact, Dunny was able to laugh at the purposefully hurried and somewhat deceptive process to get her in the army, but in the end, serving her country would help her to do something she really did love.

Dunny received her basic training at Ste. Anne de Bellevue in Quebec, and then she became an instructor at the Vermilion, Alberta, CWAC training centre. Following those two years, she had other duties elsewhere. One was as mess officer in Toronto. Though many women were well-informed about food and enjoyed cooking, Dunny was not one of them. In addition, she never knew how many would attend meals, and once, she spent the entire budget for the month and still had a week of meals yet to provide.

Having enlisted did allow her to see something of the world. She was posted to England just when Germany surrendered. Since the fighting had ended, being overseas meant good times for her.

As part of the demilitarization program, the army would pay her tuition to a postsecondary institution. For Dunny, her university years would bring some of the greatest joys of her life.

She left the army in 1946, and enrolled at university. Over the next two years and two summers, at the University of Alberta in Edmonton, she fulfilled the requirements for her Bachelor of Education, and she became qualified to teach grades 1 to 12. During that time, she stayed with a family whose father had "a whole set of Alexander Dumas books in French, and I went through them all, including *The Three Musketeers* and *The Count of Monte Cristo*. I had taken three years of French in high school, then freshman and intermediate French, and later a summer school course in French Romantics given in French, and I loved it."

After her B.Ed., Dunny taught grade nine for two years, then returned to university for postgraduate work. In the early fifties, she began a Master of Arts degree, specializing in English, and she completed a thesis. "There were six or seven of us taking a Masters in English, but I was the only woman." Once again, her education was funded as a result of her service in the army. "I received my fees and $50 a month for board, and I bought my own books....The reading and courses were most rewarding." She also lectured to freshman English classes.

With her marriage, Dunny moved back to Calgary, and before her children arrived, she lectured in children's literature at what was then the Calgary campus of the University of Alberta. Some years later, she returned to teaching, this time at the high school level. Her love for books never left her, and since her retirement in 1984, she and friends have held regular book club meetings.[11]

X. Hope Springs

Contemporary prairie women have a heritage of enjoying life, noticing and valuing positive moments, laughing and being joyful. That heritage is not unique to them, but it is worth celebrating. Leisure, recreation and pleasure were not the highest priorities, but those good times were significant contributors to the quality of people's lives.

Most history records the tragedies and difficulties in decade after decade of human experience. Happy times seem less important, and so the memories and stories of them disappear. But gathering those stories serves an important purpose in addition to documenting the lighter side of history. It means people have models of positive behavior, and that behavior leads to happier, healthier people. Those who feel some form of discomfort or guilt in hours of leisure or recreation learn it is O.K. to be happy, to enjoy oneself. No matter how much work or stress existed in the world around them, women of other generations looked for pleasure in their world, and found it.

Social history that records the lighter side of life validates that today's interest in entertainment, hobbies, sports, fashion and other cultural pursuits is not new. Those interests are not limited to the prairie provinces, but their form and content was often affected or governed by the landscape, cultural heritage and conditions of the time.

Saving the Past for Tomorrow

Individuals do set out to capture such stories, and that pursuit is no different today than it was decades ago. Sometimes, the stories are gathered just before the generation who knew and lived them passes away. In western Canada, one woman who decided to save prairie stories for posterity was already a successful journalist. The story she set out to learn was one unique to Canada and deeply rooted in prairie culture. Although once everyone on the prairies had known the information, by 1928, two mysteries had replaced that knowledge.

Elizabeth's Story

Elizabeth Bailey Price was born in Winnipeg, and in 1886, she moved with her family to Medicine Hat. After attending Normal School, she taught at Olds

Many women remember dances as their best times, but the dance styles would change. Square dancing is still popular with this crowd celebrating the Saskatchewan Golden Jubilee in 1955. <u>Star Phoenix</u> photo, Saskatchewan Archives Board, SP-B 3548-1

(Alberta), Edmonton and Calgary, where she eventually made her home. By 1911, she had shifted to a writing career. At the *Calgary Albertan*, she was editor of the women's page, but over the years and after her marriage, she sold freelance articles to the *Calgary Herald* and the Canadian Press papers. She was a member of the Canadian Women's Press Club and very involved with the Women's Institute of Alberta.

Already by the late twenties, the earliest traders, explorers and some settlers were passing away. The original words and intended meanings to the song "The Red River Valley" were uncertain and appeared to have changed. Nobody, it seemed, remembered how to do the Red River jig. But Elizabeth and a committee decided this folk history should not be lost. The detective work began. In 1928, Elizabeth published an article on the Red River jig in the *Toronto Star*. The committee also found a Métis family who remembered the jig. Elizabeth's article,

"Preserving the Red River Jig for Posterity" was also published by the same paper that year.

The rollicking, lilting, strenuous strains of the Red river jig are being preserved for posterity. For the first time, according to old timers of the west, the music has been written, the steps analyzed. This has been done by two of Calgary's most capable dancing teachers. Mrs. Agnes McDonald, and her daughter Marie who learned the tune and dance from a pioneer family of Alberta–the Kiplings.

Forty years ago almost everyone in the west could do the Red river jig. No social gathering was considered complete without it. During the long winter evening, and especially at Christmas time, all the people in the country, natives and whites, would gather at the Hudson bay forts. There in the large dining rooms they danced till dawn by the light of the buffalo fat "dips," or that which blazed from the huge logs that crackled in the fire place. It was a tune everybody knew.

One couple started off, others cut in, until the floor was crowded with merry dancers. Then one by one they dropped out until the last couple would win round after round of applause for their endurance and grace.

For several years past Calgary old timers have been scouring the country to find someone who could dance it for the annual "round ups." But for a time, it looked hopeless. The only "folk dance" of the west seemed to have vanished.

Lady Lougheed could do the women's steps, but she knew of no one who could execute the more intricate steps of the men. Old time fiddlers tried to recall the tune, but could get no further than the first two or three measures. Its notes had never been written down. Books on "old fashioned dances" did not mention it, while reminiscences of the old timers simply dismissed it with, "They danced the Red river jig."

[Finally, when asked, Mrs. Kipling]….beamed upon the committee.

"Indeed, I can," she said, "but I want my son Jim as a partner and my other son Willie to play it."

"Is it the real Red river jig and the real tune?" anxiously asked one, a member of the committee, who felt it was too good to be true.

"It surely is, " said one daughter. "We have danced it all our lives. My brother Willie has played it since he was ten years old. The old timers will know it the minute they see it and hear it."

Native sons and daughters gathered at McDonald academy to learn it. The whole Kipling family turned out–sons, daughter and grandsons–to teach it. Willie

Kipling tuned up his old fiddle, leaned back in his chair, closed his eyes and with the old time spirit of the wild and woolly west fiddled the animated, infectious tune of the Red river jig.

Grandmother Kipling, smiling and dignified, imbued with the spirit of the well-known music, led off the dance with her son Jim. A daughter and grandson "cut in." Soon the floor was crowded with native sons and daughters stepping along to the lively music. The women's steps were easy, three kinds as analyzed by Mrs. Agnus McDonald, dancing teacher. The men's were intricate, involving "double shuffles" and many quick changes, exhilarating yet exhausting, hence the cutting in.

Then Willie Kipling told the old timers he had learned the tune and dance from his father – that it had been "handed down." His children told of how they had learned to "do the jig" ever since they could walk, that their home had been a dancing centre of the community in the early days: that old timers danced till dawn while their father fiddled.

It was through the willingness of this real "old time fiddler" that the dance will now be recorded, both to music and steps. "I have never heard it played on the piano before," said Willie Kipling during the time he worked for hours with Marie McDonald, one measure at a time until she finally mastered it. She is now setting it down so that anyone who reads music may play it.

Although willing to pass along the dance[,] the Kiplings were very eager that it should be "done right." It has not the abandonment of the Charleston, or the lightness of the Scotch reels. It is more like the Irish jig, but the body is held more rigidly....

Yet it is graceful, vigorous and different. Like the settlement of the west in those early days, it is a mixture of new and old....[1]

Waiting for the Good Times

Good times did not come at one's bidding. Certainly, for many early settlers, better days came only long after they had moved to the prairies, built basic shelter, acquired essentials of life, and raised and educated their families. Along the way, most found some things to be glad about. Anger, bitterness and sadness lined the faces of those who didn't, but their stories are more often remembered.

In some families, those that had seen tough times worked harder to ensure that their children developed the capacity to see life in a positive manner, the capacity to laugh at themselves and situations, and the ability to be hopeful. They gave a gift of optimism, and to them, knowing that their children had easier or happier lives brought pleasure. Some even found joy in giving the gifts of optimism and good times to young people who were no relation.

Contemplating the vistas of western Canada's landscape brought many women pleasure and a sense of tranquility. This woman enjoys the view of the North Saskatchewan River and Edmonton before it became home to high rises.
Sir Alexander Galt Museum and Archives, P19770245017

Olga's Story

Olga Macialek Strutt was born in Brandon, Manitoba, in 1922. With 10 children in the family, there was plenty of work, but her parents seldom fought or complained around the children, instead allowing them to see life in a reasonably positive manner.

Music was one of the joys of family life, but eventually, inadequate income became a problem. In the thirties, with 12 mouths to feed, Olga's father made $48 a month, not enough for Olga to continue her education. By 1934, little more than a child, she went to work. The things she enjoyed and imaginative ways she entertained herself spoke of how truly young she was, despite her adult responsibilities. Yet in starting work at a young age, she was like the children of thousands of immigrants. Her adult life was also difficult, yet recalling the past, she recognized the humor inherent in many of the situations, even in some of the bad times.

Her health battles since the seventies have been heroic – long and difficult. She has had numerous types of cancer, including breast cancer. She suffered recurrences, surgeries and radiation treatments. Surprisingly, she has remained optimistic. She explains, "Nobody wanted to talk to me about my illness. Still stubborn, I'd say to myself, 'I'm going to make it.' I'd sing at the top of my voice. Boy that made me feel great." Somehow, she kept a sense of humor and continued to help others whenever she could. At 78, she believes she has led a balanced life, accepting the bad times but preferring to focus on the bright side.

We were just ordinary folks. Nobody landed in jail. Everything was a challenge [but] I always kept a positive attitude. I led a balanced life. There were lots of problems but I just figured that was normal life. [I enjoyed] playing baseball, knitting, sewing…singing. As a child I used to sing "O Canada" at the Remembrance Day Service and recited "In Flanders Fields." I sang a duet with a friend in a concert at the mental hospital. When I saw all those white coats, I froze. I played the violin at home for my Dad. Took lessons at a dollar each. I didn't learn the violin too well so changed to the mandolin. I played in a 15 piece orchestra at Portage la Prairie.

1932, I think, was the one I got the most laughs….Well, me and my girl friend went to this place that had all kinds of fruit, mostly wild. They had a man on a horse patrolling. We would sneak in, fill our bloomers, and if he came after us, we lifted the pant legs and got rid of most of the plums. We went in weighing 90 pounds and came out 110.

I quit school when I was 12 years old, just didn't have clothes. Went to work for a rich family in Brandon for $8.00 a month. When she would go golfing, I would pretend I was rich, so would try one of her teddy's (one-piece lingerie with top and bottom). She was 6 foot and me 4 foot 11. Then, I'd lay on their chesterfield with one of her Guinea Gold cigs, get a piece of string, and pretend I had a poodle.

As for dancing, I never did outside. Although once at a blind bowlers' "banquet" I won $2.50 for dancing. Later, on my birthday, I requested a waltz on a radio phone-in show and asked my husband to dance around the kitchen with me. He said I dance like I'm pumping water.

In 1938, my brother had a cafe on Pacific Avenue. The CPR station was just across the road. At that time, young boys 18 or older rode the box cars, coming from the west. They were hungry so I would feed them and give them a sandwich, etc. To this day, my brother didn't know I stole off him. Boy, that made me feel great. I worked seven days a week for him for $2.50....

I opened the Highway Confectionery in Brandon in 1951. It had an eight stool lunch counter. I did all my own baking and cooking. Of course, I had a girl working for me. The very best time came in 1952 at the age of 29. Looking after 10, 12, 14 and 16 year-old boys and girls. I really enjoyed them. I was a teen mother for south end community. We had a club in my basement every Saturday night. They would come to dance. I bought them a record player but they had to buy the records. They sure complained about that. Then, Sundays I would take them for a ride in a panel truck, about ten of them. One day they wanted me to turn into a side road. I got stuck. There stood a farmer with a shotgun. "Come back to steal more sheep?" I was scared. Then he started to laugh, looked at all the kids and said, "Lady you sure have been busy." He went and got a tractor and pulled us out.

In 1968, four more (adult) children came into my life when I remarried. I love them like my own, and hoped that they didn't think I was the wicked step mother.

By 1969, I had cancer on my right leg. [The doctors] removed 90 percent of my calf, also removed all the glands in my groin. Some of the family said what a horrible leg I had. It is all hollowed out from the surgery. I told them I still have my leg, and if it would make them feel better, I'd make a tough pie dough and fill it in. They told me I'd be in the hospital for at least six weeks. I said I'd be out in four, and I was. They told me I had five years to live but [later] I got a letter from the University of Manitoba saying I was cured and would I donate my blood to help others with melanoma. I donated blood in 1972 to the university and the Red Cross. Then I started to lose weight, which they did not want me to do. They put me on a high protein diet, with all kinds of vitamins. At that time there was no such thing as a support system for cancer patients.

About that time, we had a pet mallard named Natasha who got some lead poisoning. She was really getting sick. I phoned the university and they told me to forget it, she would die. I said, "No way." I would do all I could. So I gave her what I was taking: milkshakes and vitamins. She started to pick up, but then began to lose the use of her feet so I decided to take her to the vet. There I am, with people with their purebreds, and me and my sister-in-law with a duck wrapped in a towel, with only the head sticking out. The vet told me to give her calcium. I also put her in water twice a day, talking to her, "We are going to make it." Then I would tell her to move her legs up and down. She did. That old duck died of old age at 17. I phoned the university and they wanted to hire me.

I believe things always turn out. Keep your head up. Always think positive. Where would our parents be if they didn't always have a smile for everyone? We were all born equal. When you have faith, all kinds of doors are open to you. Some women today want to live too high. They should stop and smell the roses once in a while, and enjoy their children. They think they have it hard now. They create tough things for themselves. You only pass this way once, so do the best you can….Live one day at a time and be thankful for what we have."[2]

Moving On

Most women who considered themselves happy had learned when it was time to move on. Life in the West had always involved moving. Aboriginal people moved their camps with great regularity; Métis families were born out of the movement of fur traders to the north and west; settlement was all about people moving in.

Moving on and leaving behind what was not needed as the journey continued was something some people did instinctively and others learned to do. Moving on

Usually, a family travelling to a homestead met other families en route and appreciated the company. Some formed life-long friendships, and later shared many good times together. Provincial Archives of Alberta, Ernest Brown, B 669

often meant sorting what was useless from what was important, risking that something worthwhile might be discarded, having faith that it could be replaced by something more useful or more worthwhile. It meant having a realistic but hopeful perspective.

Many prairie women lived long lives, a few celebrating their hundredth birthday and more. For them, some years were happy and others were not. Women who came to the West as little girls at the turn of the century may have had their happiest years as children, teenagers or seniors. From a psychological perspective, the difficult years of financially establishing oneself or a family, of raising small children or doing well at a job would have existed whether a woman lived in the Canadian West or in Ireland, China or Scandinavia. Sometimes, those were life stages to pass before things could look brighter. It just happened that in the early settlement years of the prairies, most of the population were young adults who had or soon had young children to raise.

From a historical perspective, the lack of some amenities seen as essentials today was not considered deprivation at the time. Many of the settlers from eastern Europe, Ireland, Scotland and rural areas anywhere in the world did not have electric lights. The housing in their homeland was basic. They would have been cleaning lamps and cutting wood or peat or digging coal for their stoves whereever in the world they might be. As farmers, they would have been raising livestock, threshing, using wagons and driving horses or oxen in their homelands, and although there was that very critical time when the family had to quickly erect a home before winter, many were not worse off in the Canadian West than they had been.

Some certainly would lament the hard times but the opportunities in Canada far surpassed those in their homelands. Once war came, even those who had little, at least had homes. They were not refugees, nor were their homes and fields devastated by war. Many would want to return to their homelands for a visit. Very few wanted to return for good.

Those who held optimistic life views could see bright spots in their experiences. They dealt with the bad times and moved on, ready for better times. Still, somewhere along the way they realized difficulties are only one part of the entire picture.

Rosalee's Story

Rosalee van Stelten (nee Auger) was the daughter of Eunice Elizabeth Auger (nee Smith) and became the adult stepdaughter of Olga Macialek Strutt. Like her stepmother, Rosalee developed the ability to put life's ups and downs in perspective, and her worldly experience has given her a hopeful world view.

Photographed in London, a weary but happy Petty Officer Rosalee Auger (van Stelten) was going someplace important. Chosen from among 120 candidates, the navy woman had just arrived in England to begin duty on behalf of Canada at Buckingham Palace. She worked in the press department and returned to Canada as part of the scheduled royal visit. Lee van Stelten collection.

The oldest in a family of three girls and one boy, Rosalee spent many years in Winnipeg. She has deep Canadian roots, having travelled and lived throughout Canada, as well as in London, England. Hers was the life of an army child, frequently moving, frequently making new friends. She took on mothering responsibilities at a very early age because her mother became sick with tuberculosis.

In 1953, Rosalee followed in the family tradition and entered the armed services. Her last posting was in Ottawa. In 1968, she moved to Calgary. Her decision to marry came when she was 40 years old, and the van Steltens decided not to have children. Marriage brought a new challenge, as well as somewhere different to travel – Holland, where she became very close to her husband's family. Throughout her life, she had travelled extensively. Rosalee has a sophisticated view of what it takes to enjoy life and be happy, a view that never devalues responsibility or work. It focuses on individual choices but also acknowledges the role people play in each other's lives.

I was born in Port Arthur in 1933. We moved to Winnipeg in 1942 when Dad was stationed there with the Princess Patricia's Canadian Light Infantry. After Dad went overseas, we bounced back and forth between the two provinces.

When my mother got TB and went into the sanatorium in 1945, we spent part of a year in Red Rock, Ontario, and a part of the year in Carman, Manitoba, living with relatives. We returned to Winnipeg in 1946. I changed schools 12 times in 12 years! My mother hated Winnipeg winters and would yank us out of school in January and take us to the Lakehead until spring, when we moved back to Winnipeg. I had taken care of my siblings from the age of 14 – when my mother was an invalid – until I was 20.

During my teen years when my mother was home, my pleasures were weekend outings with my best friend's family – picnics, river rafting, horseshoes, baseball, family sing songs; also cycling with a group of friends; movies, skating – badly. Mom had learned leathercraft and copper tooling for occupational therapy in the T.B. sanatorium and taught me both of those crafts, which I did for many years. She was an avid reader, which I also became. I had an artistic streak and loved photography.

When I joined the Navy there were all kinds of sports including curling, tennis and basketball. On dates we went to restaurants, movies, ballroom dances – which I loved. And skating – badly. Once in HMCS Cornwallis, a group of us were playing crack the whip at the rink. The "New Look" was in: pencil-line skirts to mid-calf. I had one tailored with a fly front and centre seam. They cracked me into the boards and the stitches ripped from fly to hem. "Excuse me, your slip is showing," my date whispered. I tied a head scarf to my waist, points down, and carried on unconcerned.

I joined the Navy in Winnipeg in 1953, at the age of 20, and served in Cornwallis, Halifax, Shelburne and Dartmouth, Nova Scotia; Esquimalt, BC; Winnipeg, Manitoba; Ottawa, Ontario; and London, England. Joining the Navy was seen as a radical move for a woman in the early fifties. From my mid twenties to mid thirties, I was in the Wren Personnel trade, in charge of women's barracks in various establishments, mothering other people's children.

The best time I remember were the years 1954-55 when I was stationed on the west coast. The Wrens lived in a wonderful old hotel, with the upper deck converted to dormitories. We were a happy sisterhood, an enclave of women in a sea of men. I was a junior rating so responsibilities were few. Morale was high. There were movies, dances, sailing, tennis, beach barbecues and picnics, good friends. It was great.

The apex of my career was special duty in Buckingham Palace for the six-week Royal Tour of Canada, 1959. I crossed Canada with the Royal Party and sailed aboard HMY Britannia. The Department of National Defence said one of the reasons I was chosen for the job was my "capacity for work." In the last 10 years of my service life, I was in the personnel branch and mothered other people's children. So, something positive came from all that responsibility in my early years.

I don't know where my positive attitude came from. Laughter was a big part of our family heritage, even with the tragedies. For many years, when we ping-ponged between Manitoba and Ontario, my way of fitting in was to be the clown. I think it was love that held me up: from my mother and her elder sister, from my grandmother. Later, in the service, I had surrogate mothers who did the same. I am also fortunate in having a loving stepmother who joined the family when I was 35. Against all odds, she has beaten the most challenging of life's trials. She just never gives up. Also, my sisters and I are extremely close. (My brother died when he was 35.)

When circumstances were challenging, I kept a positive attitude because I was a bright student who, although shy, made friendships that have lasted a life-time. I always felt loved by my family, as though I were special. Even when Mom was in the san and we were farmed out to relatives, I felt cherished.

When things are tough I always say, "In ten years, this won't matter." In other words, take the long view of life. Everyone has ups and downs. Enjoy the good times and build up a reserve of happiness. Cherish your family and friends. When life is hard, they will uphold you. So will a strong faith.[3]

Living Legacy

The story of good times for prairie women is not one linked only to a particular era or a particular lifestyle. For some women, marriage and motherhood were very important. When these things did not fall into place as expected, women found other ways of finding that same happiness. Job satisfaction could not necessarily replace the need for family. Sports and hobbies were just enjoyable activities but did not fit the bill.

Such women made commitments by volunteering to help others in countless ways, and sometimes that commitment was a huge responsibility, and a very rewarding one. Thousands of women have volunteered their time to raise money to fund the needs of the community. They volunteered their efforts to raise money for the homeless, destitute and hungry at home and around the world. They offered unpaid hours of work to the Red Cross, cancer and heart funds, and for a wide range of culture-based groups.

But what some women have volunteered to do for other girls or women has gone beyond that. It has been a sharing of life, and it has meant offering love, acceptance and time. It meant becoming a mother or grandmother to a child without family or with family in difficult circumstances. Such women cared, and in doing so they made their own families, brought happiness to themselves and to others.

Shirley's Story

Shirley Black was born in Calgary in 1932. Although having lived in Radium, B.C., and Galloway, Alberta, when she and her mother moved to locations where her father worked, Shirley spent most of her life in Calgary. For over 40 years, she worked as a dental receptionist and enjoyed getting to know the interesting mix of patients that arrived each day.

She also explored some hobbies and took lessons in painting and ceramics. Shirley played badminton and loved golf. She began playing when she was about 18 years old at a time when there weren't many women golfers. In fact, being left handed, and with no ladies' left-handed clubs available, she got men's clubs and had them cut down for her. When she could, she played four times a week and truly loved the game. However, there was more to Shirley than playing games. Like many other women, She believed in serving her community. She volunteered for a variety of tasks at her church. Already, in her twenties, she became a volunteer with Big Sisters and continued until the organization was disbanded (it was later revived).

As the years passed, Shirley explored her interest in creative writing. She began to write stories, and she was one of the founding members of the Alexandra Writers Centre Society in Calgary. She spent endless unpaid hours working for the benefit of those interested in writing, helping them, mothering them along when they needed it, listening to their stories, making them smile or offering her ear as someone they could trust with their fictional and with their real life stories.

Along the way, Shirley had her own successes with writing. She won prizes in contests and had work broadcast on CBC. Most of her stories revealed her warm and ironic sense of humor, a trait she learned from her father. Her work makes readers want to laugh and shed a tear – in the same story. Her central characters, usually female, reveal insights into human nature, insights garnered from the people of her city. Shirley accepted and valued those people from whom she drew bits and pieces of her characters – whether they were strangers, family or friends.

Her willingness to accept, value, love and help others went beyond what most people do for individuals who are not family. Shirley never married. She had no children of her own, but that did not mean she could not love and support a child. She made a personal commitment to a young girl, and becoming her "mother" brought joy to both of their lives.

When my mother became ill the doctors thought it was her tonsils, then her teeth. Hodgkin's disease was hard to diagnose. Impossible to cure. She was given a year to live. Friends rallied around to donate blood. There was a twenty-five dollar charge for blood transfusions and it was their gift to us. Every evening my dad and I would walk across the Zoo to the General Hospital to visit for one hour, and always we took a rubber ball so we could have a game of catch on the way home. I was nine years old when she died.

My grandfather proved too old to care for a young child. "Grandmother" Hides, our tenant, was asked to "keep an eye on me." She was a stern disciplinarian, and I lived for the winter months when my dad worked in the Calgary office. [He often travelled.] Then there would be Kresge hamburgers, double features at the local movie theatre on Saturday evenings and walks along the railroad tracks. He'd tuck me into bed at night and read a story. Not *Anne of Green Gables* and Nancy Drew, rather *Dial M for Murder* or *The Postman Always Rings Twice*, books he wanted to read and I loved to hear.

As I grew older he began to live a separate life. Through the years he had become so accustomed to living in hotels, he preferred them to home. My "grandmother" and I, left alone in the big house along the Bow River, became close. I told her my secrets. She told me of dreams that had never come true. She lay awake at night listening for the sound of my key in the lock, and brought me tea in the morning. I phoned often to check on her. She met my friends and cautioned me about "respect and never giving in," and when someone I was fond of was killed in an accident, she broke the news gently, then held me as I sobbed into her lap. Both she and my dad died when I was in my early twenties and I thought that never again would I have close family.

Like many young people of my generation one of my first stops after graduation was the Unemployment Office. There I was interviewed by two middle aged women with faded brown hair and rimless glasses.

"What is it you are looking for?" they asked.

"Oh, it doesn't matter," I said. "I'll be married by next year and start having children." The fact that I didn't have a boyfriend and no prospects never occurred to me.

They glanced down at my ring finger and then up at my face. "Don't be so sure," they said. "Look at us."

Only half of their prophecy came true. Although I've never married, I did become a surrogate mother and grandmother.

Deb's family had always lived across the street from our house. When she was orphaned at twelve, her grandmother, like my grandfather before her, decided she was too old to care for a young girl, so Deb came to stay with me. It was not easy. I wasn't used to being a single "mom." Deb found it difficult to accept me in this role. Still, thirty-five years later and living eighty miles apart, although maybe not in the traditional sense, we are still family. Graduations, weddings and holidays are important to us. When Rick [Deb's son] was in his early teens, he spent many weekends with me. Now Brandon [Deb's younger son] comes with his sleeping bag and a suitcase full of games.

We call often and Deb tells me, "I get more like you every day. Someone straightened up my papers and now I can't find a thing."

And last Christmas, Nicole [Deb's daughter] paid me the ultimate compliment when she opened the gift I had given her, a trendy outfit from her favourite store.

"You are the coolest old granny in the world," she said.

Can life get much better than this?[4]

Mothers and Daughters of Hope

For some prairie women, focusing on hope and quality of life is much more than a casual commitment. Sharing the good times isn't just a matter recalling pleasant memories, telling stories with happy endings or having a few laughs at a party with family or friends. Some believe that the ability to recognize what is good in life – what is positive and hopeful – can make a difference in how lives unfold. They believe that sharing, making time for oneself and enjoying time with others can be instrumental in making good things happen.

Jacqueline's and Ronna's Story

A very special few have used their professional lives to foster such attitudes, and they created a legacy centred on those beliefs. Ronna Fay Jevne of Edmonton is one such woman. Her mother, Jacqueline Jevne (nee Lakeland) of Wetaskiwin, who passed away in 1984, was another. Neither ever denied the harsh realities and chal-

Quietly watching wildlife was a treat for many. Such times were also treasured as "Kodak moments," and often became the source of inspiration for writers and artists. Stettler Town and Country Museum.

lenges of life. However, to them, the existence of difficulties – in the past or present – did not overshadow the possibility of hope, happiness and good times. Both valued their ties to the prairie's history and landscape. Like thousands of others in the past and present, they have deeply held spiritual beliefs, rooted in humanism.

Jacqueline Lakeland was born at Medicine Hat in 1926. Eventually, the Lakelands moved with their young daughter to Calgary, and there Jacqueline completed high school. Next was Calgary Normal School for teacher training, followed by her first job. It was at Falun near Wetaskiwin, Alberta.

Not long after, she married a local farmer, Morris Jevne, whose parents had come to the Wetaskiwin area about the turn of the century and had homesteaded. At 19, Jacqueline became a farm wife with few of the city amenities she had once enjoyed. In fact, she decided to enter as fully as she possibly could into the spirit of rural life. That included supporting rural issues and initiatives.

Over the years, the couple's involvement in the rural co-operative movement meant travel across Canada and Europe. Since her husband was a leader in the movement, sometimes her husband travelled and Jacqueline stayed home, looking after the farm and children.

Not surprisingly, given her background, she began to see education and co-oper-ation as tools that could improve the quality of life for rural women and their fam-ilies. At 42 years of age, she returned to university, and subsequently, she shared her knowledge and skills with others in a wide variety of workshops for rural families. One such project was a three-year stint offering workshops in an agricultural lead-ership project. She worked with about 18 individuals to prepare them for leadership in agriculture on the provincial, national and international levels.

About 60 years after Jacqueline's birth, posthumously, she became one of the few women appointed to the Alberta Agricultural Hall of Fame. She received the honor because of her accomplishments.

Jacqueline believed a sense of humor helped to carry her though the ups and downs of farm life. Just as important, perhaps more important than the impact she had on neighbors, friends and strangers, was the impact Jacqueline had on her daughter, Ronna Jevne. In 1992, Ronna was one of the founders of Hope House and the Hope Foundation of Alberta. In her work, Ronna focuses on the importance of hope in people's lives. A joint venture of the community and University of Alberta, the Hope Foundation offers counseling, provides education and does research relat-ed to hope. The clients of the Hope House are people who face chronic or life-threat-ening physical or mental problems.

A professor at the University of Alberta, Ronna has authored eight books, four of them specifically on the importance of hope: *The Voice of Hope*, *It All Begins with Hope*, *Finding Hope* and *Hoping, Coping and Moping*. She credits first learning the pre-requisites of a hopeful attitude from her mother.

In our personal worlds we each have something, to a greater or lesser degree, that helps us move forward. There are those who seem to face the future with an unending sense of positive expectations. Others are paralyzed by the chal-lenges of life, unable to move forward. Still others seem seduced by adversity to slowly diminishing hope....

The Mothers of our hope love us. Their love gives birth to a world that can be trusted, a world where we can expect to have our needs met. We are fortunate if we have mothers who give voice to the messages, "You are okay, you can do things: you don't have to be afraid of life; females are not second class citizens; solutions are more important than who is to blame." They are our mentors, our models....They give birth to a self that is hopeful....Mothers of hope love us for who we are....My mom was, indeed, a mother of hope....[5]

As a child, I knew the gift of a rainbow. I took joy in every season, saw life in every injured bird, knew quiet in a storm. I loved to ride bareback before dawn and bask in the sweat of helping with the haying. I instinctively knew who and when to trust. I saw a world of abundance and knew it was to be shared.[6]

Sharing the Joy

As adult women, it is possible to see abundance, not every day and not in all ways, but on some days and in many different ways. Sharing the good times contributes to creating good times. Women who know how to be happy demonstrate to others how to bring joy into life. Those who watch and listen also learn.

Stories of love and laughter are part of the prairie landscape. What joy must have welled into the hearts of some women when they saw the beautiful landscape, or when they knew they finally had land or homes or jobs of their own. What a pleasure to amble along a boardwalk and window shop or stop to chat with a friend, to wear a new dress or carry a parcel of something special or for someone special. Whether women had purchased a gift or made it, whether it reflected a specific cultural heritage or not, whether it was something to make life easier or was a small luxury, gifts meant joy.

Love meant thrilling and passionate moments; and sometimes, it was quietly expressed moral support or moments of silence when just being together was enough. There would always be a million reasons for joyfulness and a million ideas of what brought joy. Hours, days, months, years, decades, a century later, the memories of good times were renewed pleasures.

Occasionally, the women of hope and happiness were remarkable. Sometimes they were ordinary women living ordinary lives, but their capacity for hope, for happiness, for experiencing and remembering good times made them extraordinary – made life special for themselves and for others.

Sometimes just being together, even if it was in a box, made the world a little brighter. Stettler Town and Country Museum.

In 1936, Joan Oliver, who grew up near Calgary, climbed from Lake Agnes to Needle Peak, above the Beehive at Lake Louise. For some women, mountain climbing got in the blood. Glenbow-Alberta Institute, NA 4868-246

Footnotes

I. Hoping for Happiness

1. W. J. Healy, *Women of Red River*, 206-207. As quoted from *Harpers Magazine*, 1860.
2. Mary Fitzgibbon, *A Trip to Manitoba*, 60-62.
3. Lovisa McDougall Papers, Provincial Archives of Alberta. As quoted by J. G. MacGregor, *Edmonton Trader: The Story of John McDougall*, 103-105.
4. Ibid., 122.
5. Ibid., 130.
6. Ibid., 199.
7. Lucy Chiesa (nee Rocchio), interview with the author, 27 March 2000.
8. Edna Quilichini (nee Larose), letter to the author, [May] 2000.
9. Peggy Holmes with Andrea Spalding, *Never a Dull Moment*, 59-60.

II. Love Lights Shining

1. For exact ratios and statistics, see J. William Brennan, *Regina: An Illustrated History*, 190.
2. Norah Matthews Driscoll, Oral History Project, City of Edmonton Archives, 11-12.
3. "To Kiss or Not to Kiss," *Modern Women*, February, 1906. Emily Murphy Scrapbooks, City of Edmonton Archives.
4. Emilie Ferguson, "Cupid and Cupidity." No source or date, Emily Murphy Scrapbooks, City of Edmonton Archives. The author has used this unusual spelling of her first name.
5. Emily Ferguson Murphy, "A Married Flirt," *Modern Woman*, Jan. [ca 1906], Emily Murphy Scrapbooks, City of Edmonton Archives.
6. Jack Peach, "a place to take your best girl," *All Our Yesterdays*, 108. As quoted from *Calgary Herald* column by Jack Peach, 21 July 1984.
7. W. J. Healy, *Women of Red River*, 210-212.
8. Bob Edwards, *Eye Opener*. As quoted by Hugh Dempsey in *The Best of Bob Edwards*, 97-99.
9. Jean Leslie, memoirs sent to the author, [May] 2000.
10. John Hawkes, *The Story of Saskatchewan and its People II*, 1110.
11. Aldis Olson, "Honeymooning on the Canadian Pacific Railway," *Memories: Roses in December*, 25-26.
12. James Farquharson Macleod Fonds, Glenbow-Alberta Institute, M776/14.

III. Every Day and Festive Days

1. F. H. Schofield, *The Story of Manitoba*, 174-176.

2. Mrs. Kennedy, *The Story of Saskatchewan and its People, Volume II*, authored by John Hawkes, 1033-1034.

3. Monica Hopkins, *Letters From a Lady Rancher*, 36-37.

4. "Hail the Province of Saskatchewan," *The Leader*, Regina, 6 September 1905. As quoted in *Saskatchewan History*, vol XXXIII, no 3 (Autumn 1990), 89.

5. Mrs. Madge Isabel Strong, Oral History Project, City of Edmonton Archives, Interview, 4 Oct 1968, Transcript, 4-5.

6. Kathleen Esch, B.Sc., *Edmonton Journal*, 13 December 1935; 3 March 1936; 10 March 1936.

7. Edith Van Kleek, *Our Trail North*, 45-57.

8. Ibid., 78-87.

IV. Impressing an Audience

1. Eugenie Louise Myles, *Tarpaper Shack Twice to Watch Royalty Disrobed in Westminster Abbey*. References for this story are based on the autobiography information of Mrs. Myles. See 24 for the fire. See 64-70 for references to the piano.

2. Beatrice Carmichael Fonds, City of Edmonton Archives, Clipping, *Edmonton Bulletin*, 2 November 1929.

3. Mrs. H. J. Kenyon, Saskatchewan Archives Board, Saskatchewan Archives Questionnaires, No. 5, Pioneer Recreation and Social Life.

4. Sheilagh Jameson, *Chautauqua in Canada*, 138.

5. Lena Yachyshn, interview with the author, 13 July 2000.

V. Women's Culture, Women's Lives

1. Ramsay Cook and Wendy Mitchinson, *The Proper Sphere*, 214-215. As quoted by the authors from *Saskatchewan Grain Growers Association Year Book*, 24-26.

2. Nellie McClung, *Purple Springs*, 282-283.

3. *Winnipeg Tribune*, 29 January 1914. As quoted by Candace Savage, in *Our Nell*, 88-89.

4. Henrietta Muir Edwards, Edwards/Gardiner Family Fonds, Glenbow-Alberta Institute, M7283. All quoted reference related to Ms. Edwards are from this source.

5. Interview with the author, Gladys Hanna Hurl, 17 March 2000.

6. Ian D. Livermore, "The Quilt of Life," *Glenbow Magazine*: 19.

7. Lillian Rediger, "Grandmother's Heirloom Quilt," *Folklore*: 18-19.

8. Jane Aberson, *From the Prairies With Hope*, 81-82.

9. Jim McLeod, "Hutterite Sweetheart Handkerchiefs," *Piecework*. All related references are from this source.

VI. What About the Outer Me?

1. Bob Edwards, *Eye Opener*, 1 January 1910. As quoted by Grant MacEwan in *The Best of Bob Edwards*, 182.
2. A. F. M. "Home Dress-making," *The Woman at Home*, 405-406.
3. Clark, Dorthy. Oral History Project. Sir Alexander Galt Museum and Archives.
4. Mary Melendy, *The Perfect Woman*, 376.
5. Ibid, 380.
6. Ibid, 203-204.
7. Queenie Palmer, *Kapasiwin*, 89-101. Information was supplied by Mrs. Palmer, August, 1987.

VII. Enjoying New Landscapes

1. Nancy Allison, interview with the author 4 July 2000. All quotes by Nancy Allison are from this source.
2. For this story see Leanne Allison, "Tobacco Road," *Canadian Alpine Journal*, 77 (1994): 18-23.
3. Elizabeth Parker, *Canadian Alpine Journal*, 6.
4. A.L.O.W. [Elizabeth Parker], "Some Memories of the Mountains," *Canadian Alpine Journal*, 17 (1929): 56-60.
5. Winnifred Lois Kloster (nee Gallop), letter to the author, [ca May] 2000.
6. Evelyn Lyster, Letters of Evelyn and Verle Lyster, Pat Lyster Fenske Collection. Except those written by Verle Lyster, all letters quoted were written by Evelyn as dated and are part of this collection. Changed handwriting style for the November 2, 1969, letter suggests the laborious process of writing at this time.
7. Verle Lyster, Letters of Evelyn and Verle Lyster, Pat Lyster Fenske Collection. Letters dated 10 October 1968 and 18 January 1970 are by Verle and both are part of this collection.

VIII. Out to Win

1. Melendy, 381.
2. Northern Alberta Curling Association Fonds, Provincial Archives of Alberta, 71.50, Box 1, File 7.
3. Trafford Tyler, *The Calgary Golf and Country Club 1897-1997*, 61-61. All statistics related to Calgary golf and Paddy Arnold are from this source. See also 32-33, 58-59.
4. Diane Ransom, "'The Saskatoon Lily':A Biography of Ethel Catherwood.," *Saskatchewan History*, 85. All measurements related to Catherwood's career are from this source.
5. Ransom, 82.

6. *Shooting Stars*, National Film Board of Canada, Publicity Sheet. Some related statistics are reported differently in newspaper articles from the Edmonton Grads Scrapbook of Daisy Johnson, City of Edmonton Archives, A93-29.

7. Jill Forsyth, excerpts from book-in-progress re: Abbie Scotts. Quotes are from 10 July - 30 August 1924, Abbie Scott's personal diaries are in the possession of her daughter Lois Forsyth (nee Kennedy).

8 "Do You Remember Way Back When," *Edmonton Bulletin*.

9. "City Girl Queen Winter Carnival Banff Next Year," *Edmonton Journal*.

10. "Edmonton Rustlers Win," *Edmonton Journal*.

11. "Title-Seekers End Training With Impressive Practice," *Edmonton Journal*.

IX. Sisterhood

1. Marjory MacMurchy, *The Woman–Bless Her: Not as Amiable a Book as It Sounds*, 61-62.

2. Wauneita Society Minute Book, University of Alberta Archives.

3. *Third Annual Announcement, 1922-1923*, 38. All quotes and information regarding the 1922-23 program are from this source.

4. *Tech-Art Record* Vol. 1, 45-48.

5. "Dressmakers Give Pageant," *The Emery Weal*, 21 November 1929.

6. Eva J. Bond, interview by John Henderson, 24 August 1977. Saskatchewan Archives Board. R-1491.

7. Mike [Elga Muriel] Hegan, interview with the author, 18 Febuary 2000. Additional information was gathered from Dick Hegan during the same interview and from subsequent visits with Mrs. Hegan.

8. Marg Gilkes, *Ladies of the Night*, 12.

9. Ibid., 20-21.

10 Ibid., 246-247.

11. Dunny Hanna (nee Robertson), interview with the author, 11 July 2000. All information and quotes in this story are based on this intervie and subsequent visits.

X. Hope Springs

1. Elizabeth B. Price, "Preserving the Red River Jig for Posterity," *Toronto Star*. Elizabeth Bailey Price Fonds, Glenbow-Alberta Institute, M 1002, F. 20.

2. Olga Macialek Strutt, memoir to the author, 20 April 2000.

3. Roselee van Stelten, memoirs and correspondence with the author, 21 April 2000.

4. Shirley Black, memoirs to the author, 11 September 2000.

5. Jevne, Ronna Fay, *The Voice of Hope*, 8-14. Quotes and further information are included in this section.

6. Ibid., 137.

Selected Bibliography

Aberson, Jane. *From the Prairies With Hope*. Edited by Robert E. VanderVenne. Regina, SK: Canadian Plains Research Centre, University of Regina, 1991.

A. F. M. "Home Dress-making." *The Woman at Home* (January-June, 1905).

A. L. O. W. "Some Memories of the Mountains." *Canadian Alpine Journal 17* (1929): 56-60.

Allison, Leanne. "Tobacco Road." *Canadian Alpine Journal 77* (1994): 18-23.

Bliss, Jacqueline. "Seamless Lives: Pioneer Women of Saskatoon 1883-1903." *Saskatchewan History XLIII*, no. 3 (Autumn, 1991): 84-99.

Bloomfield, G. T. "'I Can See A Car in that Crop': Motorization in Saskatchewan 1906-1934." *Saskatchewan History XXXVII*, no. 1 (Winter, 1994) 3-21.

Brandon Normal School, (Pamphlet). [Winnipeg, MB]: Manitoba Culture, Heritage and Recreation, 1985.

Brennan, J. William, ed. *Regina Before Yesterday*. Regina, SK: Historical Committee, 75 Anniversary Management Board, City of Regina, 1978.

Brennan, J. William. *Regina: An Illustrated History*. Toronto, ON: James Lorimer & Company and Canadian Museum of Civilization, 1989.

Cavanaugh, Catherine and Randi R. Warne. *Standing on New Ground: Women in Alberta*. Edmonton, AB: University of Alberta Press, 1993.

Cavell, Edward and Jon Whyte. *Rocky Mountain Madness*. Banff, AB: Altitude Publishing, 1982.

Conrad, Peter. "Beating the Great Depression." *Folklore 14*, no. 3 (Spring 1993) 10-11.

Cook, Grace Duggan. *Roots and Romance*. No City: Grace Duggan Cook, 1981.

Cook, Ramsey and Wendy Mitchinson. *The Proper Sphere*. Toronto, ON: Oxford University Press, 1976.

Dafoe, Christopher. *Winnipeg: Heart of the Continent*. Winnipeg, MB: Great Plains Publications, 1998.

Dempsey, Hugh, ed. *The Best of Bob Edwards*. Edmonton, AB: Hurtig Publishers, 1975.

Dewar, John. "Saskatchewan's Basketball Beginnings (1981-1922)." *Saskatchewan History 41* (1988) 99-112.

"Documents and Newspaper Scrapbook: Breaking New Ground–Sarah Ramsland, MLA, 1919-1925." *Saskatchewan History XLIII*, no 2 (Spring 1991) 52-56.

Duncan, Joy, ed. *Red Serge Wives*. No city given: Centennial Book Committee, 1974.

Edwards, Mrs. O. C. "Looking Back on Life." *Ladies Home Journal* (May, 1931).

"Elizabeth Parker, In Memoriam." *Canadian Alpine Journal XXIX*, no. 1 (1944-45).

The Emery Weal Annual, Calgary, Alberta, 1940-41.

Fitzgibbon, Mary. *A Trip to Manitoba*. London, England: Richard Bentley and Son, 1880.

The Gateway, Graduation Special Annual. Edmonton, AB: University of Alberta, Students' Union, 1912.

Gilkes, Margaret. *Ladies of the Night*. Hanna, AB: Gorman & Gorman, 1989.

Goldstrom, Marian, ed. *Fifty Years of Trails and Tales*. Calgary, AB: Skyline Hikers of the Canadian Rockies, 1982.

Gray, James. *The Roar of the Twenties*. Toronto, ON: Macmillan Company of Canada, 1975.

Griffith, Nes. *The Vision Splendid: Centennial History of the National Council of Women 1893-1993*. Ottawa: Carleton University Press, 1933.

Gutkin, Harry and Mildred Gutkin. Gazette, "Give Us Our Due." *Manitoba History*, no. 13 (Autumn, 1996).

"Hail the Province of Saskatchewan." *Saskatchewan History XXXIII*, no. 3 (Autumn, 1980) 81-89.

Hamilton, John David and Bonnie Dickie. *A Winnipeg Album*. Toronto, ON: Anthony Hawke, Hounslow Press, 1998.

Hancock, Carol. *No Small Legacy: Canada's Nellie McClung*. Winfield, BC: Wood Lake Books, Inc., 1986.

Harmiota: Grains of the Century 1884-1984. Harmiota, MB: Hamiota Centennial History Committee, 1984.

Hawkes, John. *The Story of Saskatchewan and its People II*. Chicago-Regina: The S. J. Clarke Publishing Co., 1924.

Hayden, Michael. "Women and the University of Saskatchewan: Patterns of a Problem." *Saskatchewan History 40* (1987) 72-82.

Healy, W. J. *Women of Red River*. Winnipeg, MB: Russel, Lang & Co., Ltd., 1923.

Herstory: The Canadian Women's Calendar. Sydney, BC: Gray's Publishing Ltd., 1978, 1979, 1980, 1981, 1982.

Herstory: The Canadian Women's Calendar. Regina, SK: Coteau Books, 1995, 1996.

Holmes, Peggy. *It Could Have Been Worse*. Toronto, ON: Collins Publisher, 1980.

Holmes, Peggy with Andrea Spalding. *Never a Dull Moment*. Toronto, ON: Collins Publisher, 1984.

Hopkins, Monica. *Letters From a Lady Rancher*. Calgary, AB: Glenbow Museum, [ca 1981].

Hryniuk, Margaret. *A Tower of Attraction: An Illustrated History of Government House*. Regina, SK: Canadian Plains Research Centre, 1991.

Jameson, Sheilagh. *Chautauqua in Canada*. Calgary, AB: Glenbow-Alberta Institute, 1979.

Jevne, Ronna Fay. *The Voice of Hope*. San Diego, California: LuraMedia, 1994.

Klimko, Olga and Michael Taft. *Them Days: Memories of a Prairie Valley*. Saskatoon, SK: Fifth House Publishers, 1993.

Kuffner, Lori. "Girls of Summer." *Western People* (18 September 1997) 8-9.

Leslie, Jean. *Glimpses of Calgary Past*. Calgary, AB: Detselig Enterprises, Ltd. 1994.

"Life Was Hectic Among the Rodeo Ladies in Those Days of Long Ago." *The Wild Bunch* (November 1984).

Lillian Benynon Thomas (pamphlet). Manitoba: Manitoba Department of Cultural Affairs and Historical Resources, 1983.

Livermore, Ian D. "The Quilt of Life." *Glenbow Magazine* (Winter, 1993) 19.

McClung, Nellie. *Purple Springs*. Toronto, ON: University of Toronto Press, Reprinted 1992.

MacEwan, Grant. *Eye Opener Bob*. Calgary, AB: The Institute of Applied Art, [ca 1957].

McDougall, Lovisa Jane Amey. *Letters of Lovisa McDougall, 1878-1887*. Edited by Elizabeth M. McCrum. Edmonton, AB: Alberta Culture, Historical Resources Division, 1978.

MacGregor, J. G. *Edmonton Trader: The Story of John McDougall*. Toronto, ON: McClelland and Stewart Ltd., 1963.

McLeod, Jim. "Hutterite Sweetheart Handkerchiefs." *Piecework* (July/August, 2000).

MacMurchy, Marjory. *The Woman–Bless Her: Not as Amiable a Book as It Sounds*. Toronto, ON: S. B. Gundy, 1916.

Mein, Stewart. "The Aberdeen Association: An Early Attempt to Provide Library Services to Settlers in Saskatchewan." *Saskatchewan History 38* (1985) 2-19.

Melendy, Mary. *The Perfect Woman*. [Chicago]: K. T. Boland, 1901.

Millar, Wilma, ed. *Kapasiwin*. [Calgary, AB]: No Publisher Given. 1987.

Morgan, E.C. "Pioneer Recreation and Social Life." *Saskatchewan History 18* (1966) 41-54.

Myles, Eugenie Louise. *Tarpaper Shack Twice to Watch Royalty Disrobed in Westminster*. Victoria, B.C.: Elm Editions, 1995.

Norris, Marjorie. *A Leaven of Ladies*. Calgary: Detselig Enterprises Ltd., 1995.

O' Donnell, John. *Manitoba As I First Saw It*. Winnipeg, MB: Clark Bros. & Co., 1909.

Olson, Aldis. "Honeymooning on the CPR." *Memories: Roses in December*. Calgary, AB: Kerby Centre Education Programs, 1999.

Payne, Michael. *The Most Respectable Place in the Territory*. Ottawa, ON: National Historic Parks and Sites, Canadian Parks Service, Environment Canada, 1989.

Parker, Elizabeth. "The Alpine Club of Canada." *Canadian Alpine Journal 1* (1907); 17 (1929).

Peach, Jack. *All Our Yesterdays*. Calgary, AB: Calgary Herald, 1986.

Ransom, Diane. " 'The Saskatoon Lily':A Biography of Ethel Catherwood." *Saskatchewan History 41* (1988) 81-98.

Rasmussen, Linda, et al. *A Harvest Yet to Reap*. Toronto: Canadian Women's Press, 1976.

Rediger, Lillian. "Grandmother's Heirloom Quilt." *Folklore 13*, no. 1 (winter, 1991-1992) 18-19.

Reekie, Isabel. *Along the Old Melita Trail*. Saskatoon, SK: Modern Press, 1965.

Robertson, Heather. *Salt of the Earth*. Toronto, ON: James Lorimer & Company, Publishers, 1974.

Saskatchewan Grain Growers Association Year Book. Regina: Saskatchewan Grain Growers, 1916.

Savage, Candace. *Our Nell*. Saskatoon, SK: Western Producer Prairie Books, 1979.

Schofield, F.H. *The Story of Manitoba*. Winnipeg, Vancouver, Montreal: The S. J. Clarke Publishing Company, 1913.

Second Annual Announcement. Calgary, AB: Provincial Institute of Technology and Art, 1921-22.

Shilliday, Gregg, ed. *Manitoba 125: A History* I (1993); II (1994); III (1995) Winnipeg, MB: Great Plains Publications, 1993-1995.

Shulakewych, Bohdan, ed. *Shadows of the Past*. Edmonton, AB: St. Michael's Extended Care Centre, 1986.

Silverman, Eliane Leslau. *The Last Best West: Women on the Alberta Frontier 1880-1930*. Calgary, AB: Fifth House Publishers, 1998.

Smith, Margot and Carol Pasternak. *Pioneer Women of Western Canada*. Toronto, ON: Ontario Institute for Studies in Education, 1978.

Smith, Roy. *S.A.I.T. The First Sixty Years*. Calgary, AB: The Southern Alberta Institute of Technology, 1990.

Smillie, Christine. "The Invisible Workforce: Women Workers in Saskatchewan From 1905 to World War II." *Saskatchewan History XXXIX*, no. 2 (Spring 1986).

A Stroll Down Memory Lane II. No City: the Seba Beach Heritage Museum, 1996.

Strong-Boag, Veronica. *The Parliament of Women: The National Council of Women of Canada*. Ottawa, ON: National Museums of Canada, 1976.

Strong-Boag, Veronica. *The New Day Recalled: Lives of Girls and Women in English Canada 1919-1939*. Markham, ON: Penguin Books, 1988.

Tech-Art Record: The Official Year Book of the Students' Association of the Provincial Institute of Technology and Art 1 (1927-28); 2 (1929-30).

Third Annual Announcement Calgary, AB: Provincial Institute of Technology and Art, 1922-23.

Tulloch, Catherine. "Pioneer Reading." *Saskatchewan History 12* (1960) 97-99.

Tyler, Trafford. *The Calgary Golf and Country Club 1897-1997*. Calgary, AB: Calgary Golf and Country Club, 1997.

The University of Alberta 1908-1983. Edmonton, AB: The University of Alberta, 1982.

Van Kleek, Edith. *Our Trail North*. Edmonton, Alberta: Edith Van Kleek, 1980.

Wells, Eric. *Winnipeg: Where the New West Begins*. Canada: Windsor Publications (Canada) Ltd. 1982.

Wetherell, Donald, with Irene Kmet. *Useful Pleasures: The Shaping of Leisure in Alberta 1896-1945*. Regina, SK: Canadian Plains Research Centre, 1990.

Willcocks, George. *A History of Exhibitions and Stampedes in Medicine Hat*. Medicine Hat, AB: The Exhibition, [ca. 1996].

Winnipeg–Canada. Winnipeg, MB: City Council, 1904.

Wood, Cornelia. *The Story of the Women's Institute*. Edmonton, AB: Council of the Alberta Women's Institute, 1955.

Zeman, Gary. *Alberta on Ice*. Edmonton, AB: GMS Ventures, 1985.

Interviews, Letters and Memoirs of the Author

Nancy Allison, 4 July 2000; Shirley Black, 11 September 2000; Patricia Lyster Fenske: Letters of Evelyn and Verle Lyster, 14 April 2000; Jill Forsyth: Excerpts book-in-progress re: Abbie Scott's Diaries, 19 April 2000, 21 May 2000; Marg Gilk, 5 June 2000; Gladys Hanna Hurl, 17 March 2000; Dunny Hurl Hanna, 11 July 2000; Elga [Mike] Stayner Hegan, 12 February 2000, 31 August 2000; Ronna Jevne, 6 September 2000; Winnifred Lois Kloster, [ca. May] 2000; Jean Leslie, [May] 2000; Edna Larose Quilichini, [May] 2000; Olga Macialek Strutt, 20 April 2000; Lee van Stelten, 21 April 2000.

Archival Sources

Allen, Vera, Paper, Medicine Hat Museum and Archives, M88.72.1.

Bend Little, Olive, Manitoba Sports Hall of Fame.

Canadian Chautauqua Programs, Medicine Hat Museum and Archives, M87,13.1.

Canadian Women's Press Club, Provincial Archives of Alberta, 74.56.

Carmichael, Beatrice, City of Edmonton Archives, ms.223.

Clark, Dorthy. Oral History Project. Sir Alexander Galt Museum and Archives.

Driscoll, Nora Matthews, Oral History Project, City of Edmonton Archives, 11-12.

King, Mrs. Stephen and Dorthy May King, "Early Days in Edmonton and District," City of Edmonton Archives.

Edwards/Gardiner Family Fonds, Glenbow-Alberta Institute, M 7283.

Higgins Haight, Robina, Manitoba Sports Hall of Fame.

Hockey-Women's Hockey File, City of Edmonton Archives.

Jamison, Hazel, Collection, Alberta Sports Hall of Fame.

Jevne, Jacqueline, Department of Agriculture, Edmonton, Alberta.

Johnson, Daisy, Edmonton Grads Scrapbook, City of Edmonton Archives, A93-29.

Kerr, Cay, Manitoba Sports Hall of Fame.

Macleod, James Farquharson. Glenbow-Alberta Institute, M776.

McDougall, Lovisa Jane Amey, Provincial Archives of Alberta.

Medicine Hat Community Art Club, Medicine Hat Musuem and Art Gallery, M 71.425-71-430, M82.15.7.

Murphy, Emily, Scrapbooks, City of Edmonton Archives.

Northern Alberta Curling Association Fonds, Provincial Archives of Alberta, 71.50, Box 1, File 7-11.

Pedagogical Pioneers: History of Education, Interviews by John Henderson: Eva J. Bond August 24, 1977, R-1491.

Penley Family, Glenbow-Alberta Institute, M 8058, M 8602.

Price, Elizabeth Baily, Glenbow-Alberta Institute, M 1000, M 1002, F. 20.

Ramsland, Sarah. Papers, Saskatchewan Archives Board, S-A 191.

Randon, Marie and Claire, Stettler Town and Country Museum.

Pioneer Recreation and Social Life, Province of Saskatchewan Questionaire No. 5: Mrs. D. A. Moorhouse, Mrs Richard (Lilian) Miles, Mrs. H. J. Kenyon, Mrs. Marion Anderson, Mrs. H. J. Seeman, Mrs. Jessie Elizabeth Cameron, Saskatchewan Archives Board.

Scanlan, Gladyce Ina Greene, Medicine Hat Museum and Art Gallery, Bio File, M93.54.8.

Towards a New Past, Oral History & Visitation: Anne Kratzer (nee O'Kravey), R 5445; Eloise Metheral, R 5853; Eline Morrow, R 8142-43, Saskatchewan Archives Board.

Strong, Mrs. Madge Isabel, Oral History Project, City of Edmonton Archives.

Wauneita Society, University of Alberta Archives.

Newspapers

Calgary Albertan, 16 June [ca 1913].

Calgary Herald, 9 June [ca. 1913]; 3 July 1940; 5 July 1998.

Edmonton Journal, 17 March 1933; 10 March 10, 1934; [ca Feb 1932]; [no day given],1937.

The Emery Weal, 18 March 1926; 21 November 1929; 17 December 1929.

The Leader (Regina), 6 September, 1905; 23 July 1919; 28 November 1919; 29 November 1919; 5 December 1919.

Saskatoon Star Phoenix, 26 September 1928.

Saskatoon Daily Star, 27 September 1928.

Stettler Independent, 30 August 1972.

Toronto Star, 7 April 1928.

Winnipeg Tribune, 29 January 1914; 24 August 1974.

Winnipeg Free Press, 23 December 1961.

An Index of Names and Places